An Urgent Warning for Our Time

"THE COVENANT *with* DEATH"

ISAIAH 28:15

© 2013   Copyright for English language in USA and Canada

Stephen J. Spykerman

All rights reserved. No part of this book may be reproduced in any form whatsoever, whether by graphic, visual, filming, microfilming, tape recording or any other means, without the written permission of the copyright holder, except in the case of brief passages embodied in critical reviews and articles where the title, editors and ISBN accompany such review or article.

All rights reserved under International and Pan-American Copyright Conventions

First Printing: September 2013 V1

ISBN: 978-1-937735-54-8

Legends Library Publishing, Inc
4700 Clover St.
Honeoye Falls, NY 14472

Inquiries to: info@legendslibrary.com
Phone: 877-222-1960
Website: www.LegendsLibrary.org

Book interior layout and cover design by Alisha Bishop

An Urgent Warning for Our Time

"The Covenant with Death"

ISAIAH 28:15

Stephen J. Spykerman

WITH COUNSEL FROM RABBI AVRAHAM FELD

New York

Other books by this author:

Christians and Jews – The Two Faces of Israel
Great Britain – Her Calling and Hidden Ancestry
Who Are You America? – Time to Lift Your Prophetic Veil

Soon to Be Published:

The Hidden Ancestry of America and Great Britain

Acknowledgements

First and foremost I am indebted to HaShem, the Holy One of Israel, to whom I owe all I am and ever shall be. It is the words of His prophets which gave me the inspiration for this book. The longer I live on this earth the more I understand that without Him I can do nothing.

Special thanks must go to my precious wife for her outstanding loyalty, forbearance and love. She has provided the caring environment which enabled me to accomplish this task, plus she has greatly assisted me by placing the pictures and completing the end notes.

There is no question that without the encouragement, help and advice from Rabbi Avraham Feld that this book could not have been written. I am especially grateful for his constant involvement and for the gentle way he has at times tempered my zeal and for the wise counsel he has consistently provided.

Grateful thanks must also go to Yair Davidiy for his indefatigable and dedicated work as a researcher into the history of the lost Ten Tribes of Israel. A book such as this would not have the interest or credibility without the benefit of his discoveries.

The contribution made by my dear friend John Hulley of Jerusalem, to some of the contents of chapter eight also needs to be acknowledged.

A special tribute needs to go to Rabbi Jonathan Cahn for his remarkable research regarding "GROUND ZERO:" The spiritual birthplace of America. Excerpts of an article that preceded his brilliant work, "The Nine Harbingers of Judgment," are included in chapter eleven.

A further special accolade must be given to Rodney Atkinson for his outstanding research of the hidden Nazi truth behind the formation of the European Union. His benchmark work; EUROPE'S FULL CIRCLE— Corporate Elitism and the New Fascism, is an absolute must for anyone who wishes to understand the future direction of world affairs today.

Parts of this book have been published previously in the United Kingdom under the title: "Who Are You America? Time to Lift Your Prophetic Veil!" by Stephen J. Spykerman and published by Mount Ephraim Publishing.

My special thanks must go to Rosamund Stresemann for her outstanding DEATHPACT article, which she has graciously allowed me to incorporate in this book. In her article she exposes the sinister historic and formative relationship between Nazi Germany and the Muslim Brotherhood, Hezbollah Hamas, the P.L.O. and Al Qaida. Her quest for the truth was spurred on by a DVD from the German "Spiegel TV" Channel about the history of the Middle East. She says: I watched the following scene: a high ranking officer of the SS knelt on the ground together with Muslim SS soldiers and prayed with them to Allah.

Finally, I wish to especially acknowledge the amazing work of Bat Yeor in her exposure of the secret Covenant between the EU and the Arab League, as contained in her remarkably well documented book; EURABIA: THE EURO - ARAB AXIS.

Publisher's Note

The publisher wishes to acknowledge at the outset that this book contains strong, if not controversial content. Readers will quickly discover that the author pays no homage to *political correctness* nor is he subject to group-think mentality that plagues our modern "consensus" society. The author does however strive for fidelity in declaring the *truth* according to *his* interpretation of biblical prophecy and against the backdrop of human history.

For a variety of legitimate reasons, publishers frequently seek to mute or at least soften the more strident passages in their non-fiction manuscripts. Curbing the exuberance of the more passionate writers is done with an eye toward retaining credibility and reasoned discourse.

After some consideration, however, the publisher has decided to resist the urge-to-curb this particular author and manuscript. While the publisher does not necessarily subscribe to all of the author's viewpoints found herein, he has nevertheless chosen to grant the author his "full voice."

Mr. Spykerman *is* passionate about his topic, but he wishes harm upon no one but the enemies of truth, freedom and liberty. This book becomes the vehicle through which he declares his truth to the world, free from heavy-handed editorial restraint. After all, on what authority would the publisher seek to "correct" the author's opinions?

In this book the author makes bare his testimony before the world. He has in effect walked the plank and beyond, resting his case firmly upon his own internal compass, If the author's predictions prove accurate, we can be grateful for the timely word-of-warning, if they do not, we can be grateful for that as well!

Contents

Author's Disclaimer i
  Re: "Anglo/British Israelism"

Introduction iii
  America's "Manifest Destiny!"

Chapter One 1
  Lost Key to Understanding End-time Prophecy

Chapter Two 11
  Israel Becomes Two Nations, Each With its Own Distinct Calling
  and Destiny

Chapter Three 19
  The Gentile "Birthright" Sons of Joseph are Found Within the
  British Empire & the United States of America!

Chapter Four 25
  America's Ancient Birthmark

Chapter Five 41
  The Final Words of Moses—a Lion and a Unicorn

Chapter Six 53
  Are the American War of Independence and the Civil War
  Prophesied in the Bible?

Chapter Seven 67
  The Early Seeds of Zionism

Chapter Eight 81
  If Muslims Can see it — Why Can't We?

Chapter Nine 125
  Is the EU the Mortal Enemy of America?

Chapter Ten 175
  Covenant of Death & Contract With Hell

Chapter Eleven 197
  Appeasement Leading to Divine judgment

Chapter Twelve 235
  The Divine Hand of Protection Has Been Withdrawn

Bibliography 243

About the Author 251

The Covenant With Death 253

Endnotes 257

AUTHOR'S DISCLAIMER

Re: *"Anglo/British Israelism"*

The author wishes to disassociate himself from mainstream Anglo or British-Israelism, as he believes it to be a creed that has become tarnished by the twin evils of racism and anti-Semitism. Whereas the early writers of the Anglo-Israel movement were honorable men who based their ideas on the Bible, some presented their case more responsibly than others. The danger inherent in the British-Israel movement was its core belief that its adherents were the "chosen nation." This definition sadly led many to fall into the trap of racial superiority. Yet, the real question is not so much "why" one is chosen, but rather "what" one is chosen for. To be chosen generally means that you have been selected to perform a certain task. It does not mean you are better than anybody else! The movement also fell into the usual trap of replacement theology, which is the belief that all the promises given by a Divine covenant to the patriarchs of ancient Israel have since been cancelled and reassigned to the Christian Church.

Anyone coming with a message that is even remotely associated therefore has to overcome mountains of prejudice. The broth has been thoroughly spoiled by erroneous interpretations of the Scriptures by many Anglo-Israelite writers. With the racist identity movement stealing the concept of Anglo-Israel theology and applying it to their own vile ends, the well became even more polluted. Historians and religionists have since increased the confusion. The secularization of society coupled with the pernicious dogmas of political correctness has added a further bitter harvest. Nevertheless, in this poison brew there lies buried an unmistakable grain of truth. The Scriptures declare the return of the "Lost Tribes of the House of Israel" as the major theme of all prophetic teaching in the Hebrew Bible. Even the NT of Christianity, clearly stated the purpose of their "Messiah's mission," when He said: *"I was not sent except to the lost sheep of the house of Israel."* (Matthew 15:24). The great Prophets of the Bible, such as Isaiah, Jeremiah and Ezekiel, frequently warned the people of Israel that their continuing disobedience to God's commandments would inevitably lead to them being deported as slaves and taken into foreign lands. From there they would be scattered to the four corners of the world only to be re-gathered in the last days by the hand of HaShem, back to the Land of Promise, where their Messiah will rule over them in His 1,000 year long Millennial Kingdom. Christianity has either deliberately ignored or utterly failed to take account of whole portions of prophetic writings, which speak about the ultimate restoration of the whole House of Israel. Once this truth is found, it opens up a whole new world of understanding, which needs to be treated with great care, as you have found a most precious pearl of great price! In fact you have discovered a long hidden key that will not only unlock the prophecies of the Bible, but will also make them totally relevant to our time today.

Be careful! Before you read this book the author encourages the reader to beware for:

> *There is a principle which is a bar against all information, which is proof against all arguments and which cannot fail to keep a man in everlasting ignorance—that principle is contempt prior to investigation.*
>
> —Herbert Spencer 1820 - 1903

INTRODUCTION

America's "Manifest Destiny!"

One of the most remarkable features of America is that her people have an overwhelming belief in their country. The disaster of 9/11 in New York resulted in an unprecedented outburst of patriotism throughout the United States. Modern day Americans, much like their Puritan forefathers, believe that God is still in charge of America's "Manifest Destiny." The "Pledge of Allegiance," *"One nation under God,"* expresses this same sentiment of America's "Manifest Destiny." What does Manifest Destiny mean? What does this talk of Manifest Destiny imply? In embracing this concept, are Americans not subliminally adopting an exclusively Israelite or even a Jewish concept of being "the Chosen People?" This question really is most relevant and we need to ask ourselves: "Could there possibly be an element of truth in this?" Could it be true that the American people have a Manifest Destiny in that they were "chosen" by God to fulfill a certain role in the world?

The most extraordinary truth about the nation! Are you interested? Do you want to know more? Just read on and you will discover the truth.

America has an amazing ancestry and heritage, yet it seems neither the nation nor its mainstream churches are aware of this.

In this ultra secular age it appears the majority of Americans have departed from the faith of their fathers. Pillars that have underpinned society for many generations are being shaken and overturned. America's Judeo-Christian heritage, with its Bible based standards that have so singularly contributed to the nation's greatness, is being deliberately undermined by the ruling elites which dominate the Federal government and the judiciary. Just as in the time of the Judges in ancient Israel, the majority of Americans are doing, "what is right in their own eyes." God brought His judgment upon His nation, Israel, whenever it departed from His covenant and prostituted itself with other gods. America today is in a similar position to those ancient Israelites. Sadly, most miss the connection! They miss it because Americans do not recognize that their destiny is closely connected with that of ancient Israel. The essential message of this book is that, as God judged Israel in ancient times, so He is judging America today, and we see mounting evidence of the consequences of rebellion in her society today.

Those of the Church continue to dwell in confusion, because the concept of their relationship to Israel is fundamentally flawed. The great prophetic books of the Bible convey the central role Israel is going to perform in world affairs at the end of the age. Sadly, however, it appears that the Church has failed to grasp the truth about the Israel of the covenant to which those Prophets were referring.

The Puritan Pilgrim Fathers had a better understanding. Those pioneers who founded the colonial settlements from which the United States of America was to spring forth and blossom like no other nation before it, called themselves variously as the *"Seed of Abraham,"* the *"Children of Jacob,"* and *"His Chosen People."* Did they perchance know something that has been forgotten today?

Why has America Been "Blessed" Above all Nations?

The American Declaration of Independence (1776) states that *"all men are created equal,"* and thus the illustrious founding fathers highlighted the link with the first chapter of Genesis in the Bible. These same great patriarchs of America were spurred on by a vision in which they saw themselves to be establishing an America that would be the New Jerusalem, the Republic of God. The Puritans especially felt this was their God-given purpose. When they established their commonwealth, they saw themselves replaying the sacred history of the children of Israel. To their minds the signs pointed that way even before the new country was founded. Just as the

Israelites were miraculously delivered from Egyptian oppression to establish a Godly society in the Land of Promise, so these Puritan pilgrims, escaping from religious persecution, fled from England to establish a Godly society in Massachusetts. Benjamin Disraeli, the Victorian Prime Minister of Great Britain, declared, *"The American nation is more like that of ancient Israel under the Judges than any other country."*

A most remarkable fact is that God is mentioned in the constitution of every single one of the fifty States of the Union. The Hebrew Bible has profoundly influenced America more than any other nation on earth. In the early years of America's foundation, most of its prominent statesmen and scholars were well versed in Hebraic civilisation. Hebrew and the study of Hebraic laws and institutions were an integral part in the early American colleges and universities such as Harvard and Yale. The early framers of the Constitution used the civil policy of ancient Israel as their model. It may rightly be considered the first and only national constitution that is explicitly founded on the Ten Commandments of the *Torah*.

When the Puritans celebrated the first ever Thanksgiving Day, by giving thanks to God for the harvest of 1621, they imagined it totally unlike "thanksgiving" today. Instead it was celebrated as a type of *Yom Kippur*, the solemn "Day of Atonement," full of repentance, fasting and prayer. Thanksgiving is still the day when every American worth his salt will make for home and Mom's traditional dinner of roast turkey, stuffing, sweet potatoes with marshmallow, mashed potatoes and pumpkin pie. It has become a wonderful family celebration, and certainly it ought to be a time of thanksgiving, as Americans surely have become the most blessed people on the earth. The question is: Why? Why, indeed has America been blessed above all nations?

It would be arrogant to assume that America's global supremacy has come to her because of her own merit. Her fabulous wealth has clearly not been given to her because somehow the Americans are more superior and talented than the citizens of other nations. It cannot be said that the American people have received all the stupendous blessing of their national inheritance because they deserved it. Even in these days of America's vast debts, failing economy and failing strength, the question still remains: How on earth did she come into possession of all this vast wealth and how did she attain her global supremacy in the first place?

Let Abraham Lincoln Speak

In the middle of the American Civil War (1861-65), things looked bleak, as the tide of the war seemed to favor the South, which was rebelling against the Union. As the North had suffered many early reverses, Abraham Lincoln made an urgent appeal to the nation. In his official proclamation of April 30, 1863, he called for a nation-wide day of fasting and prayer. Part of this proclamation reads as follows:

"We have been the recipients of the choicest blessings of heaven. We have been preserved, these many years, in peace and prosperity. We have grown in number, wealth and power as no other nation ever has grown; but we have forgotten God! We have forgotten the gracious hand which preserved us in peace, and multiplied and enriched and strengthened us; and we have vainly imagined, in the deceitfulness of our hearts, that these blessings were produced by some superior wisdom and virtue of our own. Intoxicated with unbroken success, we have become too self-sufficient to feel the necessity of redeeming and preserving grace, too proud to pray to the God that made us."

President Lincoln's words ring as true today as they did then. He knew America's great material blessings had not been earned. He understood that the God of Abraham was the divine source of these blessings. His parents had named him after that great Patriarch of Israel and he was proud to carry the name of the, *"father of the faithful,"* which to him was the greatest of all names. As the people obeyed Abraham Lincoln's call to prayer and fasting, God heard their pleas and the tide of war turned until final victory was sounded for the Union.

Before we can address the prophetic scenario that now lies immediately ahead for America, we must first of all discover the long hidden ancestry of the nation. The time has come for the removal of the veil that for centuries has lain over the face of America. Recognizing the *"Israel of the Covenant,"* that the Prophets of the Bible were addressing is the one key capable of unlocking our understanding. It is also the key to future survival as a great nation and people. That key question is... **Who are you, America?**

CHAPTER ONE

Lost Key to Understanding End-time Prophecy

A major key that enables the diligent enquirer to unlock the secrets hidden within the prophesies of the Tanach (the name used in Judaism for the canon of the Hebrew Bible), is the understanding that after King Solomon's reign, the Kingdom of Israel separated into two distinct nations, with the Kingdom of Judah in the south, and the kingdom of Israel in the north. The key that will unlock the prophesies of the Bible is the knowledge that when the prophets speak about Israel, they almost invariably refer to the northern Kingdom of Israel.

DID YOU KNOW: According to the Bible, ten out of the twelve tribes of Israel split away to form their own kingdom? (1Kings 12:16; 19-20.) That those ancient Israelite secessionists called their new nation, "Israel," located within the boundaries of their tribal territories, to the north of "Judah?" That the Assyrians subsequently invaded their country and took them into exile? (2 Kings 17:5-18.)

HAVE YOU HEARD: How those Israelites over time forgot their identity and became known as the Lost Ten Tribes? (Isaiah 1:3; Hosea 1:9; 7:8-10, Isaiah 42:16-20; 49:15-16, Yevamous 3, Kol HaTor.)

WERE YOU AWARE: Those lost tribes never returned to their ancestral lands, but that in the future they are destined to reunite with the Jews of "Judah?" (Ezekiel 37:19-22; & Zechariah 10:6-9). That in the meantime God has given them an important role to fulfil?

DID YOU REALIZE: The prophets indicated that major concentrations of the ten tribes of Israel were destined to be located at the coastal extremities of the earth such as North America, the British Isles, the coastal nations of North-western Europe, and Australia, New Zealand and South Africa? (Isaiah 11:12; 41: 1, 5, 8-9; 42:4, 10 & 12; 49:1, 6.) [See Yair Davidiy's books, as listed in the bibliography for exact details]. The Oral Torah has many references to all of this, for example see the book of Ovadyah, see comments of Rashi, Arbarbenel, Tanchuma, Targum Yonatan etc.)

DID YOU EVER PERCEIVE: America was prophesied to become the richest and most powerful nation on the earth and was destined to control most of the major strategic bases in the world? If you don't believe it, check it for yourself by looking up these Scriptures! (Genesis 27:28-29; Deuteronomy 33:13-17; Hosea 2:8; Numbers 24:5-9; Micah 5:7-9; Genesis 22:17-18.)

DID YOU ALSO UNDERSTAND: That every heraldic symbol or emblem on America's Great Seal, the Presidential Seal, as well as the famous U.S. dollar bill, point directly to America's Israelite origins?

FINALLY, CAN YOU COMPREHEND: That all the above points, plus many more, confirm that the people of America are among the descendants of those Lost Tribes of Israel?

There you have it in a nutshell! The Bible, undisputedly the world's most widely published book, and the one book we can find in almost everyone's bookcase, has said it all. The irony is that in its pages there lies hidden a key which has remained undiscovered for most of its readers, yet it is this key that points the diligent enquirer to the present day whereabouts of the lost tribes of Israel. Thus the Bible, that most neglected of all books, has laid it all out for us. It is only when we understand the true ancestry of the English speaking peoples that we can possibly recognize the end-time prophecies of the Bible, as they refer to the future of America in conjunction with the State of Israel!

None of the above contradicts the fact that there are also great haters of the nation of Israel mixed in with 10 Israel! The Ten Tribes of Israel themselves anciently were at odds with, and became fierce enemies to the southern kingdom of Judah during its long history. It must be said that even today being of ancient 10 Israel stock is not a guarantee of fair mindedness and love of the present day Jewish State of Israel!

The pages of the Bible explain the reason for America's extraordinary prosperity and universal influence, as being due to the long hidden ancestry of her people. Her cultural, economic, technological and military dominance lies in the simple fact that she is descended from those lost Israelite sons of Jacob, with Manasseh, the son of Joseph, the thirteenth tribe of Israel being the most dominant and ruling tribe! She has come to her success as a direct result of the "Birthright" Covenant which the God of Israel, the Rock of Ages, made with the Patriarch Abraham, the ancestral father of the vast majority of all American citizens.

American society, both Christian and secular, perceives Israel as one nation! The truth is that the Bible, Israel's unique history book, tells us that the Israel of King David and King Solomon became TWO NATIONS! (1 Kings 12: 19-24).

After the ten tribes of Israel had rebelled and seceded from the House of David: *Rehoboam came to Jerusalem, and gathered the entire House of Judah and the tribe of Benjamin, one hundred eighty thousand choice warriors, to fight against the House of Israel, to return the kingship to Rehoboam son of Solomon. The word of God then came to Shemaiah, the man of God, saying, "Speak to Rehoboam son of Solomon, king of Judah, and to all the House of Judah and Benjamin and to the rest of the people, saying, Thus said HASHEM:*

"Do not go up and fight with your brethren, the children of Israel; let each man return to his home, for this matter was brought about by Me!" (1 Kings 12:24, emphasis added).

HASHEM wanted a separation between Judah and Israel because He had a separate role for each nation to fulfill. Hence the prophetic word: "THIS MATTER IS FROM ME!" However when the northern Kingdom went into exile the Bible clearly shows how they had broken the covenant and in direct consequence, their status as official Hebrews was severed. From here on they would have the legal status of sons and daughters of Noah's covenant, albeit of Israelite stock. Over time those xiles progressively forgot their own Hebrew origins. The Hebrews who survived, namely the Jewish people, maintained their Hebrew identity simply because, unlike 10 Israel, they largely remained faithful to the Sinai covenant of their fathers. The fact that God had a separate destiny for the two nations of Israel is overlooked by most Bible scholars and historians. Nevertheless, this truth is one of the most important keys to understanding our times.

It is a matter of historical record that King David's United Kingdom of Israel, after the reign of Solomon, was divided into two parts. In the South was Judah with Jerusalem as its capital, and in the North the other ten tribes, known as Israel, were located. The two kingdoms were to fulfill their separate destinies with a great purpose being worked out in each nation. A further vital key to understanding end-time prophecy is that the covenant God made with Abraham is comprised of at least two distinctive parts. God swore an oath by Himself that the blessings he had pronounced would come to all future descendants of Abraham. These blessings can therefore from one viewpoint be simply divided in two sections:

1. *The Promise of the Sceptre*

2. *The Promise of the Birthright*

The Promise of the Sceptre

This blessing was referred to in the words: *"And all the families of the earth shall bless themselves by you"* (Genesis 12:3), and also: *"and kings shall descend from you"* (Genesis 17:6). Yet the full meaning of the promise only becomes clear two generations later when Jacob, whilst on his deathbed, pronounces the following prophetic blessing on his son Judah:

"The sceptre shall not depart from Judah, nor a scholar from among his descendants until Shiloh [that is to say, the Messiah] arrives; and his will be an assemblage of nations" (Genesis 49:10).

From this we see that Judah's commission was to bring forth, *"Shiloh,"* the Messiah, from a royal line of kings and to be the *"lawgiver,"* by preserving the Law of God, (the Torah), for the benefit of all of mankind. By this promise of the sceptre, Judah is given an awesome *"spiritual"* calling. The Jewish people today are the modern descendants of that tribe, as well as the inheritors of that great *spiritual* calling. Judah was charged with the preservation of God's Word. This is the meaning of *"a scholar from among his descendants,"* which the King James Bible translates as: *"a lawgiver not departing from between his feet."* The word *"lawgiver"* perhaps does convey the calling of Judah more clearly, as it is only Judah which has preserved the Torah from the day it was given at Mount Sinai right down to our time today. It is only the Jewish nation that has "walked the walk" so to speak, as they have walked in the Torah. Without the diligence of the Jews we would have never heard of the Ten Commandments upon which America's constitution and laws are based. As history is our witness, without the Jewish nation the world would not have the benefit of God's Word. After all, it is the Jewish scribes who meticulously preserved and recorded the Torah (the books of the Law of Moses containing God's instruction to mankind) and most meticulously copied the Torah scrolls with incredible diligence and devotion throughout all their generations. They also perfectly preserved the Writings and the Psalms, as well as the testimonies and pronouncements of the prophets of Israel. The prophet Isaiah gives a prophecy which sums up the conclusion of a process that has been going on for thousands of years:

"For from Zion will the Torah come forth, and the word of HASHEM from Jerusalem." (Isaiah 2:3).

In those brief words Isaiah sums up the *"HOPE OF ISRAEL!"* This Messianic hope is the establishment of the Kingdom of God on the earth. It speaks of the restoration of Israel with all its twelve tribes being re-gathered into one Kingdom of Peace with the Messiah of Israel, the "Sar Shalom," (Prince of Peace), reigning from Mount Zion in Jerusalem for a thousand years. (Ezekiel 37:21-28) 1

It is this glorious Messianic vision of hope that stands at the very center of the spiritual mission which the Patriarch Jacob passed on to Judah nearly four thousand years ago. The truth is that without the Jews the world would have missed out on the immeasurable blessing of the Bible. Even the New Testament is essentially a Jewish book, although not accepted by the Jews as a divine document. Its central character of

Nazareth, according to its story, was a Jew, and so were all of the apostolic writers and authors of the new (renewed) Testament. John confirms the spiritual calling of the Jews when he informs us that: *"Salvation is of the Jews"* (John 4:22 KJV). In other words even according to the NT, the Jews are of salvation and in no need of missionary intervention. They simply need to keep the Torah that was entrusted to them under the loving guidance of their pious sages. (See: Deut. 17).

The Promise of the Birthright

The lives of the patriarchs are meant to be spiritual role models. Abraham was called the *"father of the faithful,"* and every move he made and every word he spoke carried prophetic significance for his descendants. This was true of all the patriarchs of Israel.

The blessing of the birthright was contained in God's further words to Abraham, *"I will make you most exceedingly fruitful, and make nations of you; and kings shall descend from you."* (Genesis 17:6). Notice it says, "I will make nations of you!" Thus if we were to find the illustrious inheritors of this Birthright Promise we would have to look for *exceedingly fruitful "NATIONS,"* (plural), rather than for "A NATION." * [1]

A key promise contained in the covenant of the "Birthright Blessing" was that the descendants of Abraham would be exceedingly numerous. *"I shall surely bless you and greatly increase your offspring like the stars of the heavens and like the sand on the seashore!"* (Genesis 22:17).

Most of us are familiar with the biblical account of Esau, the firstborn son of Isaac, selling his birthright to Jacob for a bowl of stew (Genesis 25:31-34). Jacob on his deathbed passed on the blessing of the birthright to Joseph. (Genesis 49:22-26.) This blessing was an exceedingly special blessing to have, as the words, *"I will make you most exceedingly fruitful,"* implied a promise of great physical wealth, as well as great strength and a position of leadership. When we examine the evidence later on we will find that Joseph, too, fulfilled his divinely ordained commission. The fact that this blessing went to Joseph is subsequently confirmed in the book of Chronicles, where it states:

"The sons of Reuben, the firstborn of Israel. (He was the firstborn, but when he defiled his father's bed his birthright was given to the sons of Joseph, son of Israel, although not to receive the hereditary right of the firstborn, for Judah prevailed over his brothers, and the ruler was to come from him; but the firstborn's portion was Joseph's)." (1Chronicles 5:1-2).

If we are to recognize the descendants of Joseph in the world today we need to look for many exceedingly fruitful, most populous and incredibly blessed nations, who in turn have been a blessing to all the nations on the earth. The nations who were to inherit the "birthright" would have to become the most powerful nations and achieve exceptional success in all their endeavors, if they were to be the source of physical blessings to all the peoples of the world.

A Dual Covenant

Judah's Sceptre calling is primarily of a *"spiritual"* nature, and this commission remained with the kingdom of Judah. The Jewish people today are the modern day descendants of that kingdom, as well as the inheritors of that great calling.

Joseph's Birthright commission appears to be of a more *"physical"* kind. Joseph's calling is to become *"many nations"* that are to become *"exceedingly fruitful"* and *"as the stars of the heaven and as the sand which is on the seashore,"* and a source of physical blessing to all the nations of the earth. Here we can deduce from God's promise that through Abraham's seed *"all the families of the earth shall be blessed"* has a dual application. Firstly it speaks of a *"Spiritual"* blessing coming through the *"Sceptre,"* and secondly it speaks of a *"Physical"* blessing flowing from the *"Birthright."* Already here in the book of Genesis we see conflict with the commonly held beliefs of the Church regarding Israel. The Christian Church at large, and much of the world besides, maintains Israel to be only one nation, whereas the Bible informs us that the descendants of Abraham are to become one nation subdivided into many nations! (Genesis 17:19). Judah too will be found amongst those nations descended through Abraham's son Isaac.

Abraham's wife, Sarah, to be "a Mother of Nations"

Identical promises were given separately to Abraham's wife, Sarah, in Genesis 17:16, *"I will bless her; indeed, I will give you a son [Isaac] through her; I will bless her and she shall give rise to nations; kings of peoples will rise from her."* Notice, she is not to become "a mother of A NATION," but that she is to become *"A MOTHER OF NATIONS,"* (plural)! The Bible states that the matriarch Sarah is to become "a mother of nations," (plural), clearly inferring many nations. It is only as we understand the reality that Israel split into two kingdoms, each going its separate way, that this prophecy can possibly make any sense. Everyone knows where the Jewish people are located. However, the question is, "Where are Sarah's other nations today?" Is it not reasonable to want to know more about those nations?

Abraham's Descendants to Become an Innumerable Multitude

Where is this "great multitude" the divine covenant speaks of? Israel today is a tiny country surrounded by hostile Arab nations. Only some five-and-a-half million Jews live in Israel, and the other Jews in the world number no more than ten million. Where then are these innumerable multitudes promised to Abraham's descendants through his son Isaac? Surely a population of only fifteen million cannot count as being *"descendants as the stars of the heaven and as the sand which is on the seashore?"* Perhaps it means that over the span of thousands of years they would be counted a tremendous multitude. The verse may very well also mean something in addition! Even allowing for the use of metaphor or hyperbole, these expressions lead one to think of huge numbers.

The "replacement theology" endemic in the Christian Church has tended to spiritualize this promise away, by stating that the Christians are this innumerable multitude. Strange as it may seem, the irony is that there may possibly even be some truth in this, as when we read Genesis 48:14-16, we find that Jacob speaks of, *"an angelic messenger who redeemed him from all evil."* He then crosses his arms to bless the two sons of Joseph. As he does so, he makes the sign of the Hebrew letter *"Tav"* over his grandsons, and in that ancient script it pictographically means "seal, covenant, or sign of the covenant." He then prophesies that they are to grow into a multitude in the midst of the earth, or as the original Hebrew text puts it: *"May they proliferate abundantly like fish."*

Notice, that just prior to the astounding blessing upon the two sons of Joseph, Jacob saw Joseph's sons, and said, *"Who are these?"* This is not a happy or positive hint of possible future signs of identification. For his question, *"Who are these?"* is surely strange. For he knew that there in front of him stood the two sons of Joseph. In this we have an indication that the Divine Spirit helped him to see prophetically how some terrible evil kings would emerge from those two lads, causing his descendants to break the covenant leading to exile, loss of identity and dispersion amongst the pagan nations of the world. His query indicates that he did not recognize their future descendants, as he saw evil kids coming from his presently wonderful grandchildren. Maybe, he hesitated as he saw something that made him doubt if the blessing should be given to them!

Nevertheless, the question remains, who are these multitudinous descendants who have a sign of the cross and the fish as their symbols and who speak of a Redeemer, [angel/messenger] who saves them from all evil? The implication we can derive from Jacob's words and actions, as he blessed his two grandsons, is that the lost tribes may very well be coming out of a Christian background and may well be numbered among the numerous gentile descendants of Ephraim and Manasseh, those two sons of Joseph. Great sages of the Jewish people, [Rashi, Arbarbenel etc.], have written that the western European peoples have roots in the HEBREW LOST TRIBES. Again, examine Yair Davidiy's research, [i.e. his book Ephraim], for further details.

However, this still leaves us with the problem that this theory does not explain God's specific promise that Abraham would become *a father of many nations,* and his wife Sarah would become *a mother of nations.* From what we have seen so far we can reasonably conclude that those nations are likely to be Christian. We are dealing here with one of the greatest unsolved mysteries history has bequeathed us. Where are those other nations and innumerable non-Jewish mainly Christian descendants of Abraham? *2

The secret lies with the twelve sons of Jacob

After years in exile, Jacob had an encounter with God, during which his name was changed to Israel. His new name "Israel," means, "prevailer" or "champion of God," and it reflected his new character and identity. This same Jacob was the father of twelve sons, the children of Israel, who subsequently grew into the Twelve Tribes of Israel. After the conquest of the Promised Land, each of these tribes was awarded its own territory and each of them maintained its own tribal identity and leadership. To discover the present day whereabouts of those hidden Israelite nations and those missing innumerable multitudes of the Abrahamic Covenant we need to look among those tribes of Israel. The question is: what has become of them?

CHAPTER TWO

Israel Becomes Two Nations, Each With its Own Distinct Calling and Destiny

The Sons of Joseph to Inherit the Birthright Blessing

In about 1700 BCE Jacob/Israel pronounced the promise of the Birthright blessing upon the heads of his two grandsons, Ephraim and Manasseh, the two sons of Joseph. We read in Genesis 48:14-21 about the blessing pronounced by Jacob upon these two lads. Ephraim, the younger son was accorded the privileges of the firstborn. This in terms of status made Ephraim the primary leader or Chief of the Tribes of Israel. What we need to realize is that every move the Patriarch Jacob made and every word he spoke held prophetic significance for his descendants. This is true of the lives of all the patriarchs of the Hebrews.

Many centuries later, following Solomon's death in 931 BCE, division occurred and the Sceptre of Judah and the Birthright of Israel were separated. (See: 1 Kings 11:28-35 & 1 Kings 12:1-24). Coincidentally, the American nation too was forged in the heat of war, rebelling against British rule in the name of freedom and self-government. The catalyst for that War of Independence was the issue of taxation. Here history was repeating itself, as the Ten Tribes of Israel also rebelled over this same issue of taxation, and they too seceded from their mother country to form their own kingdom. This is how the SCEPTRE family of Judah and the BIRTHRIGHT family of Joseph each became the head and representative of a distinct nation, or commonwealth. Each nation now developed independently of the other to fulfill their separate respective destinies.

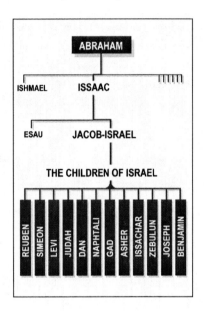 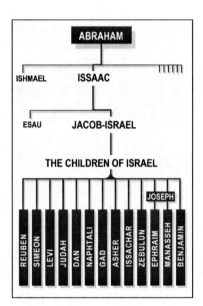

The Name Israel Belongs Partially to the Sons of Joseph

Each of the two nations, Judah and Israel, thus had their own distinct role and purpose in the world. The greatest irony is that the Jewish nation today is called Israel, whilst the actual Nation and Kingdom of Israel, in direct fulfillment of the covenant, has become gentile *"many nations"* and goes by various other names. The Jewish State that we see in the Middle East today does not constitute "all" of Israel, as it represents only a small proportion of the full house of Israel. The name Israel actually belongs to the descendants of the two sons of Joseph, Ephraim and Manasseh, as emphasized in the Birthright blessing which Jacob pronounced over the two lads, when he said: *LET MY NAME be declared upon them"* (Genesis 48:16). Thus the two sons of Joseph INHERIT the name "Israel." The Jewish people are primarily comprised of the tribes of Judah and Benjamin and some of the tribe of Levi. Simeon, whose tribal territory was located south-west of Judah, also partially merged with Judah. The name of their kingdom was called Judah, with Jerusalem as the capital. The other ten tribes seceded from the House of David to establish the kingdom of Israel, with Samaria as the capital city. Israelite refugees from the Assyrian invasions also joined Judah, whilst at the same time some of Judah's territory became occupied by the Assyrians and consequently many from Judah fell into captivity and were exiled together with the northern kingdom of Israel. Both nations together comprise the twelve tribes, and all are Israelites, descended from the patriarchs Abraham, Isaac and Jacob.

Judgment Upon the Kingdom of Israel

During the approx. 210 years of Israel's independent existence from approx 931 BCE until absorption by the Assyrian Empire in around 721 BCE, her ten tribes were ruled by a succession of evil kings who repeatedly broke their covenant relationship with God. They led many of the nations into moral depravity through the worship of false pagan gods, which led to a proliferation of the occult and witchcraft. The land became lawless and filled with violence, and the people practiced the most grisly non-Hebrew rites, even the forbidden Moloch cult. God sent many prophets to warn them of His impending judgment. This finally came as the warlike Assyrian Empire made its third and final attack in 721 BC when the remaining population of the Kingdom of Israel was taken into captivity. The Scriptures faithfully record the event:

"Then HASHEM became very angry with Israel and removed them from His Presence; none remained except the tribe of Judah alone" (2 Kings 17:18).

Shalmanezer III, the King of Asyria, receiving tribute from Jehu King of Israel—Black Obelisk, British Museum

Judgment Upon the Kingdom of Judah

Over a century and a quarter later, the Kingdom of Judah suffered the same fate as her northern neighbor, the reason being that many of them too had departed from their sacred covenant with God by embracing pagan gods and consequently sinking into a hedonistic morass of depravity and lawlessness. Once again, many warnings had been given, and during 604-581 BC Judah suffered three successive invasions and was finally overthrown by the King of Babylon. Almost the entire population was taken into captivity to Babylon.

Judah Returns to Her Ancestral Land

The Jews were to suffer seventy long years of captivity in Babylon, but their plight was considerably eased after the Persians defeated the Babylonians. By the special dispensation of King Cyrus of Persia, some 50,000 Jews returned to Jerusalem to rebuild the Temple under the leadership of Ezra and Nehemiah. Thus a remnant of the House of Judah returned to the land to fulfill their *"spiritual Sceptre"* commission of becoming a source of *"Spiritual" blessing* to all the nations of the world.

Israel Never Comes Back

The Bible, which is the history book of God's dealings with His chosen nation Israel, does not record the House of Israel ever returning to its tribal lands to the north of Judah, and neither does secular history. Thus the Ten Tribes of Israel have become known as THE LOST HOUSE OF ISRAEL or THE LOST TEN TRIBES! The reason they were not permitted to return to their ancestral lands is because they too have yet to fulfill their divinely ordained prophetic commission. They are to become the prophesied, *"innumerable multitude"* walking in their *"Birthright"* destiny, to bring untold *"physical" blessings* to all the nations and families of the world.

A most important spiritual requirement for the return to the Land of Promise by 10 Israel is that above all other considerations, they need to return to their Hebrew Roots and the pure faith of their patriarchal fathers, Abraham, Isaac and Jacob. Before they even attempt to return to their older brother Judah they need to repent in the full realization that they are the ones who have broken the Divine Covenant. They need to deeply repent also of the myriads of heinous crimes committed against their brother Judah by their Christian ancestors throughout the past two thousand years. They cannot return demanding this or that, as the only proper way for them to return is with a humble heart and a contrite spirit and by showing the right kind of respect towards Judah, their senior brother.

The NT Writers Knew Where the Lost Sheep of the House of Israel Were

In the New Testament, when it tells of the Nazarene sending His disciples out preaching, He specifically told them NOT to go to the Gentiles, NOR to the cities of the Samaritans, *"but go rather to the lost sheep of the house of Israel."* (Matthew 10: 6). Both the Nazarene and His disciples clearly knew where the *"lost sheep of the house of Israel"* could be found! This same NT figure—when accosted by a Gentile woman seeking deliverance for her daughter—said to her:

"I was not sent EXCEPT to the lost sheep of the house of Israel" (Matthew 15: 24, emphasis added).

By this He revealed the actual purpose of His mission. He was sent to rescue the *"lost sheep"* of the house of Israel. He was *primarily* referring to those ten lost tribes of Israel who never returned from their captivity, as well as to those of the house of Judah amongst whom He performed His ministry. In John 10: 16 Jesus said:

"And other sheep I have which are not of this fold; them also I must bring, and they will hear My voice; and they will be one flock and one shepherd."

Notice, He yearned for those other sheep, (*the lost sheep of the house of Israel*), with whom He was in covenant relationship through God's word to Abraham, the *"fold"* being the Jews of the tribes of Judah and Benjamin! His reference to both folds becoming one flock with one shepherd was a reference to the prophesied reunification of the two houses of Israel.

Future reunification of Israel and Judah is prophesied

This ultimate restoration of Israel and Judah is referred to a number of times by the prophet Jeremiah:

"For behold, days are coming—the word of HASHEM—when I will return the captivity of My people Israel and Judah, said HASHEM, and I will return them to the land that I gave to their forefathers, and they will possess it." These are the things HASHEM spoke concerning Israel and concerning Judah" (Jeremiah 30:3-4, emphasis added).

The prophet refers to two distinct sets of captives saying:

"And I will return the captivity of Judah and the captivity of Israel, and will rebuild them as at first" (Jeremiah 33:7, emphasis added).

Jeremiah also prophesies a New Covenant at the end of days in the future that will apply to both covenant nations:

"Behold, days are coming—the word of HASHEM—when I will seal a new covenant with the house of Israel and with the house of Judah." (Jeremiah 31:30, emphasis added).

Ezekiel prophesies the ultimate future reunification of the two houses of Israel:

"Thus said the LORD HASHEM/ELOHIM: "Behold, I am taking the wood of Joseph, which is in the hand of Ephraim, and the tribes of Israel, his comrades, and I am placing them and him together with the wood of Judah, and I will make them into one piece of wood, and they will become one in My hand..... will make them into one nation in the land, upon the mountains of Israel, and one king will be a king for them all; they will no longer be TWO NATIONS, and they will no longer be divided into TWO KINGDOMS, ever again" (Ezekiel 37:19,22, emphasis added).

The wood in the hands of both Ephraim and Judah mentioned by Ezekiel above may well be a reference to the Torah itself, as may be implied by the prophet in verse 20:

"The pieces of wood upon which you will write shall be in your hand, before their eyes."

After all, there are two pieces of wood, or two sticks in each Torah scroll, furthermore both houses of Israel have access to the Bible, where in hundreds of places the ultimate restoration between the long separated houses of Israel and Judah is mentioned. Thus they both have the evidence [*the wood/sticks*] before their eyes. Ezekiel may possibly even have been referring to his own statement, as it refers to the pieces of wood being in his own hand! He no doubt was aware, as he was writing those prophetic words about the reunification of the two houses of Israel, that his words would be preserved for all time and for all future generations.

Flavius Josephus Also Knew Where Those Lost Tribes of Israel Were

An authoritative testimony comes from the Jewish historian Flavius Josephus, who said that: *"The Ten Tribes are beyond Euphrates till now,* [approx. 100 AD], *and are an immense multitude and not to be estimated by numbers!"* [*1] Notice that even in those days Josephus describes those missing ten tribes as an *"immense multitude."* Josephus also wrote: *"The entire body of the people, (the ten tribes), of ISRAEL remained in that country, wherefore there are but Two Tribes, (Judah and Benjamin), in Asia and Europe subject to the Romans."*

Here we have a renowned secular historian of the time confirming more than 600 years after the return of the Jews to the Promised Land from their exile in Babylon that the Ten Tribes of Israel had still not returned from beyond the Euphrates River. Josephus knew that their population had become too numerous to estimate, and that the Euphrates River served as their western border. History records that they never did return, and, as we have already seen, the New Testament through the words of the Nazarene Himself confirms the fact. So, where are these missing Israelites? What has become of them?

Lost Forever?

Clearly, the Israelite populations beyond the Euphrates River, which Josephus described as an *immense multitude,* cannot simply have vanished into thin air. After the Assyrian empire was destroyed in 612 BCE by

Babylon, ably assisted by Scythian, e.g. Israelite tribes, the captive tribes of Israel freed themselves and over time established kingdoms and empires of their own. [*2] The prophet Amos tells us of God's intent for them:

"For behold, I decree that I will SHAKE OUT the House of Israel among all THE nations, as [grain] is shaken in a sieve, and not a pebble falls to the ground" (Amos 9:9, emphasis added)

Here we have a sure promise that God would "*SIFT*" the massive populations of the Israelite tribes through the nations of the earth, but that He would preserve them as a people. They might lose their identity but they would be kept intact even when mixed with other peoples. Moreover, not one of them would be lost to God. All serious students of the Bible recognize that Israel features as a key player in God's purposes, as evidenced by end-time prophecy. This begs the question: "Where are these mysterious and multitudinous Israelites today?"

Chapter Three

The Gentile "Birthright" Sons of Joseph are Found Within the British Empire & the United States of America!

The Covenant Promises Were Meant for Our Time

A vital key to identifying these lost Israelite tribes is to understand that the promises of the Birthright covenant were to be realized in our time. Jacob commanded that his name, "Israel," be placed on Ephraim and Manasseh, the two sons of Joseph (Gen 48:16). He made it clear that the words he was about to speak were to be fulfilled at the end of the age.

"Then Jacob called for his sons and said, "assemble yourselves and I will tell you what will befall you in the End of Days." (Genesis 49:1-2).

Bible scholars agree that the reference to the *"END of DAYS"* refers to modern times and the end of the age. To determine exactly when these "End Days" come into being for the prophetic promises to be fulfilled, we need to look for another clue.

Israel Was to Become a "Nation and a Company of Nations"

After Jacob's vision, known ever since as the vision of *"Jacob's ladder"* (Genesis 28), he had yet another encounter with God, in which the Abrahamic covenant was further amplified.

"Your name shall not always be called Jacob, but Israel shall be your name." And God said to him: "I am El Shaddai. Be fruitful and multiply; a nation and a congregation of nations shall descend from you, and kings shall issue from your loins" (Genesis 35:10b–11, emphasis added).

At the end of his life the Patriarch Jacob pronounced this same blessing on the heads of the two sons of Joseph. Jacob spoke as follows:

"He [Manasseh] too will become a people, and he too will become great; yet his younger brother shall become greater than he, and his offspring's [fame] will fill the nations." So he blessed them that day, saying, "By you shall Israel bless, saying, "May God make you like Ephraim and Manasseh!—and he put Ephraim before Manasseh"" (Genesis 48:19-20).

Here we see the "Birthright" blessing being placed upon the heads of the two sons of Joseph. One of these, in *"the last days,"* is to become a "congregation" or commonwealth of "nations," whilst the other is to become a *great people* or *great nation*.

The most remarkable possible fulfillment of Bible prophecy in modern times was the sudden arrival of the two mightiest world powers in the history of our planet. One was a Commonwealth of Nations that became the greatest empire the world has ever seen. The other, having been birthed by her, was to become the wealthiest and most powerful single nation that has ever existed on the earth.

This is the remarkable real-life story of the British Empire and the United States of America. The British Empire was utterly unique in that there has never been a "Commonwealth" of nations, in all of world history. Likewise, America's global power has no historical precedent. It is in these two nations that the two sons of Joseph stand identified before the world today. Great Britain represents gentile Ephraim, as she became that great "congregation of nations," whereas America represents Manasseh, who was to become a "great people or nation." It is upon these two peoples that the extraordinary "Birthright" blessing has been bestowed, and it is they who have given the world the language of liberty and freedom. The name Joseph literally means *"let him add"* and is synonymous with prosperity.

Great Britain and America alone have walked in the footsteps of Joseph, in that they have brought unheard prosperity and advancement to the world.

The extraordinary ancestry of Great Britain and America is confirmed even in the Hebrew language, as "BRIT" is the Hebrew word for "COVENANT," whereas "ISH" is the Hebrew word for "MAN." Thus the term "British" literally means "COVENANT MAN" or "MAN of the COVENANT."

In the case of America we have a similar situation, as the Hebrew term for the "UNITED STATES OF AMERICA" is "ARSOT HABRIT," which literally stands for "STATES OF THE COVENANT."

Jacob's Last Will and Testament

Jacob, the great Patriarch of Israel, passed on the "Blessing of the Birthright" to Ephraim and Manasseh, the sons of Joseph, jointly, whilst he was on his deathbed. The fact that this was pronounced on the deathbed of Jacob gives the blessing extra power and spiritual authority. This deathbed blessing was in effect Jacob's last will and testament, and it was legally binding in God's sight.

They Were to Become Great Colonizers

Jacob prophesied over his son Joseph, "A charming son is Joseph, a charming son to the eye; each of the girls climbed heights to gaze." (Genesis 49: 22 - Stone Edition Chumash). Others interpret this verse as comparing Joseph to a prolific vine or tree growing luxuriantly by a spring, whose boughs or vines surge upward over the surrounding walls. This alludes to Joseph's offspring or to Joseph himself.*1 The KJV interprets it as follows:"Joseph is a fruitful bough, a fruitful bough by a well; his branches run over the wall." The term, "A fruitful bough by a well" indicates an enormously productive and prosperous people who live in close proximity to the sea, whereas the phrase, "His branches run over the wall" indicates that the sons of Joseph would not be a stay-at-home kind of people. They were to be a colonizing people, their colonies branching out from their shores to the four corners of the world. This aspect has been especially fulfilled by the British, who have been the greatest colonizers the world has ever seen.

Britain and America are Brothers!

The relationship between siblings is always a special one—"*blood is thicker than water.*" Is it not interesting to note that ever since America gained its independence, the world has perceived "A SPECIAL RELATIONSHIP" between America and Great Britain? Once having understood who these two brothers are, is it any wonder that there is indeed a special relationship? History testifies that in times of great crisis America and Great Britain have invariably come to the aid of each other to defeat the threat. This occurred in the First and the Second World Wars, the Cold War, both Gulf Wars, as well as in the present ongoing conflict against the Taliban in Afghanistan. A most intriguing aspect is that in each conflict destiny has produced leaders in both nations, who were not only especially compatible to each other, but also men made for the crisis. This is true for the unique partnership between Roosevelt and Churchill in the Second World War, and for J. F. Kennedy and Harold Macmillan during the Cuban Missile Crisis at the height of the Cold War, as it was for Ronald Reagan and Margaret Thatcher in defeating the evil communist empire of the former Soviet Union. We witness the same pattern in more recent times in the extraordinary partnership between President George W. Bush and Tony Blair. It is by divine providence that these brother nations have this "special relationship."

Sadly, with the election of President Obama the picture has changed dramatically, as time and again he has shown his personal antipathy towards Britain by taking great pains to insult and affront America's closest friend, strongest partner, and most reliable ally. For sheer offensiveness it's hard to beat the incredible statement on the Falklands dispute with Argentina, where the State Department declared itself to be neutral over the Falklands. "The US recognizes de facto UK administration of the islands but takes no position on the sovereignty claims of either party." Considering the fact that 255 British soldiers died retaking the islands in 1982, this latest announcement surely takes the biscuit as the most brazen betrayal of an US ally. The Special Relationship has been downgraded by the Obama administration where London is treated in Washington, as though it were the same as any other European power, albeit less charitably than either Paris or Berlin. Then there is the deliberate undermining of British influence in NATO, this despite the fact that Great Britain provides more troops for NATO operations than any member apart from the United States. This is evident by the fact that there is currently not a single British General in charge of any of the big five supreme and operational commands (in contrast to two Frenchmen and a German). On top of this there is the refusal to recognize Britain's sacrifice in Afghanistan. It is especially galling that the president cannot even be bothered to acknowledge the sacrifice made by over 384, (as at 11/7/11), British servicemen on the battlefields of Afghanistan alongside their American allies. This casualty figure represents not less than 66% of the total number of deaths suffered by the coalition excluding the U.S.A. President Obama's attitude was especially evident during his lacklustre speech at West Point in December 2009. Britain has currently as many soldiers stationed in Afghanistan (10,000), as all the other major European powers combined. In contrast to George W Bush, who frequently thanked the British armed forces and people for their role in the War on Terror, Obama has spectacularly failed to do so. The list of deliberate slights get longer by the day and varies from the bust of Winston Churchill being thrown out of the Oval Office, to the embarrassing treatment meted out to the British Prime Minister at the White House in March 2009, which can be summed up by the mocking statement by a senior State Department official, who said: "There is nothing special about Britain. You're just the same as 190 other countries in the world, and you shouldn't expect special treatment."*2

Chapter Four

America's Ancient Birthmark

America's Great Seal is one of the clearest and most potent symbols of her heritage as a gentile nation with Israelite roots. Just as the Royal Coat of Arms of Great Britain, with its famous supporters of the Lion and the Unicorn, conveys her lost Israelite ancestry, so likewise do the arms of the United States of America. America's Great Seal is tantamount to a birthmark on a human body. Now you may be able to take on a false name, obtain a bogus birth certificate and carry a fake passport, but you cannot forge an indelible birthmark. In the case of having to report a missing person the police will invariably ask for a recent photograph and general description of the person. They will want to know what clothing he or she was wearing, when last seen, etc. Yet, what will help them the most in their search are any significant marks of identification such as scars, tattoos or birthmarks. Of all of these identifying signs, a birthmark is considered the clearest of all because it is indelible.

The historians of this world have largely ignored the significance of heraldry in its role of identifying the origins of the person, nation or institution. Nevertheless, heraldry is the most consistent and accurate form of identification. This is because its successive owners jealously guard the rights to their heraldic property. The Great Seal of America is not only a badge of identity—it is much more than that, as it serves as the inescapable and indelible birthmark of the United States of America. It tells the world exactly who you are!

Significance of Number Thirteen in American Heraldry

Ephraim was the leading tribe of the sons of Joseph, as God declares through his prophet Jeremiah: *"Ephraim is my firstborn"* (Jeremiah 31:9). What then of the United States? The fact that America began with 13 Colonies is highly significant. This number 13 is stamped all over the heraldry of the United States.

It was on July 14 1777 that Congress officially sanctioned the American flag. The Congressional resolution stated: *"Resolved that the flag of the United States be 13 stripes, alternate red and white; that the union be 13 stars, white on a blue field."*

Some 84 years later, in April 1861, at the battle of "Bull Run" in Manassas, at the beginning of the Civil War, the Confederate flag was given a red background with two crossed blue stripes containing 13 stars. Remember, that heraldry is the most consistent and accurate form of identification. Could it possibly be that this number 13 is in some way connected with Manasseh, the thirteenth tribe of Israel?

It is a well-known almost universal superstition that the number thirteen is an unlucky number. Hotels, motels and guesthouses avoid listing their rooms as number thirteen and you will never find a hotel with a thirteenth floor! Yet, we find the number thirteen occurs all over American heraldry. Just think about this: thirteen original colonies, 13 signers of the Declaration of Independence, thirteen stripes on the U.S flag, thirteen rods in the National Mace, thirteen letters in America's national emblem, the "American Eagle." And for minorities: the 13th Amendment! The irony is that only those familiar with Jewish numerology, also known as gematria, know the significance of the number thirteen. Clearly, the founding fathers of America did understand the significance of this number and they especially chose to apply it, first to the thirteen colonies, and subsequently to most of the other visual images that together convey the identifying heraldry of the United States.

In the Hebrew language each letter of the alphabet, (alef bet), doubles up as a number, as there is no separate system of numbers. Thus the Hebrew letters are themselves the numbers, so Aleph (A) is 1, Bet (B) is 2 and so on. This means that each number or combination of numbers has a particular meaning. The number thirteen is the numeric value of the Hebrew word "ECHAD," which means "ONE," just as is highlighted in Deuteronomy 6:4, the verse that declares the eternal Mosaic pledge of Israel:

"Hear O'Israel: HASHEM is our God, HASHEM is the One and Only."

This immediately gives a completely different meaning to the number thirteen. It is also happens to be the numerical value of *"Ahava,"* which is the Hebrew word for *"love."* No doubt the founding fathers intended to convey Oneness and Unity, when they especially singled out number thirteen. Once you start looking for links you will find them in all sorts of places. For instance the country was founded on *"July the Fourth,"* this date too is spelled with thirteen letters. The year the country was founded in was "76: 7+6=13. In the eagles right talon featured on America"s Great Seal there are thirteen leaves on the olive branch and there are also thirteen olives. When we add 13+13, we get a sum total of 26, which just so happens to be the numerical value of YHVH, God's Holy Name. This is made up of the Hebrew letters Yod (Y)=10, Hey (H)=5, Vav (V)=6 and Hey (H)=5. With the number 26 thus concealed in the right talon of the eagle and the number 13 in the left, it would seem there is a hidden message saying that the God of Israel (26) is ONE, e.g. (13)! In this too the founding fathers were indicating the Israelite origins of the nation.

Heraldry—an Ancient and Most Accurate Science

In the legends and works of art in ancient Greece, there is a record of the emblems used by both sides in the Trojan War. In Israel's biblical history we find that each of the Twelve Tribes of Israel had an emblem and that by HaShem's command these were in regular use during the forty years of wandering in the wilderness after their Exodus from Egypt. This is clearly stated in Numbers 2:2: *"The Children of Israel shall encamp, each man by his banner according to the insignias of their father's household, at a distance surrounding the Tent of meeting shall they encamp."* These badges were a means of identification, as their primary purpose was to distinguish between the different families, clans and tribes. So much for our heraldic experts who pronounce that heraldry originates in the Middle Ages, [around a thousand years ago], with the advent of the knights and their armor. Here we have clear evidence that these Israelite tribes stood by their tribal standards and their fathers' ensigns some three and a half thousand years ago! The Camp of Israel was divided into Four Brigades, with Judah in the east, Reuben in the south, Ephraim in the west and Dan in the north. To sum up the heraldic emblems of the Four Heads of Israel's Brigades: the standard of the Brigade of Judah was a Lion, the standard of the Brigade of Ephraim was an Ox, the standard of the Brigade of Dan was an Eagle, and the standard of the Brigade of Reuben was the Face of a Man.

Remember: the paramount purpose of heraldry is to identify! From the most ancient times, families, clans, tribes, cities and nations have used emblems and symbols as a means of identification. In the course of time, the world of heraldry evolved with banners, badges, shields and colors, not to forget Coats of Arms, all designed to promote particular identity and affiliation. Heraldry is not only one of the most ancient, but also one of the most accurate, sciences in the world. Thus we have family crests, coats of arms, clan and tribal emblems, tartans, national emblems and flags, religious symbols, church emblems, corporate logos and even football club emblems. They are all designed as badges of identity. The right to use these emblems invariably was jealously guarded, as it passed from generation to generation, and rarely, if ever, was the emblem of one family, tribe or city adopted by another. Because of this, the courts in both Europe and America have long since recognized the importance of heraldic emblems in tracing heirs and in identifying the ancestral roots of families. Had our historians, and especially the ethnologists among them, deigned to use this knowledge to track the history and movements of the lost ten tribes of Israel from their places of exile below the Caspian and Black Sea, their present day whereabouts would be common knowledge by now.

The Great Seal Declares America's Israelite Origins

The Great Seal of America shows the face of an eagle holding in its right claws an olive branch signifying peace, having 13 leaves and 13 olives, which taken together represent the ineffable and unutterable Name of the God of Israel. Notice also, that the "Olive Tree" is a symbol of

Israel, which ranks in importance with the seven-branched Menorah and the Star of David. In its left talons, the Eagle is holding 13 arrows portraying its power to fight. An Olive Branch and a Bundle of Arrows were the official emblems of the tribe of Manasseh, the elder son of Joseph (Genesis 49:22-23). Furthermore, on the Eagle's breast is a shield, having 13 bars and stripes, which represent the 13 original British Colonies. Above the Eagle's head are 13 stars arranged in the shape of the Star of David positioned within a cloud of glory. This cloud of glory is a representation of the mysterious "Pillar of Cloud" that hovered above the Tabernacle at the center of the "Camp of Israel" in the wilderness. This same Pillar of Cloud preceded the ancient Israelites in their forty years' sojourn through the desert after their exodus from Egypt. In the dry air of the Sinai wilderness of western Arabia this cloud would have been visible for many miles. To a distant observer it would have indicated the presence of Israel, even though the huge encampment itself could not be seen. Consequently, this cloud symbol in effect indicated the presence of Israel. The question surely is, "Why would America's Great Seal so emphatically indicate her Israelite heritage, if the nation's roots were not from ancient Israel?" Why does the Great Seal use those Israelite symbols? Why feature the name of HaShem, the Holy One of Israel? Why does the Star of David feature in it? Why is the "Pillar of Cloud" so prominently displayed above the eagle? Why would any nation convey its Israelite/Hebrew origins in this demonstrable way, if there is no truth to it?

The Star of David on U.S. Marine & British Officer Swords

The six-pointed star commonly known as the Star of David is a unique Israel symbol which, as the name implies, has royal connections with King David of Israel. Its correct name is "The Shield of David" or, in the Hebrew language, *"Magen David."* This symbol is thought to have its roots in the Ancient Paleo-Hebrew alphabet, very similar to the present Hebrew alphabet. In this old alphabet the equivalent of the English letter "D," *e.g.* the Hebrew letter *Dalet*, was shaped like a triangle. Thus this ancient, triangular shaped *Dalet* was used at both the beginning and the end of the name "DAVID." King David was the great warrior king of Israel, and the Israelite armies that were led by him bore the Star of David —two interlaced *Dalets* to signify the first and last letters of their King's name. In this we may surmise the origins of the term the "Shield of David" or in the Hebrew language the *"Magen David."*

The national flag of the State of Israel and the Israeli Armed Forces such as the IDF and IAF portray the Shield of David. This is an indication that they look upon it as a mark of Israelite identity and as clear support for their claim of descent from the people over whom the House of David reigned. Thus even in our modern times we can see that this emblem has been, and still is, used as evidence of a claimed relationship to ancient Israel and the Throne of David. This raises a stark question . . . .

If the State of Israel uses it as evidence in support of claimed continuity of the nation and people over which the House of David ruled, then "WHY DO THE UNITED STATES AND GREAT BRITAIN USE IT?"

"What do you mean, Why do the United States and Great Britain use it?" you may well ask. Incredible though it may sound, both the armed forces of America and Britain use the Shield of David all the time! The plain fact is that in the armed forces of both nations, officers receive their commission and their authority from the President in the case of the U.S., and from the Sovereign in the case of Great Britain. They are in effect an instrument and an extension respectively either of the President's or Sovereign's authority. The curious thing is that in both the United States of America and in Great Britain, the symbol of that authority is the Shield of David. In the United States only the officers in the Marines Corps receive this distinction. U.S. Marine Corps advertisements often display a fearsome Marine in a dress uniform drawing a beautiful sword. If you look carefully, you can clearly see the Star of David just below the hilt of the sword. If in doubt, ask any Marine! In Great Britain, all officers who pass out at Sandhurst, their military college, are given a sword, as a symbol of their commission. The emblem of the Star of David appears below the hilt of the sword of all commissioned officers in the British army owing allegiance to the British Crown.

America's Ancient Birthmark

The Covenant With Death

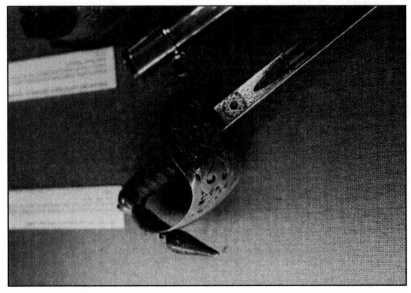

Note: the Star of David below the hilt of the sword

One Nation From Many People

It was this "Pillar of Cloud" symbol that reflected Israel's relationship with God. The fact that we see the outline of the Shield of King David of Israel within this cloud, further confirms the truth of America's Israelite roots as a nation. Finally, from within the Eagle's beak there flows a scroll bearing just 13 letters—"E PLURIBUS UNUM," meaning *"one nation from many people."* The fact that we find the number 13 appearing no less than eight times in the Great Seal is obviously very significant.

Although, as we have already seen, this number thirteen is indelibly associated with the Oneness of the God of Israel, there is, as has already been hinted at, a further important meaning attached to this number, which has a particular application for the United States of America. The ownership of this number especially belongs to the tribe of Manasseh, as in order of precedence Manasseh was the thirteenth tribe of Israel. Jacob had twelve sons of whom Joseph was the 11th and Benjamin the 12th. When Joseph's descendants were divided into two tribes bearing the names of his two sons Manasseh and Ephraim, this increased the number of the tribes to thirteen. As Jacob on his deathbed gave the primary birthright to

Ephraim, this made Manasseh the thirteenth tribe of Israel. Ephraim, having been placed ahead of his older brother Manasseh, thus succeeded Joseph in the 11th position in the roll of the tribes. As Benjamin already held the 12th position, this then places Manasseh 13th.

The Founding Fathers Designed the Great Seal

The American Great Seal was designed by the founding fathers of the Republic. Benjamin Franklin, Thomas Jefferson, and John Adams comprised the original committee for creating an official national seal for the new nation. George Washington too played an important part in the early years. Thomas Jefferson originally proposed that the obverse side of the seal portray the children of Israel traversing through the wilderness, led by a divine cloud during the day and a pillar of fire by night. Benjamin Franklin's design for the seal showed Moses lifting his rod and dividing the sea, while in the background Pharaoh's armies were overwhelmed by the returning waves. These visionary men truly had a Hebraic mindset which they clearly applied in their designs. Although Franklin's design was not adopted, the rays emanating from the pillar of fire in his design survived to find expression in the seal that was ultimately selected. What is clear is that the founding fathers of America saw a parallel between the Israelite experience of Egyptian bondage and their own perceived colonial bondage under the "tyranny" of an English king. The Harp of King David of Israel was included in three of the early designs. The final version of the Great Seal emerged after no less than sixteen drafts were made over a period of some 159 years. This means that it took the combined efforts of over four generations of prominent American leaders to produce this unique and most potent emblem of America. It surely cannot be down to mere coincidence that, wittingly or unwittingly, these great men came up with an emblem that in its every detail reveals America's Israelite ancestry and its true origin as Manasseh, the birthright son of Joseph. The Great Seal therefore is America's "birthmark" - an indelible mark - that cries out: *"I am Israel!"*

America's Memories of Ancient Egypt

Ancient Israel's experience in Egypt truly was a formative one. This was especially so for Joseph, as he was instrumental in saving the whole household of Jacob by establishing them in Egypt. Joseph also was the only one of the sons of Jacob who married an Egyptian woman, and thus the blood of Egypt as well as the blood of Jacob/Israel is intermingled in the descendants of Joseph. It was in Egypt that the 12 sons of Jacob and their families grew into a great multitude (Exodus 1:7).

It should not surprise us therefore to find Egyptian symbolism in American heraldry. In fact, without this reference to Egypt, the heraldic evidence would not be complete. Egyptian imagery was also on the mind of many who contributed to the creation of America's symbolic emblems. Thus on the reverse side of the Great Seal, as portrayed on the back of a US dollar bill, we find displayed the Great Pyramid of Gizeh with 13 steps; and on top of this pyramid is an, *"all-seeing-eye,"* representing the very, "eye of God." Above the pyramid and the, *"all-seeing-eye,"* is the motto, *"Annuit Coeptis,"*—literally meaning, *"he has prospered our undertakings."* This is highly significant, as in this motto we have a direct reference to Joseph, whose Hebrew name, *"Yosafe,"* meaning, *"let him add,"* is a name that implies prosperity. The words of Genesis 39:2-3 & 23 indicate that God made all that Joseph did to prosper in his hand. Here we have the same words describing the prosperity of Joseph used in this, "Annuit Coeptis," motto. Could this really be down to mere coincidence? Another point of interest is that this motto is composed of 13 letters, the number that is the signature of Manasseh, the 13th tribe of Israel. Is this another coincidence?

The Influence of Freemasonry

The cult of freemasonry has abrogated a number of the above symbols. The usual explanation for the emblems in American heraldry is that they originate in masonry. It is a well-documented fact that George Washington, as well as some of the other founding fathers of the Republic, were indeed masons. The, *"all seeing eye,"* is today commonly recognized as a Masonic symbol. Yet masons falsely claim their craft originates with Solomon, that great king of Israel, who was the builder of the first Temple in Jerusalem. Therefore it should not surprise us to find Israelite or even Egyptian symbols in Masonic regalia. Another little-known fact about masonry is that they had a certain knowledge of the Kabbalah, which is commonly considered to be a form of Jewish mysticism. Kabbalah is the Hebrew term for *"that which is received."* The teachings were first published in thirteenth century Spain in a book called the Zohar, which previously had been part of the oral mystical dimensions of the Torah. The book contains sublime concepts on morality, social justice and even human rights. These teachings have had a tremendous influence on the development of western philosophy especially after the 17th century, and we may surmise that the founding fathers of America too were clearly influenced by some of its high-minded primarily Jewish concepts.

After its publication in Spain, the Zohar was circulated outside Jewish circles and much of its content was copied by non-Jews, mostly from within the Roman Catholic Church. These churchmen were prone to put their own Christian interpretations on the teachings. In fact, even today, the Vatican library houses the greatest collection of Cabbalistic texts in the world. Over time this Christian adulteration of the authentic Jewish Cabbala, led to its teaching being adopted by European schools of the occult and magic. As we consider this general background, we need to understand that Satan's role is to be the author of confusion, and that he is always out to counterfeit anything that is of God. He takes that which is holy and corrupts and pollutes it by creating a fake counterfeit of the real thing. The fact that there are certain occult associations with the symbol of the *"all seeing eye,"* does not take away its true origin as a representation of, *"the all seeing eye of God, the Omnipresent and Omnipotent Creator of the universe."* Satan is the fallen angel, whose job is to be the declared adversary of God's purpose, and also to tempt His nation Israel. He wants to besmirch and destroy anything that belongs to His chosen people Israel.

Promise of a New Messianic Age

Beneath the Pyramid there is yet another motto which reads, *"Novus Ordo Seculorum,"* meaning, *"New Order of the Ages."* This is a most interesting choice, as what we see here is an analogy that compares the establishment of the American nation with the ultimate restoration of the United Kingdom of Israel, as God's supreme and model nation during the millennial rule of her Messiah. The enemies of God have hijacked this motto too, as they interpret it to mean "New World Order," which represents man's vain and futile attempt to create a perfect world. Man's attempt to create a "New World Order" is doomed to abject failure, and is set to end in a totalitarian tyranny that is destined to engulf the whole world in war.

"I Have a Dream!"

Dr Martin Luther King did what the prophets of old did in ancient Israel—he disturbed the conscience of the nation. He died, much like those same prophets, a martyr's death. He is remembered most for his famous "I have a dream" speech in which he drew on the words of Isaiah, the prophet of ancient Israel. His words struck a chord with the people, as the passage spoke of the coming of Messiah, and as Martin Luther King recited those words with his sublime eloquence, he gave hope to the nation.

"I have a dream today! I have a dream that one day every valley shall be exalted, every hill and mountain shall be made low, the rough places will be made plain, and the crooked places will be made straight; and the glory of the Lord shall be revealed, and all flesh shall see it together" (Isaiah 40:4–5).

Martin Luther King continued: *"This is our hope. This is the faith that I will go back to the South with. With this faith we will be able to hew out of the mountain of despair a stone of hope."*

What Martin Luther King subliminally expressed, as he quoted from the book of Isaiah, was a vision of the Two Houses of Israel re-united under the rule of a righteous King and the whole world benefiting from His glorious reign. The much prophesied messianic age to come is the true meaning of a *"Novus Ordo Seculorum," a new and righteous order of the ages,* that is to witness the establishment of the "Newly Restored Messianic Kingdom" of Israel, in one single garment of destiny. One day in the not-too-distant future this vision will become a reality, and there is not a power on the earth that can prevent its occurrence.

The New World Order that is such a hot subject for the conspiracy theorist on the Internet, and which on occasion you hear the politicians talk about, is merely a human counterfeit of the real thing. It being a human endeavor, you can be sure there will be nothing new or righteous about the kind of New World Order they propose. The writing is already on the wall, as all recent political trends indicate increasing government control. Their system of global governance will bring the nightmare of George Orwell's 1984 global control freak society into terrible reality. Man's attempts to bring a New World Order and One World Government will lead the world into the Great Tribulation, also known as the "Time of Jacob's Trouble" and the End of the Age, culminating in the final battle of Armageddon spoken of in the Book of Revelation. (Revelation 16:16).

The American Bald Eagle

According to the author and researcher Steven Collins, the eagle and the war sign of a clump of arrows was one of the primary emblems of the Massagetae tribe that ruled over the Scythians. This tribe dominated the Scythian Empire.*[1] Greek historians gave them this tribal name and it was in fact the Greek way of referring to Manasseh, the descendants of the elder son of Joseph. The eagle symbolism was not nearly as evident in the adjacent Ephraim-controlled Parthian Empire. Consequently, the eagle and the clump of arrows symbol identified Manasseh, not Ephraim. It is therefore no coincidence that we find this powerful eagle symbol in the Great Seal of America, rather than in the Royal Coat of Arms of Great Britain. Recently, the Israeli scholar Yair Davidiy made a further fascinating discovery when he researched this subject. He found evidence that a bald eagle symbol was used to represent a group of Israelites being exiled by the Assyrians from the tribal territories of Judah and Benjamin,*[2] These were the last captives to join the other ten tribes in their exile and captivity.

The bald eagle with its white head and tail is the national bird of the United States, and as such it has become a protected species. This magnificent bird of prey is also the symbol of the United States of America. By now it should not come as a surprise to know that the American bald eagle too is a symbol of the ancient Israelites who went into captivity. The prophet Micah in Israel's consummate history book confirms this fact. The prophet, speaking of the rebellious house of Israel, exhorts them to; *"make your baldness broad like an eagle's, for they have departed from you."* (Micah 1:16b).

Joseph's Dream in the Presidential Seal

Joseph was a visionary, and even as a young teenager he was set apart from his brothers who disparagingly referred to him as a dreamer. They considered him as someone who did not dwell in the real world, and they thought he had ideas beyond his station. The Bible records Joseph's dreams and one of the most important of these is recorded as follows:

"'Look, I dreamt another dream: Behold! The sun, the moon, and eleven stars were bowing down to me." And he related it to his father and his brothers." (Genesis 37:9-10).

In a previous dream, Joseph had talked of eleven sheaves of grain bowing down to his sheaf. His eleven brothers hated him for his words, as to them they seemed to indicate that their little upstart brother was going to rule over them. When Joseph came out with this second dream his brothers envied him all the more. That Joseph's dreams were about his ruling over the whole family of Jacob is made very clear by the way that Jacob himself interpreted them. Jacob's very words are recorded for us, and this is what he said:

"What is this dream that you have dreamt! Are we to come—I and your mother and your brothers—to bow down to you to the ground?" (Genesis 37:10).

It is clear from this that in Joseph's dream, Jacob saw himself as symbolized by the sun, and his wife Rachel as the moon, whereas Joseph's eleven brothers were symbolized by the eleven stars. Thus in this prophetic dream, the sun, the moon and the stars appear as the symbol of the whole Jacob/Israel family with the exception of Joseph himself.

Yet Joseph was also a son of Jacob and therefore part of the Israel family. Consequently, if each of the sons of Jacob were to be symbolized by a star, then Joseph too needs to be added to complete the picture. As Joseph's two sons Ephraim and Manasseh were made equal in status with the other tribes, the result would be 13 stars representing the whole family of Israel. Therefore, any symbol or heraldic emblem portraying the sun, the moon and thirteen stars must be regarded as an emblem of Israel! Where in the world do we find such an emblem today? There is only one place and that is on the official Seal of the President of the United States.

Thus we find Joseph's dream, representing the whole family of Israel, portrayed in the Presidential Seal! We find this same emblem also on the flag of the President of the United States. WAS AMERICA ALSO NOT CALLED, THE LAND WHERE DREAMS COME TRUE?

The fact that every official national and presidential emblem of the United States has its origin in ancient Israel simply cannot be mere coincidence. Instead it provides us with further evidence that the original Anglo-Saxon and Celtic immigrants of America, together with others from many nations, are the modern day descendants of the lost house of Israel. From the fact that the 13 stars on the Presidential Seal represent the whole family of Israel, we can also conclude that within the American population are found representatives of each of the 13 tribes of Israel with Manasseh being the leading or ruling tribe. Moses in his day solemnly warned the ancient Israelites of the dire consequences they would suffer if they were to break the covenant they had entered into at Mount Sinai. His warning contained the following statement:

"You will be torn from upon the ground to which you come to possess it. HASHEM will scatter you among all the peoples, from the end of the earth to the end of the earth, and there you will work for gods of others." (Deuteronomy 28:63b - 64).

The Covenant With Death

THE PRESIDENTIAL SEAL

The present eagle-and-arrow symbol of America's Great Seal is derived from the Scythian Massagetae. The Massagetae tribe dominated the Scythian Empire. Various Greek historians gave them this tribal name and it was in fact the Greek way of referring to Manasseh, the descendants of the elder son of Joseph. The American bald eagle is a symbol of the ancient Israelites who went into captivity. *"Enlarge your baldness like an eagle, for they shall go from you into captivity"* (Micah 1: 16).

The 13 phases of the moon, a symbol of the matriarch Rachel, the mother of Joseph

13 letters - 'E PLURIBUS UNUM'. Meaning: - 'One nation from many people'

13 Olives on the olive branch

13 Leaves on the olive branch

Olive tree - A symbol of Israel

The rays of the sun, a symbol of the patriarch Jacob, the father of Joseph (Genesis 37:9 - 10.)

13 stars representing the whole family of Israel: 13 tribes including two tribes descended from the two sons of Joseph.

A shield having 13 bars and stripes

A bundle of 13 arrows in the eagle's talon

50 stars representing the 50 States of the United States of America

© Mount Ephraim Publishing

Joseph's dream in the Presidential Seal

"Look, I have dreamed another dream. And this time, the sun, the moon, and the eleven stars bowed down to me.' So he told it to his father and his brothers" (Genesis 37:9-10). Jacob answered, *'What is this dream you have dreamed? Shall your mother and I and your brothers indeed come to bow down to the earth before you ?'* (Genesis 37:10).

CHAPTER FIVE

The Final Words of Moses—a Lion and a Unicorn

Moses, just as Jacob before him, pronounced a prophetic blessing upon the assembled tribes of Israel just prior to his death. And of Joseph he said:

"A sovereignty is his ox-like one—majesty is his, and his glory will be like the horns of a re'eim; [unicorn;] with them he shall gore nations together, to the ends of the Land; they are the myriads of Ephraim, and the thousands of Manasseh" (Deuteronomy 33:17).

Joseph here is characterized as the firstborn son of a bull with the horns of a unicorn. Notice the double emphasis placed upon the word *"horns."* Maimonides, commonly known as Rambam, considered by many Jewish scholars the greatest of all the Jewish sages, gives a most revealing interpretation to the word *"they"* in the final sentence of the above verse. *And "they" are the myriads of Ephraim, and "they" are the thousands of Manasseh.* The term *"they,"* refers to the two horns that figuratively represent the two branches of Joseph, Ephraim and Manasseh. It is with these horns that *"they,"* [the two sons of Joseph], would gore the nations and push the people together to the ends of the earth. Thus the horns of the unicorn represent awesome military power.

The Jews historically have never had the national power to gore the nations, let alone to push or pursue them to the ends of the earth. Yet, this was certainly true for the once mighty British Empire, and today it can only be applied to the United States of America.

The Hebrew word for "unicorn," as used in *Israel's History Book,* (the Bible), is "RE'EM." Most "modern" translations of the Bible literally render this correctly as a wild Ox. However, this beast has been identified as an Oryx, (a type of straight horned deer), and as a kind of auroch or wild Ox now extinct. This wild Ox was the ancestor of domestic cattle. Jewish *Midrashic* sources apply the term "RE'EM,"[*1] to both the deer and the bull. This could explain why the heraldic representation of a unicorn looks more akin to a horse-like deer than a bull. Like the unicorn in the Royal Arms of Great Britain, the Oryx was white in color. In profile the white Oryx appears as if it has only one horn.

The Lethal Power of the Unicorn

A good example of the power of the United States can be seen in the aftermath of Japan's treacherous attack on Pearl Harbor in the early morning of December 7th 1941. Until that moment, America had been extremely reluctant to become embroiled in any foreign wars with isolationist forces having the upper hand. Pearl Harbor dramatically changed the national mood and the day after the attack, war was declared on Japan and the Axis powers. Just a few months prior to this, with the whole of the European continent engulfed in the flames of war, the American army amounted to very little. It was comprised of small poorly-trained volunteer forces, which according to the then Army Chief of Staff, General George Callett Marshall, equated with the standing army of Sweden. Much of its once mighty Pacific Fleet had been either damaged or destroyed in the Pearl Harbor attack, and its Air Force by all accounts was a very minor player in the world league. After the U.S. declaration of war, Hitler expressed his concern to Air Marshall Goering about the reputation of those American masters of mass production. Goering assured Hitler that there was nothing to fear from American industry. He replied, *"The Americans cannot build airplanes. They are very good at refrigerators and razor blades."* Yet, what we see then is an awesome shift in American power with the whole nation galvanized into action. Forty-eight thousand warplanes came off the assembly line in 1942 alone! A year later this number increased to a staggering 86,000 warplanes. So much for Goering's derogatory comment about fridges and razor blades! Then there is the remarkable story about the World War II Liberty ships; no less than

2,751 box-standard, mass produced ships were launched in just over three years. These ships could carry 2,840 jeeps, 440 tanks, or 230 million rounds of ammunition, and they became the mainstay of the supply lines across the Atlantic to England, as well as transport to the Pacific theater of war. The first of these ships took 245 days from assembly to launch. The frenetic challenge was to reduce this timeframe and progressively it was reduced to sixty days, until a shipyard in California got it down to just four and a half days.

The Unicorn Grows a New ("American") Horn!

In just one year after Pearl Harbor, America had outstripped the total war production of Germany and Japan! In a matter of a few years, America, the reluctant warrior, had become the most powerful military giant the world had ever seen. It was an extraordinary feat bordering on the miraculous! It can fairly be said that this was the time when the "unicorn" grew a new horn! The center of global power was shifted from the British Empire to the United States of America. The mantle of Joseph's power and authority to rule the world was transferred from Ephraim to Manasseh! It is by their actual history that the world can tell those two sons of Joseph apart.

We also find in the Bible the account of the king of Moab hiring a false prophet to curse Israel. The plan backfired, as God forced him to bless Israel instead. God compelled him to speak:

"It is God who brought him out of Egypt according to the power of His loftiness. He will consume the nations that oppress him and crush their bones, and his arrows shall pierce them. He crouched and lay down like a lion, and, like a lion cub - who can stand him up? Those who bless you are blessed and those who curse you are accursed." (Numbers 24:8-9).

Notice once again how those two sons of Joseph represent formidable military power capable of eating up the nations, by crushing their military bones and piercing them through with arrows.

In the immediate aftermath of 9/11, the world once again witnessed the awesome power of JOSEPH, as it *crushed the bones* of the terrorist-sponsoring Taliban government in Afghanistan and *twice pierced* Saddam Hussein's forces in Iraq *with his arrows/missiles.*

Let Nations Bow Down to You

Part of the "Birthright blessing" was: *"Peoples will serve you, and regimes will prostrate themselves to you;"* (Genesis 27:29). This has certainly come to pass both in war and in peace. Many nations have bowed down to Great Britain especially in the heyday of her empire. Since that time, many nations have had absolutely no choice but to prostrate themselves before her brother and successor, the United States of America.

In Great Britain's case, a relatively recent example occurred at a time when the British fleet was much depleted, and had become a mere shadow of its former self, yet even so, she still was able to enforce her will by force of arms. The case in question was Britain's daring recapture of the Falklands Islands in the 1982 Falklands War, when Britain by force of arms forced the Argentine government to concede defeat.

More recently was the Gulf War, where Saddam Hussein and his Iraqi occupying forces *"were made"* to leave Kuwait. The two sons of Joseph, America and Great Britain led the grand military alliance that comprised Operation "Desert Storm." Ever since that victory, for the following twelve years, and despite Saddam's defiance, his air force was forbidden to fly over much of his own country, as a result of a "No Fly Zone" order by these same two sons of Joseph.

Then, in the aftermath of 9/11, they overthrew the Taliban terrorist supporting regime of Afghanistan. The fact that they wasted that victory through their subsequent involvement in the Second Gulf War, does not take away the astounding feat of arms they accomplished in that first campaign. The Second Gulf War too was a flawlessly executed text book case of blitzkrieg by those same two sons of Joseph, in the teeth of the most ferocious global diplomatic opposition, and once again Joseph had intervened to force his will upon Iraq's evil regime. Once more, the allies suffered massive setbacks in the aftermath of their campaign due to appalling lack of foresight on the part of their military planners. Their mindlessly stupid decision to dismiss Saddam Hussein's army, Police

Force, as well as the entire Baath Party Civic Service left the conquered nation with a total leadership vacuum, which was soon filled with lawless and terrorist forces at a terrible cost to the allied forces.

Victorious Brothers in Arms

To continue the subject of other nations bowing down to the sons of Joseph, let us look at the last century. An especially graphic example is to be found in the Armistice followed by the humiliating Treaty of Versailles at the end of the First World War in 1918, when Germany was forced to bow down to Great Britain and the United States of America, as well as to France. Thus the ancient prophecy the Patriarch Isaac pronounced over his son Jacob's descendants was fulfilled in our time.

At the end of World War II, after the hard-won victory of the Allied Forces over Hitler's Third Reich and Japan in 1945, the greater part of the world's population was subject to either the British Empire or the United States of America. During World War II, the British Marines wore a badge depicting half the globe, whereas the American Marines wore a similar badge that pictured the other half. Between them these two brother nations-in-arms controlled much of the world either as colonies and protectorates or as occupied territories. Thus virtually the whole world bowed down to those intrepid sons of Joseph. Nations such as Germany, Austria, Italy and Japan "bowed down to them." Yet, surprisingly, the allied Anglo-Saxon brothers-in-arms in their victory demonstrated the most extraordinary mercy towards their conquered and vanquished enemies. Without knowing it, they exhibited one of the key characteristics of their forefather Joseph.

Anglo-Saxon Mercy

There is a further modern-day parallel here, as Joseph's descendants Ephraim and Manasseh, alias Great Britain and America, saved their Israelite brothers in the Second World War. Norway, Denmark, the Netherlands, Belgium, Luxembourg and France are all nations of mainly Israelite descent. The Nazi war machine had overwhelmed them all. They had lost their independence, and their only hope of deliverance lay in the mighty efforts of their Israelite brothers, America and Great Britain, ably assisted by her Commonwealth compatriots. Joseph in his day had saved his brothers from starvation and certain death in the global seven year famine that raged throughout the Middle East, by allowing them to settle in the Nile Delta, (the land of Goshen), the most productive region of Egypt. His latter day American, British, Canadian, Australian, New Zealander and South African descendants saved their brethren from their bondage under the Nazi yoke.

In the same spirit of Joseph, the most outstanding example of mercy and magnanimity was America's act of restoring the damaged economies of her former enemies, Germany and Japan, through her Marshall Aid plan. People say the Americans only did it out of pure self-interest, as a defense against the onslaught of the Communist juggernaut to the east. This might have been true had there been no alternative! However, there were many other options available, one of which would have been the ruthless subjugation of the German and the Japanese people through permanent occupation. The Allies most certainly had the power, as both Germany and Japan were totally at their mercy. They could have easily annexed Germany at that time. It is what the Germans themselves would have done! The Japanese too, had shown that they had no qualms about doing just this to the countries they overwhelmed. The Russians also demonstrated that they would hold on to conquered territory and turn them into Russian satellites. The Allied Forces not only had the military might but also the right in international law to do so!

America's act of giving her defeated enemy her own territory and government back was an extraordinary act of mercy and magnanimity. She thus was truly walking in the footsteps of the Patriarch Joseph, who magnanimously forgave his brothers, who, when filled with envy and hatred for him, sold him into slavery. The unprecedented decision by the U.S. government to pour in billions of her own dollars to restore her enemy's economy had never been heard of before, in all the history of the world. Never before had victorious conquerors treated their vanquished foe in such a benign way.

Furthermore, after America and Britain had conquered much of Germany in World War II, allied airmen from Britain and America flew their mercy missions 24 hours around the clock to feed their former mortal enemies in the Berlin Airlift of 1948. The Russians had cut the corridor into West Berlin, which was situated deep in Russian-occupied East Germany. Nothing could get through overland to the citizens of West Berlin, who faced starvation and inevitable surrender to the Communist giant to the east. The American and British pilots risked their lives flying the Berlin Corridor in the face of Russian threats to shoot them down. They did this for their defeated German enemy just three years after the bitter war against the Nazis had ended. They did this to save Berlin of all places, the very seat of Hitler's evil empire! They did this at a time when the whole world stood aghast after the true horrors of the Holocaust had become public knowledge! President J F Kennedy came to Berlin to make his famous declaration: *"Ich bin ein Berliner!"* Thus he "drew a line in the sand," making it crystal clear to the Soviet Union that the Western Alliance, led by Joseph's modern day descendants, America and Great Britain, would resist Russian attempts to take over West Berlin. In direct consequence the Russians were forced to back down from the confrontation they had started. Thus the Russians too, like the Germans, Japanese and the Italians before them, were forced to "bow down" before the modern day sons of Joseph.

There was nothing magnanimous in victory about the conduct of the Communist partner in the wartime Western Alliance. The Russians in Eastern Europe behaved in stark contrast, as the nations they liberated from their Nazi conquerors soon discovered to their cost that they had exchanged a Nazi yoke for a Communist one. The Soviet Union held on to its conquered satellites, including East Germany, for over 45 years, until through economic necessity she had no choice but to let them go. The contrast between Israelite and Gentile mindset could not have been greater.

Another more recent example of this extraordinary character trait of Joseph's magnanimity has been the handover of the British Crown Colony of Hong Kong to Communist China on July 1st 1997. When the British originally acquired Hong Kong, it had been an opium and malaria-infested rat-hole that was going nowhere. Under British rule it became one of the greatest financial and commercial centers of the world. Hong Kong prospered under the freedom-loving and free market administration of the enlightened British colonial government to become one of the most successful economies in the world. Yet when the British government handed over their colony to the Chinese in a marvelously dignified ceremony, they left over sixteen billion Pounds sterling in the colonial exchequer. It was a rare and most superior gesture of magnanimity and Imperial largesse that is so quintessentially British. It was a gesture that portrayed the "oh so British" belief in fair play and doing the decent thing. I dare say the Chinese could not believe their good fortune. As the Communist regime in Beijing at the time could not by any stretch of the imagination be described as a friend of Britain, one would be hard pressed to find any nation that would have been quite so generous to an enemy.

The World's Only Superpower

At the end of World War II America and Great Britain were in possession of the greatest collection of military hardware and power the world has ever seen in all of its recorded history. In the D-Day invasion of Normandy, an awesome armada of over 5,000 warships sailed from British ports to the Normandy beaches. At the close of the war, America had no fewer than 122 aircraft carriers to project her awesome might. Thus as the power of the British Empire began to wane after the Second World War, a new Anglo-Saxon military superpower arose to take her place. Britain's brother, Manasseh, the American fellow Israelite people, had already come to her rescue twice in both world wars, and both times her intervention saved the day. With the fearsome explosion of the atom bomb on Hiroshima in 1945, a new, militarily awesome powerful nation had made its terrifying début on the world stage. Ever since that time, the American brothers of "good old England" have militarily dominated our planet. The US Navy, with her giant aircraft carriers like floating cities in the sea, her nuclear submarines, her Tomahawk and Attack cruise missiles and huge fleet of warships, patrols the great oceans and seas of the globe. No army in the world can withstand her invisible Stealth bombers and her precision-guided Joint Direct Attack Munitions and bombs, as well as her fearsome fleets of deadly Drones and her Apache Attack helicopters with their lethal Hellfire missiles. Her technological lead over the other nations in the development of new weapons is constantly increasing by leaps and bounds leaving the rest of the world way behind in her wake. Her highly sophisticated satellites can tap into all the secret plans of her enemies at will.⁵

More recently, in the late 1990s Kosovo conflict in the former Yugoslavia, she demonstrated that she could even win a war without suffering any casualties, by utilizing her overwhelming air power alone. Today, after the break-up of the former Soviet Union in the early nineties, she is the sole military superpower in the world. Her defense budget is a staggering 10 times larger than that of Russia and 6 times larger than China's. U.S. Arms spending in 2008 at $711 billion was a full 48% of the world total and this was excluding the cost of the Iraq and Afghanistan wars estimated at about $170 billion.*² When you include those figures, U.S. Defense spending amounts to a staggering 54% of the world's total. The Defense Budget total for fiscal 2010 is projected at a massive $896.2 billion.*³ Just as it was in the days of his brother Ephraim's British Empire, when Britannia "ruled the waves," so now we find that with Manasseh's U.S.A. there is no one around who dares to "militarily" challenge her awesome might. Could all of this just be happenstance? The words of Sir Winston Churchill come to mind:

"He must indeed have a blind soul who cannot see that some great purpose is being worked out here below!"

England is Portrayed as a Young Bull

The prophet Jeremiah also describes Ephraim as a *"young bull,"* or to be precise, as an *"Aegel"* in Hebrew. According to Rashi, (one of the paramount Jewish sages and commentators), *"Aegel"* was a nickname applied to Joseph. Yair Davidiy, the Israeli author and historian, cites a Hebrew Midrash,*⁴ in his works that says that the bull represented Ephraim, Joseph's younger son, and it is interesting to note that England is nicknamed, "John Bull!."*⁵ Thus even today, England is known by the pet name given to his ancestral father Joseph. *"Aegel"* is also the root word from which the word "Angle" has been derived, and the Angles' original name was *Aegeli*. It was the Angles who gave their name to England. Incredible as it may sound, even England's name refers to Joseph's *"young* *bull"* nickname! "The Bull," is also one of the most popular names for an English pub.

According to yet another Midrash,*6 quoted by Yair Davidiy, a Unicorn, (Re'eim in Hebrew), was represented on the tribal standard of Manasseh, whereas Ephraim's standard carried the image of an Ox or Bull.*7

The metaphor of Ox or Bull alludes to power, whereas the term "firstling" or "firstborn," in Hebrew can also refer to, "greatness," or to, *"sovereign ruler."* Thus both Ephraim and Manasseh represent great power and sovereignty. Manasseh, symbolized by the re'eim or unicorn, was to become the most powerful tribe and the ultimate expression of Israelite might. Is this not exactly what we witness today in the awesome power of the United States of America? The only question is: for how much longer will America be able to maintain its universal supremacy?

The important thing to remember is that both the lion and the unicorn are emblems that originate in ancient Israel. It is surely an extraordinary coincidence to find both the lion of Judah and the Unicorn of Joseph as two main pillars supporting the Royal Arms of Great Britain!

Joseph's Brothers do not Recognize His Disguise

Remember the biblical account of Joseph's brothers, how they sold him into Egyptian slavery? After twenty-one years had passed, their father Jacob ordered them to go to Egypt to purchase food to alleviate the terrible famine in their land. They never thought they would meet Joseph again. They assumed that after all this time their brother was dead. Yet, as providence would have it, there they stood before Joseph, in official audience with the all-powerful Viceroy of Egypt, and they did not recognize him. They stood right in front of their brother and they simply did not recognize him because he was dressed in Egyptian clothes. They also could not imagine that their brother, whom they sold as a slave, could possibly have become the effective ruler of Egypt. The whole thing was just too crazy to imagine. This same analogy can be applied to America, Great Britain and (her) daughter nations, as they too have adorned themselves with foreign "Egyptian" or Gentile clothes, and consequently the whole world perceives them to be of Gentile stock. Even their Jewish brothers do not recognize their Hebrew origins anymore!

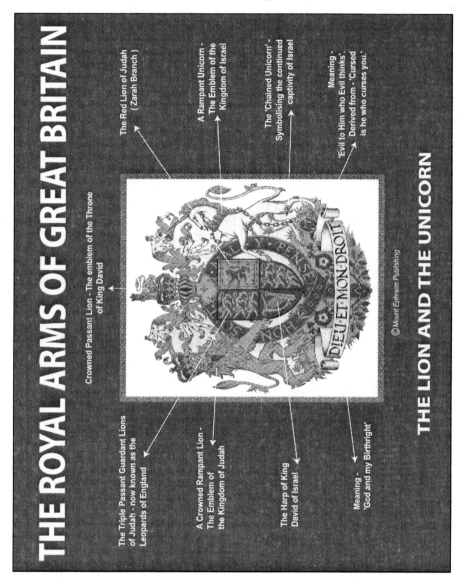

Just Like Manasseh, America has Forgotten Her Origins

Joseph named his firstborn son Manasseh, because his birth and the marriage to his Egyptian bride had "caused him to forget" his pain at being rejected by his own brothers. The meaning of Manasseh is most revealing, as the true meaning of the name is: "CAUSING TO FORGET!" Joseph had become ruler over the world-dominating Egyptian Empire, and he had become so engrossed in the great affairs of state, that any thought of his own origins were buried deep in his past. Today, his modern American and British descendants have forgotten their Israelite origins also. They have forgotten their patriarchal fathers Abraham, Isaac and Jacob and their matriarchal mothers Sarah, Rebecca and Rachel. They, just like Joseph before them, are orphans cast out of their land. Just as Joseph made a great success of his life in his Egyptian exile, so have his modern descendants today also made a great success of their lives in exile. They have become great nations which, much like Joseph before them, became rulers in the world.

CHAPTER SIX

Are the American War of Independence and the Civil War Prophesied in the Bible?

In the Book of Isaiah there is an extraordinary prophecy about the two sons of Joseph, Ephraim and Manasseh. On the face of it the meaning is totally obscure and it seems completely impossible to explain. The reality is that it is only those who understand the ancestry of the modern day birthright sons of Joseph, who can possibly understand the meaning of this prophecy. It is only once you have become aware of the true origins of America and Great Britain that you have the key to unlock the meaning of this remarkable prophecy. Yet, even if you were armed with this key it would still be pretty difficult to understand exactly what this prophecy means, as you also need to have a fair knowledge of American history to get the whole picture. Nevertheless, by this prophecy we can further discern the modern day identity of the two sons of Joseph. Let us carefully examine the chilling prophecy spoken by the prophet Isaiah:

"By the wrath of HASHEM, Master of Legions, the land is charred. The people has become like fuel for a fire; they have no mercy one for another. He snatched from his right and remains hungry; he consumed on his left, but they are not sated; everyone will eat the flesh of his own arm. Manasseh is against Ephraim, Ephraim is against Manasseh" (Isaiah 9:18-20).

What on earth can this mean? Isaiah clearly speaks out a prophecy for the future. Could it be that the Isaiah prophecy has already occurred? The prophet is referring to a yet future time when Manasseh and Ephraim, the two sons of Joseph, are devouring each other. He is speaking of a time when these two brother nations will be at war! The question is has this already happened? To get the answer we need to look into the history of Great Britain and America. It is only when we examine the history of these two nations that we discover that Isaiah's ominous prophecy has already been fulfilled.

The Catalyst for Rebellion

The British exchequer, after Britain's victory over the French in the Seven Years War (1756-63), had become heavily depleted and was in sore need of funds. Westminster was looking for ways to raise the extra revenue needed to replenish its coffers. Some in the British government reasoned that, as much of the war effort had been for the benefit of her American colonists, it would be only fair to have some of those rich colonials bear some of the burden. Thus the decision was made to levy a special stamp tax on the Americas. The Stamp Act of 1765 was the first direct tax imposed by Parliament on their American brothers. In reality the Americans were only being asked to pay a share of their own defense. As it was, the new tax, even though it effectively doubled the low local taxes the American colonists had to pay, still only came to a flat rate of two shillings per person. Furthermore, the colonial Americans enjoyed a higher level of prosperity than the people back in the mother country. The British on average paid ten times the amount in tax the colonists were being asked to pay. However, the English colonists did not see it that way. They felt strongly that the British parliament had no right to pass laws on Englishmen in the Americas, who did not have elected representation in that government! Very soon the cry went up: *"No taxation without representation!"* This then became the popular war cry throughout the thirteen Colonies.

History Repeats Itself

Here we see history repeating itself in the most remarkable way, as in ancient times the division of Israel into two separate nations was over exactly the same issue. It is interesting to note that when the Ten Tribes of Israel split away from Judah the cause for the division was the onerous taxation plans of King Rehoboam. It was the king's introduction of higher taxation that drove the Ten Tribes of Israel to rebel against their duly constituted monarch. This same Rehoboam was a very stubborn king who simply would not budge or compromise. Thus in ancient Israel the same cry had gone up: *"No taxation without representation!"* Although the Bible, (Israel's ancient history book), expresses the same sentiment somewhat differently, nevertheless it amounted to the same thing. The Scriptures record the incident as follows:

"What share have we in [the House] David? [We have] no heritage in the son of Jesse! Back to your homes, O Israel! Now see to your own house, O [kingdom of] David" (1Kings 12:16).

With wisdom and willingness to compromise, conflict could quite easily have been avoided in both cases but, primarily through the stubborn folly of King George III, who without knowing it was walking in the footsteps of King Rehoboam, the whole situation got completely out of hand. It was all so unnecessary, as the Colonists looked upon Britain as their mother-country. They talked of her as "home," and now, for want of a little "give and take" on both sides in a spirit of compromise, both mother-England and her own colonial children were fighting each other. Thus, just as Isaiah had prophesied in Isaiah 9:21, Manasseh was devouring Ephraim.

The founding fathers of America clearly recognized the Biblical connection between the Israelite experience of coming out from Egyptian bondage and their own battle against the colonial bondage under the "tyranny" of an English king. For example, Thomas Jefferson originally proposed that the reverse side of the American Seal portray the liberated "children of Israel" in the wilderness being led by a divine pillar of cloud during the day and a pillar of fire by night. Jefferson's own motto engraved on his personal seal was borrowed from Oliver Cromwell's famous words of justification: *"Rebellion to tyrants is obedience to God."*

Manasseh Devours Ephraim—the War of Independence

When in 1775 the first shots were fired in anger, the two brothers, Manasseh and Ephraim, were fighting and devouring each other just as the prophet Isaiah had prophesied. Fighting began at Lexington and also, rather ironically, at a place called Concord. William Pitt, the great war time Prime Minister of Britain during the Seven Years War, now old and somewhat ill, warned the nation at the time that Britain's enemies would take advantage of this unnecessary family squabble. When he talked of enemies, he had the French especially in mind. William Pitt, by then elevated to the peerage and known as Lord Chatham, had worked tirelessly to stop the conflict. He said: *"You cannot conquer America. They are of our own blood. If I were an American, as I am an Englishman, I would never lay down my arms—never, never, never!"*

The plain fact is that there are no two other nations on the earth that fit the prophecy so absolutely. *"Every man shall eat the flesh of his own arm—Manasseh is against Ephraim, Ephraim is against Manasseh* (Isaiah 9:20. This prophecy gives a very vivid picture of what occurred during the American War of Independence, as when brother fought against brother they were hurting themselves. They were indeed, metaphorically speaking, eating the flesh of their own arm.

Born Out of the Womb of Great Britain

William Pitt's warning came true, as France, England's perennial enemy, saw her chance to get her revenge for her crushing defeats during the Seven Years War. She supplied most of the weapons and gunpowder for the American revolutionaries and, come 1777, French "volunteers" were arriving in Virginia to assist in the fight against England. One year later, the French became formally allied to the Americans and, soon afterwards, the Spanish and Dutch too declared war on Britain. In no time at all Great Britain was pressed on all sides, as she was fighting an imperial war against most of Europe, as well as against her own thirteen colonies in America. Parliament demanded an end to the war. Lord North, the British Prime Minister, resigned, and in September 1783 the Treaty of Paris was signed at Versailles, with Britain recognizing the independence of her thirteen "rebellious" colonies. It was a hard blow for the "Old Country," as, apart from Canada, she had lost all her hard-won possessions in North America. Yet out of this very conflict a new nation was born—the United States of America—that Great Nation that was primarily descended from Manasseh, the son of Joseph, the son of Jacob, whose name was changed to Israel. Thus, in the most extraordinary way, that ancient promise of the "Birthright" blessing was coming to its ultimate fulfillment.

If we go back a little further in history and look at the emergence of the Puritans in the 1500s, we can discern that the internecine strife between Ephraim and Manasseh began even earlier with the people of the yellow ribbon. In the English Civil War the Puritan cavalry officers and the soldiers wore yellow ribbons and sashes. The yellow ribbon was used to identify and distinguish them from the royalist forces on the battlefield. Thus the yellow ribbon became an established part of Puritan heraldry. This same yellow ribbon has ever since played an important role in American history, especially in a time of war. The Puritans would fight under a great banner stating, *In God we trust!* Until recently we have seen the very same phrase on the U.S. dollar bill! The Puritans were the great change-agents of the Reformation and in the early 1600s they were able to take control of the English Parliament. The situation culminated in the Puritan war against King Charles I, otherwise known as the English Civil War. After the execution of the king for treason against Parliament and the people, Oliver Cromwell, as the "Lord Protector," became the effective ruler of the nation. The question is: Was this strife between the Puritans and Royalists another example of Manasseh devouring Ephraim and Ephraim devouring Manasseh? Is it perhaps conceivable that even some 130 years prior to the Revolutionary American War of Independence, embryonic America was struggling to escape from the womb of England?

Britain and America—a Special Relationship

It cannot be denied that the United States of America was born out of the womb of Great Britain, and just like any birth, it had been accompanied by much pain. The relationship between a mother and a child is always a special one—as the saying goes: "blood is thicker than water." Yet, is it not interesting to notice that ever since America gained its independence, the world in political circles has never stopped talking about what they perceive as "A SPECIAL RELATIONSHIP" between America and Great Britain? Once you understand who these two brothers really are, is it any wonder there should be a special relationship? In Joseph, the son of Jacob/Israel, they share the same patriarchal ancestral father, and in Asenath, the Egyptian wife of Joseph, they share the same ancestral mother. Of course, with that common pedigree, background and experience, it would be very strange indeed if there were not a special relationship between them.

Yet, just as the Patriarch Jacob had declared, the time had come when the two brothers should walk separate paths. The prophecy had to be fulfilled, and it was always inevitable that it would be fulfilled within God's perfect timing. For this reason it was necessary for Great Britain to lose the American War of Independence, as his elder brother Manasseh had to go his own way in the world to become a great nation prophesied by the Patriarch Jacob/Israel. If Britain had not lost that war in the resounding way she did, the prophecy would not have been fulfilled, and the credibility of the great God of Israel would have been put into question. It was God's purpose that Britain should lose that war. Ephraim was meant to lose it, as it was to be the instrument in bringing the blessing of the "Birthright" to his older brother Manasseh, e.g. America.

George Washington - A Man of Destiny

George Washington sits astride American history almost as a patriarchal figure, and he is looked upon as the father of the nation. Physically, he cut an impressive figure as, at six feet and two inches tall, he towered above most of his contemporaries. He had a straight military bearing and was a man with natural authority. He was a superb horseman who loved country pursuits such as hunting and shooting. He was the natural choice of the American Colonies as their Commander in Chief, as he was a fearless soldier who, whenever faced with danger, always kept a cool head.

George Washington's Inauguration

Inevitably, after a further three years of bloody war, on October 17, 1781, the British forces under General Cornwallis surrendered at the famous siege of Yorktown. That the final battle should take place at a town called "Yorktown" is highly significant in that the original meaning of York is "Castle or stronghold of the Hebrews." It is at this "Castle of the

Hebrews" that Ephraim, the younger Hebrew son of Joseph (GB), is forced to surrender his sword to his elder gentile former Hebrew brother Manasseh (USA). To add to the humiliation, the English troops were forced to march out of Yorktown with their colors, (the red ensign), encased. They went out with great dignity in true British grit style. The British military band played *The World Turned Upside Down*, a most appropriate tune, as it described exactly how the British felt. For them the world truly had been turned upside down, as their outstanding record for many centuries was to win wars rather than lose them.

The formal peace treaty was signed in Paris on September 3, 1783, accompanied by much gloating in France over England's misfortune at having lost the war. The French had come to the aid of the Patriot Continental cause, not because of any regard for the Americans, but simply to thwart and spite the English from gaining their place of destiny as the prime inheritor of the "Birthright." Finally, after eight and a half long years of bitter battles, the war had come to an end.

It is not generally appreciated that the American War of Independence was in effect America's first civil war. The fact is that nearly a third of the population had supported the king of England in this epic struggle. Those who sided with England were almost certainly from the tribe of Ephraim, whereas those who supported the revolution consequently were from the tribe of Manasseh. Thus Isaiah's prophecy, that no man shall spare his brother, and that, metaphorically speaking, every man shall eat the flesh of his own arm, was fulfilled in every sense in this titanic struggle, in which Manasseh devoured Ephraim, and Ephraim Manasseh (Isaiah 9:19-21).

At the end of the American War of Independence, the people of America, having thrown off their colonial shackles, had become Americans. Nevertheless, there was as yet no unified American Republic. The peace treaty with England was made between the 13 Colonies that had succeeded in becoming 13 independent states. The Declaration of Independence only implied a league of friendship between 13 small independent countries. It did not imply union. The reality at the time was that it was the emergency of the war that had created the necessity for the states to bind together. Once the war was over, the bond was practically dissolved, and every State did its own thing and went its own way. Had this scenario continued, America would never have walked in the destiny of her Birthright, and she never would have become the "Great Nation" the Patriarch Jacob had prophesied she would become. Once again it was George Washington, who together with other leaders became the catalyst for change, as he presided over the drafting of the Constitution for the United States of America. He was subsequently elected unanimously as the first President of the United States. To date he still holds the unique record as the only unanimously elected president in the history of America.

The inauguration took place significantly in New York, (the "New" Stronghold of the Hebrews), near the spot now marked by Ward's statue of him in Wall Street. Once in New York, he travelled to the city in a special barge festooned with the Stars and Stripes and was greeted by a joyful crowd *en route*. Looking back at this event we realize what a momentous occasion it was, as George Washington took the oath of office before a cheering crowd. He thus became the first American president under a democratic governmental system that has provided for the peaceful transition of power for more than two centuries.

Did George Washington Understand the Significance?

Washington took his oath of office with his hand placed on an open Bible. Ever since Washington's inauguration it has been the president's prerogative to choose his own Bible passage for his oath of office, and different presidents have selected various passages. Washington's selection was highly significant, as while he gave the oath, his hand rested on the King James Bible opened at Genesis 49. This is the very place in the Bible text where the Patriarch Jacob blessed his twelve sons. More significantly this is the very place that records Jacob's prophetic and most beautiful words to his son Joseph, the inheritor of the Birthright:

"A charming son is Joseph, a charming son to the eye; each of the girls climbed heights to gaze. The God of your father and He will help you, and with Shaddai—and He will bless you [with] blessings of heaven from above, blessings of the deep crouching below, blessings of the bosom and womb. The blessings of your father surpassed the blessings of my parents to the endless bounds of the world's hills. Let them be upon Joseph's head, and on the head of the exile from his brothers" (Genesis 49:22 & 25-26).

This raises the question of whether George Washington understood the enormous significance of those words as he took his oath of office on that auspicious day on April 30 1789. One cannot but wonder whether Washington realized that he was God's appointed instrument in bringing those prophetic words into reality. As the great man is not with us any more to give us the answer, we can only surmise what was in his heart at the time. Nevertheless, it is fascinating to think that Washington consciously chose this particular passage of the Bible because he understood that America was descended from Joseph, the chosen "Birthright" son of Israel. According to some accounts, Washington kissed this very Bible passage at the end of his oath of office, as the first President of the United States of America.

It was the birth of a new nation. It was also a prophetic moment of the highest order, as the descendants of the tribe of Manasseh inherited their divinely apportioned sovereign territory in the New World. It was the pre-ordained moment when gentile Manasseh was to claim his share of the "Birthright" covenant God had made with Abraham. The birth process itself had been exceedingly painful, as the nation was born in the crucible of fratricidal war, when the two brothers Ephraim and Manasseh fought each other almost to a standstill. Ephraim fought to maintain his dominance, whereas Manasseh fought for his freedom. After the victory, that untamed spirit of freedom has forever imbued America, and she has ever since become known as *"the land of liberty and the land of the free!"*

Ephraim Devours Manasseh—the Civil War

In the American Civil War we have yet another occasion where the Isaiah prophecy seems to come to its partial fulfillment. We need to bear in mind that it was the gentile Englishmen, descended from the tribe of Ephraim, who first established their colonial settlements in America. This means that at that point in history large segments of America's white population, perhaps as much as a third, were from the tribe of Ephraim. The American Civil War may well be seen as Manasseh, the older son of Joseph, asserting himself over Ephraim, his younger brother. We have already seen that in the War of Independence nearly a third of the colonial population took up arms on the side of the king of England. Most of those would have been of English descent, meaning that they had descended from Ephraim, the younger son of Joseph. It appears also that in the south of the USA the dominant element was composed of the tribe of Ephraim. In the Southern States the aristocratic landowners of mainly English stock operated the feudal system of England. They managed huge plantations spread over vast territories requiring the work of thousands of slaves. The chief crop grown in these plantations was cotton, to fulfill the almost insatiable demand from the great cotton mills of England. It is a well documented fact that the British favored the South in the Civil War.

In the Revolutionary War of American Independence it was Manasseh who started the conflict against the rule of Ephraim, as the American colonials rebelled against the rule of England. Ironically we see exactly the opposite occurring in the American Civil War, where Ephraim in the South started the rebellion against the Union. In this context it can well be argued that in the American War of Independence it was Manasseh who devoured Ephraim's arm, whereas in the American Civil War it was Ephraim who devoured Manasseh's arm. From this we can see that Isaiah's prophecy may well have been fulfilled more than once. It is uncanny how well the prophecy describes what happened during the American Civil War, as Manasseh devoured Ephraim and Ephraim devoured Manasseh, these two brothers and sons of Joseph truly were "devouring the flesh of their own arm." They were inflicting the most ghastly self-harm upon their nation with an unspeakable ferocity that cost the lives of 620,000 soldiers and an undetermined number of civilians. This has proved by far the bloodiest conflict in all of American history in which 10 percent of all northern males 20-45 years of age died, as did 30 percent of all southern white males aged 18-45 years.[*1]

A fascinating point is that the symbols associated with the very first battle in the conflict pointed directly to Manasseh and Ephraim. The first battle of the American Civil War took place at, "*Manassas,*" Virginia! Furthermore, the Northern forces (the Yankees), referred to this first battle as, "*Bull Run.*" "Bull Run" was named after a creek that was in the vicinity of the town of "Manassas." The paramount symbol of Ephraim is the bull, and the English characteristically refer to themselves as, "*John Bull.*" The Southern Confederate forces on the other hand called the battle, "*Manassas,*" after the nearby town. When you place these statements side by side we see a subliminal acknowledgement to the battle by the two brother tribes of Israel by both the North and the South. The North was fighting Ephraim, the "Bull," whereas the South was fighting Manasseh at a place called Manassas. As a point of interest, even the nickname, "Yankee," is derived from a Hebrew form of Jacob.

It was at that first major battle at Manassas, (Bull Run), that General Beauregard decided to change the Confederate flag to avoid confusion on the battlefield between the Union and Confederate forces. The Confederate flag was given a red background with two crossed blue stripes containing 13 stars. Eleven of these stars represented the secessionist states, whereas the other two symbolized the states of Missouri and Kentucky claimed by the Confederation. Thus even in Confederate heraldry we once again see that most significant number thirteen!

The American Civil War can also be referred to as a "War of Rebellion," as in effect the Southern States rebelled against the North and the Union. In this respect we see yet another parallel with ancient Israel. When the great split occurred in ancient Israel, it was the tribe of Ephraim which led the rebellion, resulting in the breakaway of the ten tribes of Israel to set up their own independent kingdom to the north of Judah. What we witness in the Civil War is a kind of replay. Here again we see the tribe of Ephraim leading the secessionist rebellion of the Confederate States of America. In the first rebellion in ancient Israel it was the tribes of the North led by Ephraim that seceded from the South e.g. Judah. In the second rebellion the reverse was the case, as the tribes of the South, once again led by Ephraim, seceded from the North.

In the American Civil War, Jefferson Davis, the President of the Confederation, led the South. The meaning of the name Davis is, "Son of David," and thus by his very name we see here a reference to King David of Israel. At the same time, a man of Jewish birth named Judah Philip Benjamin was the Secretary of State for the Confederate States of America (1862-1865). There is a high degree of irony in this, as in the first division in ancient Israel, the northern tribes led by Ephraim split away from Judah and Benjamin under the House of David. In the second division, i.e. in the American Civil War, Ephraim under Davis with Judah Benjamin attempted to split away but was prevented from doing so by Abraham Lincoln, a man named after Abraham, the first Patriarch of Israel. Can we not see the Hand of God in this amazing irony?

Thus several thousand years prior to the actual events, the Prophet Isaiah had prophesied in the most descriptive way, exactly what was destined to happen to these two sons of Joseph. He prophesied that Manasseh would devour Ephraim and that Ephraim would devour Manasseh, not only in the War of Independence, but also during the subsequent Civil War. Thus these two brothers and sons of Joseph truly were, *"devouring the flesh of their own arm,"* as, with brother killing brother, they were inflicting excruciating self-harm upon their nation, not once but twice in their history.

Sadly, prior to the Civil War, between June 1812 and February 1815, there had been yet another occasion when these two sons of Joseph found themselves at war, this time over Canadian territory. The United States declared war on England on June 18th 1812, whilst the English were still heavily involved in their war against Napoleon's France. U.S troops entered Canada unopposed on July 12th, only to be subsequently forced to retreat to Detroit, where they suffered defeat at the hands of the British. Much of the fighting on land thereafter takes place around the Canadian lakes with the battle over the next two and a half years ebbing to and fro with respectively 8 victories to the British and 6 to the American forces. Yet, the United States Army suffered terrible humiliation when after the Battle of Bladensburg, the British were able to march into Washington D.C. The President and Mrs Madison only had a few hours to pack their bags to escape from the Presidential Mansion, or face capture by General Ross, the British Commander. The troops under his command then proceeded to burn the White House, the Capitol Building plus many other buildings in the city. On the lakes and on the seas however, the Yankee captains were able to greatly humble his Majesty's invincible Royal Navy. This was especially the case in the Battle on Lake Champlain, when the Americans were able to defeat the superior British fleet by giving the Brits a terrible pasting. American Privateers and Buccaneers in the meantime relentlessly pursued the merchant convoys of the British Empire on the seven seas at a huge cost to the Kings treasury. Then on February 17th 1815 President Madison officially declared an end to the War of 1812.

Clearly therefore, Isaiah's prophecy about these two brother tribes was actually fulfilled not twice but three times! Thus this one prophetic utterance written down and recorded in the Book of Isaiah provides us with evidence that America and Great Britain and her Commonwealth daughters are descended from Manasseh and Ephraim, the "birthright" sons of Joseph. Isaiah's prophecy thus adds to the reams of additional evidence that America and Great Britain are Israelite nations, as only in American and British history this prophecy finds its most perfect fulfillment not once, not twice, but three times!

A Federal Union of States by God's Design

A most important point to consider is that the Southern States believed that secession was a matter of right for each state. They believed that when a government fails to fulfill the compact that created it, then the people have the right under the Constitution to withdraw from it. It is perhaps significant that the central government released Jefferson Davis, President of the Confederacy, without trial after keeping him in prison for just two years. The question is: Why didn't they try him for treason? Might it be because the legal experts of the day knew that they did not have a case, as secession was a right for each state to choose? Whatever the case, it is clear from all of subsequent history that America was destined to become a Federation of United States. It was only through this means that America, e.g. Manasseh, the older son of Joseph, could come into his position of supreme power, as prophesied by the Patriarch Jacob. Remember Jacob, while on his deathbed, pronounced the "Birthright" blessing on the two sons of Joseph. According to the blessing (Genesis 48:14-20), the younger son Ephraim received the primary blessing, and in the latter days of this age he was to become a "Company" or "Commonwealth" of nations, whereas Manasseh, the elder son, was to become a "great people" or "Great Nation." The Sovereign Creator God had, in his predetermined council, decreed that this group of people, in the North and the South, would coalesce into one unified nation. In this respect the attempt by the Southern States to secede was against His divine purpose, and consequently it was bound to fail.

We need only to look at the 20th Century and into the early part of this 21st Century to see this "Birthright" purpose fulfilled in the history of America. The United States, as a cohesive whole, prevailed in World War I, in World War II and in Korea. While she was humbled in the Vietnam War, she did subsequently prevail in the Cold War, etc., to emerge as the only superpower on the earth. America, the older son of Joseph, has become the dominant force in the world, while Ephraim (Great Britain) has become a second-class power. Although Ephraim today still ranks as the seventh largest economy in the world, she has become powerless and unable to act militarily without the assistance of her older brother Manasseh. Manasseh was to separate from Ephraim and become the greatest, wealthiest and most powerful single nation of earth's history. Thus the Birthright promise has been fulfilled, as Ephraim, who came to his place of global prominence and dominion first, has handed his baton of leadership to Manasseh, his elder brother. These two brother nations most certainly are a most remarkable pair.

Having come thus far in this book the reader will by now understand that the reason for America's extraordinary prosperity and universal dominance is due to the hidden ancestry of her people. The reason for America's incredible cultural, economic, technological and military dominance lies in the simple fact that she is ruled by Manasseh, the thirteenth tribe of Israel. She has come to her inheritance as a result of a promise given by the Covenant-keeping God of Israel to the Patriarch Abraham, who is the ancestral father of all Anglo-Saxon and Celtic Americans. America's global supremacy has decidedly not come to her because of her own merit. Neither has her fabulous wealth been given to her because somehow the Americans are better and more talented people than those of other nations.

CHAPTER SEVEN

The Early Seeds of Zionism

Despite all the negative propaganda and controversy associated with Zionism, the truth is that YHVH, the God of Israel and Creator of the Universe, is the ultimate Zionist, as "Biblical" Zionism originates with Him. Zionism reflects the eternal bond that links the Covenant our Creator made with the Patriarchs, Abraham, Isaac and Jacob, with the nation of Israel, the land of Israel, the people of Israel and the Messiah of Israel. Zionism therefore forms an intrinsic part of Hebrew culture. In fact the word "Sion" or "Zion" is mentioned in the Bible no less than 164 times. It is the mountain upon which King David built his citadel and where the magnificent Temple of Solomon once stood. Whereas "Sion" means summit or peak, the Hebrew root for "Zion" is "SIGN' or "WAYMARK." Zion therefore is a "sign" that points the world to YHVH, the GREAT GOD OF ISRAEL.

This is the very reason why Zionism is hated by the world at large. It is also why the politicians and nations rage against it, and why they will do anything to besmirch the term Zion in order to make Zionism appear to be something intrinsically evil. The simple truth is that rebellious man does not like to be reminded of the absolute and total AUTHORITY OF THE GREAT GOD of ISRAEL, who is the Author and Creator of all things.

At the same time it also must be said that the founders of the Jewish State created their own political form of Zionism, which is based upon secular humanism. In effect, theirs is a total departure of Biblical Zionism. Every Israeli government since the foundation of the State of Israel has practised a Zionism without God! Thus, even the leadership of the State of

Israel shares that same spirit of rebellion with the rest of mankind, as they too refuse to be subject to the authority of the Creator of the Universe.

Ever since the Romans expelled the Jewish people from their Holy Land, after the second Jewish revolt led by Simon Bar Kochba in 135 AD, the Jews have longed to return to their ancestral land. In Psalm 137 we find the well known lament of the Jews who had been taken into captivity in Babylon, who wept *"by the rivers of Babylon"* and declared, *"If I forget you, O Jerusalem, let my right hand wither."*)Some thirty years ago Boney M, the German disco band, immortalized this same yearning of the Jewish captives with their all time hit single titled, *"By the rivers of Babylon."*

The ancient dream of being a free people, once again gathered in their own land, has for the past 1900 years come into special focus on each Passover night. It is in that night they remember their great deliverance from captivity in Egypt. The Jews the world over would at the end of each Passover Seder recite: *"L'shana ha'ba-ah b'Yerushalayim."* Even to this day, as they raise their glasses at the Seder, the toast is: *"Next year in Jerusalem"* Throughout the ages, the Jews have understood that Jerusalem is connected with their future destiny. Encapsulated in this phrase, *"next year in Jerusalem,"* is the messianic vision of the great Prophets of the Hebrew Bible, which speaks of the restoration of the Whole House of Israel. Zionism therefore is rooted in the Bible, and its spirit has been subliminally embedded in the heart of every Jewish person for at least the past nineteen centuries.

Effects of the Protestant Reformation

It was the Protestant Reformation in Europe which, for the first time in centuries, made the Bible available to the common man. Thus the words of the great Prophets of the Bible, which spoke so eloquently about the ultimate restoration of Israel, soon began to strike a chord with those who had thrown off the yoke of the Roman Church. This was especially the case in the Netherlands and England. Thus the early seeds of Zionism began to take root even within Christianity in the first part of the 17th century, and this at a time whilst the long wars of the Reformation were still going on. Christian Bible believers had begun to wonder what they could do to speed the coming of the promised Messiah. Their focus was on the prophecies in the books of Zechariah and Isaiah, together with multiple others which declared that Israelites were to re-conquer the Holy Land. They were excited to discover that the re-conquest of the land of Israel was spoken of by the prophets:

"For HASHEM, Master of Legions, has remembered His flock, the HOUSE OF JUDAH, and He will make them as a horse whose glory is in war... They will be like warriors trampling [their enemies] in the mud of the streets in war... EPHRAIM will be like a mighty warrior... I will bring them to the land of Gilead and Lebanon..." (Zechariah 10:3, 5, 7 &10, emphasis added).

Notice how Zechariah describes those conquering Israelites as two separate houses, e.g. Judah and Ephraim. Isaiah continues the same theme as he prophesies that:

"He will raise a banner for the nations and assemble THE CASTAWAYS OF ISRAEL [Ephraim] and He will gather in THE DISPERSED ONES OF JUDAH from the four corners of the earth. They will fly in unison against the Philistines to the west, and together they will plunder the people of the East; their hand will extend over Edom and Moab, and their discipline over the Children of Ammon." (Isaiah 11:12 & 14, emphasis added).

Important Clue as to the Identity of Ephraim

Notice how both prophets quoted above make no reference to the intervention of any foreign powers to assist the Jews in reclaiming their Land of Promise, and neither do they speak of any non Israelite power protecting them whilst there. They refer instead to action by the two houses of Israel, (Judah and Ephraim).

This is highly significant, as the prophets speak of a combined effort by both houses i.e. Judah and Israel. They do not refer to any other nations being involved! So the question is, who has been working alongside Judah to put the nation of Israel back on the map and then to make it stay there? Whoever they are, that body should be Ephraim!

So what does history tell us? The record of history shows the British government at the forefront in assisting the Jews in their quest to return to their land, with the Americans closely behind.*1

In this we are given an important clue as to the identity of Ephraim. After all, it was the British Army, assisted by the Anzac forces of Australia and New Zealand, including a number of Jewish brigades, who liberated the Holy Land in December 1917. Then in early 1918, the Turkish forces of the Ottoman Empire were expelled from the region by the British Expeditionary Forces led by General Edmund Allenby, whose nickname ironically was *"the Bull"* (the symbol of Ephraim), and from that moment, the door to Jewish settlement of the Holy Land was prised wide open.

Great Britain was the first great power to do something practical by formally recognizing that the Jews had national rights, helping to facilitate the creation of the Jewish state. The year 2007 marked the 90th anniversary of the famous Balfour Declaration of 1917, in which the greatest empire in the world recognized the right of the Jews to have their own homeland in Palestine. Winston Churchill laid a foundation stone in Jerusalem for the Hebrew University and stood publicly against the betrayal of Britain's promises in the 1939 White Paper. In early 1942, the Nazi-German juggernaut lead by Rommel's desert army broke through the British lines and took the strategic city of Tobruk. Rommel's forces then continued their eastward thrust to the Suez Canal. Had they taken possession of the Canal nothing would have impeded their conquest of the Holy Land, which would have meant certain death for its nearly half-million Jewish population. The Jewish leadership, considering the possibility of defeat by the British, decided to remain in the land and fight the invading Germans as best they could. It was decided to establish a fortress on Mount Carmel, and to bring the entire Jewish population of Palestine there, and to hold out against the Germans for as long as possible. Had the British and Anzac forces not been able to hold the line, the world might have come to know of a Masada Mark II, with some half a million Jews committing suicide, rather than submitting to certain death at the hands of their fascist Nazi enemies.

As Providence would have it, the German onslaught was finally halted at a little place called El Alamein in July 1942. The final battle of El

Alamein in Egypt against Rommel's forces began on October 23rd 1942. The future of the entire region and much of the rest of the world depended upon the outcome of this battle. After ten days of intense conflict in which thousands of men from both sides fought and died, the German line was broken, and the allied British and Anzac forces streamed through and continued to chase the retreating Germans. The degree of gratitude which the Jewish people had for these heroes is epitomized in a gift which the Jewish leadership of Palestine, the Vaad Leumi, later presented to General Montgomery, the British Commander of the allied forces. It was a beautiful Bible, and with it was the following inscription in English and Hebrew:

"To Field Marshall Viscount Montgomery, the gallant leader of the victorious British forces, by whose hand God has placed salvation in Zion in the days of El Alamein."

History shows how, after many setbacks, letdowns, (including some major British ones), trials and tribulations both within and without the Land, the Jewish State of Israel emerged from the hideous ashes of the Holocaust in May 1948.

Ever since that auspicious moment, the new country had no truer friend in the world than the American people. It is a fact of history that ever since the foundation of the State of Israel the United States of America has stood by her as her "big brother" protector.

When we thus observe the joint involvement, first of all of the British and her Australian and New Zealand Commonwealth brothers, and secondly of the mighty United States, we are given an indication of who, *"the outcast castaways of Israel," (the house of Ephraim)* really are.

We must also never forget that it was those same nations who stood resolute in a great alliance against the evil Axis powers, and it was through their combined strength that they were able to defeat Hitler's Third Reich. Even though they were not able to prevent the unspeakably brutal horrors of the Holocaust, they nevertheless were able to bring it to an end, and thus save the remaining Jewish population of the world. As the saying goes, "Actions speak louder than words," or, loosely, as the Bible puts it: *"You judge a tree by its fruit!"*

The Judah Connection

Clearly the British and American peoples' historic involvement with the State of Israel presents us with another remarkable indicator of their true Hebrew origins. The fact is that these two leaders of the House of Israel helped to re-establish their older brother Judah back into the Land of Promise, just as was prophesied by the prophets Zechariah and Isaiah. Incredibly, it was at the Jewish Feast of Hanukkah, the feast that signifies deliverance, that the British, together with the Jewish brigades, and the Australian and New Zealand Anzac forces liberated the city of Jerusalem on December 9, 1917. A few years later in 1920, Max Nordau, the co-founder of the Zionist movement, was quoted in the London Evening Standard as having said: "We thought that the Messiah would be an individual, but I feel now as if it were a collective entity, and that its name might be the British nation." In the same year, the League of Nations gave the Mandate to rule Palestine to Great Britain. From here on the Jewish people were on a countdown to the establishment of their own State. In all of this we can see the hand of Providence at work through His people Israel.

Did perhaps the prophet Isaiah prophecy the rebirth of the State of Israel some 2,700 years ago, when he pronounced the following?

"Who has heard such as this? Who has seen such as these? Has a land ever gone through its labor in one day? Has a nation ever been born at one time, as Zion went through her labor and gave birth to her children?" (Isaiah 66:8). Perhaps this prophecy was fulfilled on May 14, 1948, when *"in one day"* the State of Israel came into being.

Nowadays, Israeli schoolchildren are given a rather hostile view of the role of the British in the restoration of their country. The latter are portrayed as malefactors, not benefactors. It is as if the Jews had won the land *from* Britain, rather than having it handed to them *by* Britain. Nations generally pass on to the young a rather glorified version of their own history. And the historical revisionism of Israeli education could be passed over in silence, were it not for the fact that it may well be blocking perception of the lost tribes of Israel. Consider the facts! For nearly two thousand years the Jews had looked forward to the fulfillment of prophecy on the return to Zion, but they lacked the power to do anything about it.

Under Turkish rule the country had become a wasteland, where vegetation was scarce and Jews were scarcer. A mere 6,000 survived in Jerusalem, subsisting mainly on charity from other Jews abroad.

During the Protestant Reformation a Zionist movement arose, aiming to restore the Jews to Israel. These Christian Zionists hoped thus to prepare the way for the coming of the Messiah. But at first they were unable to do anything about it. By the 19th century however, the British had become the greatest power on Earth. Helping defend the Turks against the Russians, they succeeded in 1840 in getting permission to establish a consulate in Jerusalem, empowered to assist Jews there in their quest for legal rights. In this more encouraging atmosphere the Jewish population of Israel increased. By the time of World War I it had grown to 60,000 -- ten times larger than before.*2

Meanwhile the U.S. also was rising to world power. In the 19th century, American Zionist William Blackstone, an evangelical leader, launched a petition for the U.S. to restore Palestine to the Jews. It was signed by 413 eminent Christians and Jews and in 1891 the petition was circulated by the U.S. Department of State to the leading nations of the world.*3

Few people realize the enormous part that British Christian Zionist played in bringing the vision of a Jewish homeland into reality. The famous Balfour Declaration was the ultimate culmination that had flowed from nearly a century of pro-active interaction between the Jewish community and British society. The British Movement for the Restoration of Israel is a totally unique event in all of the recorded history of the world. Never before had one nation shown such continuous interest in the destiny of another people. This interest was led by eminent British figures from Queen Victoria on down to King Edward VII, Prime Minister Lloyd-George, Lord Palmerston, Lord Shaftesbury and Arthur Balfour, all of them enthusiastic proponents of Zionism. Michael Polowetsky, the author of "Jerusalem Recovered," asserted that the Balfour Declaration represented the culmination of half a century of active preoccupation with Jewish culture among British political and intellectual elite. Just as Britain had been the mother country that had brought about the births of America,

Canada, Australia, New Zealand and South Africa, she now became the midwife assisting in the birth of the State of Israel.

In 1893, an Austrian Jew named Theodore Herzl wrote a landmark book, *The Jewish State,* arguing that the Jews could cope with anti-Semitism more effectively if they had a country of their own like other peoples have. He then organized a series of Jewish conferences in Basel in support of the idea. Representing only a minority of Jews, however, the participants lacked the power to do much. Most of the Jews with any political influence lived in the western nations, and in those nations the majority of Jews were firmly anti-Zionist. In Britain the Jews were enjoying a comfortable way of life, with doors of opportunity opening in many directions, including access to political positions in the titled nobility. The question soon arose whether Zionism might undermine these favorable conditions. If a new Jewish state came into existence, might it cast doubt on the patriotism of British Jews? Hence, British Jews objected strongly against the Balfour Declaration, which formally expressed His Majesty's Government's wish for the establishment in Palestine of a national home for the Jewish people. Like the Majority of American Jews, they feared that suspicions of dual loyalty might endanger their acceptance in the nation they now inhabited. Furthermore, within the British government the Declaration was persistently opposed by a Jewish member of the cabinet e.g. Edwin Montagu, the Secretary of State for India. The question had also been submitted to the leading Jewish organization in Britain—The Board of Deputies, and the Board had voted against it; indeed it continued to be anti-Zionist until 1939. It took the menace of Hitler to change its collective mind.*4

The American Jews waited even longer. It was not until several years after World War II, as the facts of the Holocaust sank in, that they abandoned their anti-Zionism. But the Christian Zionists were long accustomed to the misgivings of Jews who felt threatened by their ideas. Even when dealing with Zionist Jews they had often led the way. In this case the British Government simply chose to listen to the Jewish minority, led by secular Zionists such as Chaim Weizmann, who was destined to become the first ever President of the State of Israel. In effect the Christian Zionists launched the Jewish state over the objections of the majority of British Jews.

Christian Zionism had long been the most effective force for the restoration of Israel. Of course it was an easier path for them that that of Jewish Zionism. The Christian need not fear the accusation of dual loyalty. Furthermore, they had little or no idea that they themselves might be Israelites, as they almost certainly were! Thus they did not have to trouble themselves with thoughts of actually leaving their country to settle in the impoverished land of Palestine.

The small minority of Jewish Zionists were only able to play a role in the restoration of Israel because the British government made it possible for them to do so. The British involvement was primarily brought about by Bible-reading evangelical Protestants, who overrode the objections of the Jewish majority who were vehemently opposed. Their contribution to the restoration of Israel has been greater than that of any other people, including the Jews. The Americans were in close support of the British. The result is what might be expected if these nations include the tribes of Ephraim and Manasseh. For those two sons of Joseph are prophesied to be larger and more powerful than Judah (Deuteronomy 33:13-17). Indeed they have been fulfilling the role of redeemer, prophesied for the sons of Joseph—Ephraim and Manasseh. These holders of the birthright, (the right of the first born), became the effective head of the family of Israel at the death of their father Jacob. They were given a double portion of the inheritance, which they received for the maintenance of his widow, sons and unmarried daughters so long as they remained in the household. By restoring their brethren from the tribe of Judah to the land of Israel, they fulfilled that sacred trust.

America, much to her credit, has ever since 1948 consistently protected the Jewish nation. Thus by the actions of Great Britain and the United States of America we can see the outworking of prophecy in history, as these two "Birthright" sons of Joseph are used by God to help their older brother Judah back on his feet as an independent nation. History itself testifies that without Great Britain's initial assistance, the Jews would never have got their national independence. It is also a fact of life that without the continued protection and support of the United States it is doubtful whether the State of Israel would still exist today.

Name of the "Jewish" State was Changed to "Israel!"

The common perception of all the parties involved in the process was that the name of the new nation was to be called the State of Judah. After all, this name perfectly confirmed its ancient historic pedigree as the Kingdom of Judah. It also overwhelmingly reflected the origins of its people from the tribe of Judah. Yet on that fateful day when David Ben Gurion made the formal Declaration of the Establishment of the State of Israel, he declared the following:

"WE DECLARE that, with effect from the moment of the termination of the Mandate being tonight, the eve of Sabbath, the 6th Iyar, 5708 (15th May 1948), until the establishment of the elected, regular authorities of the State in accordance with the Constitution which shall be adopted by the Elected Constituent Assembly not later than 1st October 1948, the People's Council shall act as a Provisional Council of State, and its executive organ, the People's Administration, shall be the Provisional Government of the JEWISH STATE, TO BE CALLED "ISRAEL."

David Ben Gurion, the man destined to become the first Prime Minister of the new State of Israel, then goes on to make a statement of astounding prophetic significance. It seems most curious that even today almost no one has noticed the profound meaning of his words. The second part of his historic declaration is as follows:

"THE STATE OF ISRAEL will be open for Jewish immigration and <u>FOR THE INGATHERING OF THE EXILES</u>; it will foster the development of the country for the benefit of all its inhabitants; it will be based on freedom, justice and peace as envisaged by the prophets of Israel; it will ensure complete equality of social and political rights to all its inhabitants irrespective of religion, race or sex; it will guarantee freedom of religion, conscience, language, education and culture; it will safeguard the Holy Places of all religions; and it will be faithful to the principles of the Charter of the United Nations."

Did you get it? Not many people realize that the very foundational Declaration which brought the State of Israel into being calls not only for Jewish immigration e.g. the return of Judah, but that it also calls for THE INGATHERING OF THE EXILES e.g. the return of Joseph and his companions of the Lost Ten Tribes of Israel. Is this not truly amazing. Those prophetic words spoken by Prime Minister David Ben Gurion were no accident, as the reunification of the two Houses of Israel is THE ultimate "DIVINE" goal behind the reestablishment of the nation.

As we examine the final two paragraphs of the official "Declaration of the Establishment of the State of Israel," we discover further prophetic pointers to Israel's future.

"We appeal to the Jewish people throughout the Diaspora to rally round the Jews of Eretz-Israel in the tasks of immigration and upbuilding and to stand by them in the great struggle for the realization of the age-old dream—THE REDEMPTION OF ISRAEL."

"PLACING OUR TRUST IN THE "ROCK OF ISRAEL," WE AFFIX OUR SIGNATURES TO THIS PROCLAMATION AT THIS SESSION OF THE PROVISIONAL COUNCIL OF STATE, ON THE SOIL OF THE HOMELAND, IN THE CITY OF TEL AVIV, ON THIS SABBATH EVE, THE 5TH DAY OF IYAR, 5708 (14TH MAY 1948)."[*5]

DAVID BEN-GURION

Plus forty-one other signatories

Published in the Official Gazette, No. 1 of the 5th, Iyar, 5708 (14th May 1948).

Israel Ministry of Foreign Affairs.

Did you notice those profound words about the REDEMPTION OF ISRAEL? This is so meaningful, as the "Redemption of Israel" can only occur once the Two Houses of Israel have become re-united! (Check it out for yourself by reading Ezekiel 37:16-22). It can only come about after the INGATHERING OF THE EXILES has taken place. As is confirmed by numerous prophecies in the Bible—just look at these Scriptures; how they speak primarily about the House of Israel, (as opposed to Judah), being gathered back to the land of their fathers:

"Therefore, thus said the Lord HASHEM/ELOHIM: Now I will bring back the captivity of Jacob and show mercy to the <u>"entire house of Israel"</u> and be zealous for My holy Name. When I return them from the peoples and <u>gather</u> them in from the land of their enemies and I become sanctified

through them in the eyes of many nations. Then they will know that I am HASHEM, their God, for I have exiled them to the nations, and I will bring them to their land, and will not leave any of them there. Then I will not hide My countenance from them again, for I will pour out My spirit upon <u>the house of Israel</u>—the word of the Lord HASHEM/ELOHIM." (Ezekiel 39:25; 27-29, emphasis added).

"LISTEN, to me, O ISLANDS, AND HEARKEN, O DISTANT REGIMES: HASHEM summoned me from the belly; He mentioned my name from my mother's womb. And now HASHEM Who formed Me from the belly to be a servant to Him, I [should] return Jacob to Him, so that <u>Israel</u> would be <u>gathered</u> to Him; so I was honored in God's eyes and my God was my strength. He said: It is insufficient that you be a servant for Me [only] to raise up the tribes of Jacob and to restore the ruins of Israel; I will make you a light for the nations, so that My salvation may extend to the ends of the earth." (Isaiah 49:1; & 5-6, emphasis added).

"Hear the word of HASHEM, O nations, relate it in distant islands, and say, 'The One Who scattered <u>Israel, He</u> <u>shall gather him in</u>, and guard him as a shepherd [guards] his flock. For HASHEM will have redeemed Jacob, and delivered him from a hand mightier than he.'" (Jeremiah 31:10-11, emphasis added).

"For behold, days are coming - the word of HASHEM—when I will return the captivity of <u>My people Israel and Judah,</u> said HASHEM, and I will return them to the land that I gave to their forefathers, and they will possess it." These are the things HASHEM spoke concerning <u>Israel</u> and concerning <u>Judah"</u> (Jeremiah 30:3-4, emphasis added).

'Thus said the Lord HASHEM/ELOHIM:"When I <u>gather</u> in the <u>house of Israel</u> from the peoples among whom they were scattered, then I will be sanctified through them in the eyes of the nations, and they will dwell on their land that I gave to My servant Jacob." (Ezekiel 28:25, emphasis added).

Did you also notice that the official Declaration of the Establishment of the State of Israel held that this, *<u>INGATHERING OF THE EXILES,</u> [would be an essential part],* IN, *[bringing about],* THE REALIZATION OF THE AGE OLD DREAM FOR, *<u>THE REDEMPTION OF ISRAEL,</u>*

[which], CAN ONLY BE ACHIEVED IF WE *PUT OUR TRUST IN THE "ROCK OF ISRAEL."*

Can you believe it? All of this is stated in the foundational declaration which brought the State of Israel into being. Oh that the leaders of the present State of Israel would again embrace those same ideals!

Thus in their declaration the founding fathers of the State of Israel, perhaps even without understanding the deep spiritual significance of their words nevertheless, clearly enunciated the Divine purpose for the creation of the Jewish State. The Jewish people in Israel do indeed need to live up to the realization of the age old dream spoken of so eloquently in the Declaration of the Foundation of the State of Israel. Remember it said that the, *"Ingathering of the Exiles,"* and the, *"Redemption of Israel,"* can only happen if we put our trust in, *"The Rock of Israel."* The "Rock of Israel" is none other than Mashiach Ben [Son of] David—The *HOPE OF ISRAEL— He will bring about a reunited Israel once again comprising the Twelve Tribes of Israel.* This means the House of Joseph has to return to join the House of Judah to become The Whole House of Israel once again. In fact the *"age old dream"* spoken of so eloquently in the Declaration, is to witness the reunification of the Two Houses of Israel into one UNITED KINGDOM OF ISRAEL ruled by Mashiach Ben David. Ever since the Ten Tribes of Israel rebelled against the House of David, those two nations comprising Joseph and Judah, have been apart now for some three thousand years. If you think the establishment of the State of Israel was a miracle, wait until you witness the House of Israel and the House of Judah becoming ONE NATION once more! As this prophetic event now lies in the near future, its actual realization will have the whole world in utter astonishment.

CHAPTER EIGHT

If Muslims Can see it—Why Can't We?

The jihadist fanatics of the Islamic world have come to refer to America as the *"Great Satan"* and to Israel as the *"Little Satan."* Ayatollah Khomeiny of Iran was the first to coin the phrase in the late seventies, and thus he castigated the U.S. as the embodiment of all evil in the world. The fact that America has become the focus of Islamic anger was made abundantly clear to the world with the appalling terrorist attack of 9/11 on the twin towers in New York. America is seen as Israel's "big brother" protector, and a common cry of the Muslim demonstrators is to equate America with Israel! "AMERICA IS ISRAEL" they cry! Even in Iraq, the Sunni insurgents commonly referred to American soldiers as "Jews!" *"The Jews are coming,"* they would shout, as they see U.S. troops approaching in their Humvees. A key characteristic which especially manifested itself in the infamous terrorist outrage in Mumbai India in November 2008, was that the Muslim terrorists were looking especially to kill British, American and Jewish citizens. The Islamists crowds in their hate-filled flag burning rituals, invariably burn the Stars and Stripes alongside the Israeli flag and the Union Jack. By the way, Union Jack means, *"the Union of Jacob."* Today, it is common-place for America and Great Britain to be lumped together with the Jewish State of Israel, as the chief enemies of Islam. Do these people perchance know something we don't? The question surely is: If the Islamic world can see who you are, why can't you see it? If not as Israelite descendants of the 10 Tribes, then at least as the righteous of the 70 nations who subscribe to the Judeo-

Christian heritage, or, as conscious sons and daughters of Noah. In addition to this there are countless millions of Gentiles who are inspired by this giant of faith, the patriarch Abraham.

Moses, in his final message to the children of Israel, uttered dire warnings and prophesied what would befall them if they failed to turn from their idolatry and disobedience:

I had said, "I will scatter them, I will cause their memory to cease from man." (Deuteronomy 32:26).

The prophet Isaiah sums up America's condition of amnesia brilliantly:

"An ox knows his owner and the donkey his master's trough; but Israel does not know, My people does not comprehend." (Isaiah 1:3).

The Ox was the tribal standard of the tribe of Ephraim, and it was Ephraim who was the leader of the Northern Kingdom of Israel. The prophet Isaiah is clearly referring here to the sad state of the "Ox," i.e. the Lost House of Israel, (including America), which does not know its owner and which has forgotten its Israelite origins. Americans are oblivious to their Hebrew ancestry and the Scripture here states that in this respect even a dumb ox is more intelligent that the average American citizen. At least the ox knows its owner, whereas Americans do not know where they are from!

The Secret is Sealed Until the Time of the End of the Age as our Oral Torah Has Explained

The Prophet Daniel was instructed to shut up the words and seal the book containing the many revelations he had been given, until the time of the end. He was told that at that time: *"knowledge shall increase!"* Does this sound like the days we are living in today? Just a hundred years ago the choice of travel was by horse and buggy or maybe, when going a long distance, by steam locomotive or ship, whereas today we can reach every part of the globe by jet, and the car is a must for every one, allowing us to run to and fro each and every day of our lives. With the invention of computers and the Internet, knowledge has increased at a phenomenal rate. *The equivalent Hebrew word for Internet literally translates into*

"KNOWLEDGE INCREASE" in English, which are the very same words the prophet Daniel used to describe our time today.

Scientists claim that today, in the early years of our 21st century, the sum of all human knowledge is doubling every 2-3 years and is soon expected to double every year! As of today, this trend is still accelerating at breakneck speed. The term *"Let knowledge increase,"* is a reference not only to the unprecedented explosion of material knowledge but it refers to a similar dramatic unveiling of spiritual knowledge as well. The Prophet Daniel, when told to, *"obscure the matters and seal the book,"* asked again for further revelation as to when the end of these things would be? He was told the following: *"Go, Daniel! For the matters are obscured and sealed until the time of the End."* (Daniel 12: 4 & 9).

Today, we live in the days when the seals of the book, (the Bible), are being removed and when the words that have been closed up and hidden may finally be revealed and brought out into the open. The revelation that Israel has two identities and is comprised of two distinct nations is part of this process. This is the time when the veil, which HASHEM, the God of Israel, has placed over the face of the house of Israel, will finally be removed. The world will come to marvel at the recognition that Judah has hundreds of millions of Israelite relatives, who are his brothers, even though they are not Jews! These are, *"the lost sheep of the house of Israel."*

The time has come for America and the rest of the English speaking world to wake up to their true ancestry and recognize themselves as possibly from Israelite roots.

Battle Between the Followers of Moses and Mohammed

The Islamic nations refer to the establishment of the Jewish state as the "Nakbah," "the Catastrophe" This is because Islam is a territorial religion. It sees the establishment of the state of Israel on the former Islamic territory of the Ottoman Empire as the greatest single reversal in its quest for global domination. The fundamental rule of Islam is that any territory that comes under Islamic rule cannot be de-Islamized. Even if at one time or another, the (non-Moslem) enemy takes over the territory that formerly was under Islamic rule, in Islamic thought, it nevertheless is considered to be perpetually Islamic. This is why Moslems see the presence of the State of Israel in the Middle East as a setback so serious as to affect the honor of Allah, its god. To the Muslim mind, this most catastrophic blow to their religion simply has to be reversed. For them, having the Jewish state established on territory they consider belongs to Islam, is a humiliation worse than that of the Crusades. They simply cannot live with the presence of Israel in the midst of Islam's very heartland. For them there is only one path possible, and this is the total destruction, annihilation, eradication, and conquest of the State of Israel. Thus Islam and the modern day descendants of Joseph in the West, as well as the sons of Judah in the Middle East are on an almighty collision course. It is a battle between the followers of Moses and the Bible, and the followers of Mohammed and the Koran. A battle neither side can afford to lose. Nevertheless, the ultimate outcome is certain - Israel will prevail, as HASHEM, the Almighty Creator of the Universe and One and only true God of Israel, is not going to break His Divine Covenant with the descendants of Abraham, Isaac and Jacob. Therefore, it is only through His Divine intervention that this battle will be won. On the other hand, if Islam were to go back to its own Hebrew roots, it would embrace Jews, Judaism and Israel as friends. Sadly, we do not see any signs of this happening in our world today.

Jews & Anglo-Saxons Tarred With the Same Brush

We have already seen how, in Islamic circles, phobic hatreds of Jews and Anglo-Saxons occur together. In fact they are frequently tarred with the same brush. This same resentment has also manifested itself at the heart of the European Union.

Ever since the 1973 Yom Kippur War and the resultant OPEC oil embargo, the target of European opinion is Israel. It was in the heat of that crisis that Europe allied itself with the Arab League, primarily in pursuit of stable oil supplies. As a result of this abject capitulation to Arab blackmail, the EU has become subservient to the Arab League's demands. Thus, behind the scenes, secret agreements were made which created the concept of Eurabia. In effect this is a political axis between Europe and the Islamic world. It is destined in the near future to become the ultimate "AXIS OF

EVIL!" This political realignment has in turn, since 1973, led to large scale Muslim migration to all EU countries and has resulted in the creeping islamization of Europe. The secret covenant between the EU and Islam has been brilliantly and comprehensively documented by the Israeli author Bat Ye'or in her book entitled "EURABIA—The Euro-Arab Axis."

A total of fifty-four million Muslims now live in Europe, and most of them refuse to integrate. Consequently, endemic anti-Semitism has now morphed into a new guise. The demonization of the individual Jew has now become the demonization of the Jewish nation. With much of the world's media virulently pro-Palestinian and anti-Israel, the Jewish nation in much of Europe is now regarded as a pariah state. Endemic anti-Semitism is fuelled by the Islamic spirit of *jihad,* and it is being reignited in Europe today, where it has reached 1938 proportions. It served as a precursor to war then, and it serves as a precursor to war today! In the wake of the recent "Cast Lead" Gaza War, hate-filled protesters at anti-Israel rallies up and down Europe were chanting the obscene chant: *"Jews back to the ovens!"*

Watch out for an imminent Breach between the U.S. and the EU

Anti-American resentment fuelled by envy over America's superpower status is on the increase and powerful forces are working behind the scenes to bring an end to America's hegemony. More and more people are becoming aware that the European Union is purposely set up as a rival to the United States of America. Intelligent political observers have for some years been able to see the writing on the wall. The transatlantic partnership between America and the nations of Europe is showing severe strain. A breach between these two power-blocks already appears all but inevitable. The German dominated European Union is now openly discussing her global ambitions—challenging America on numerous fronts, sometimes, as over the invasion of Iraq, directly in the open glare of world publicity. Most of the time she engages in covert Franco-German moves behind the scenes. Her politicians are weaving a worldwide web of alliances designed to ensnare as well as check American power.

Americans and Britons generally appear totally unaware of the looming threat the EU, alias Eurabia, presents to the present democratic Anglo-Saxon world order. On May 1, 2004, a further 10 states were added to the EU conglomeration making for 27 nations with a total population of 455 million. This enlargement has also given the EU a larger population than the United States. At the same time more states are clamoring to join the EU colossus in the making. According to the CIA World Fact book of 2007, the European Union's Gross Domestic Product first surpassed the GDP of the United States by some 600 billion USD. The purpose behind the formation of the European currency in 1998 was to confront the hegemony of the almighty US dollar, and turn the European Union into a monetary superpower. The ultimate aim is for the Euro to replace the U.S. dollar as the world's reserve currency. Ten years, on the project clearly has been a triumph, as the Euro has since become an essential part of the daily life for 330 million people. The stark reality is that already in 2006 Euro notes in circulation surpassed the value of all US dollars in circulation. It is no coincidence that the Euro, the European single currency, has spread almost as far as the Denarius of the Roman Empire, the first truly pan-European coin.

Nevertheless, the European currency with its flawed "one size fits all" monetary policy determined by the EU Central Bank, does suffer from a major Achilles heel which looks set to cause the whole system to become unglued. The problem centers around inequality between the monetary discipline of the economies of the Northern EU member states led by Germany and those of the Mediterranean nations, and the situation is fast becoming untenable. The sovereign debts of nations such as Greece, Portugal, Italy and Spain place a big question mark over the future of European Monetary Union. Already, with the bailouts of Greece and Ireland, the handwriting is on the wall and the dominoes will soon begin to fall causing financial and civil chaos throughout the Euro Zone. Nevertheless, the shadowy unelected elites behind the German led EU project and their carefully chosen placemen have long since prepared a Plan B, taking into account the near certainty that the Euro may come unstuck in the near future.

When the Euro falls it is bound to create total chaos in the world's financial markets. However, worst affected of all will be the nations of the European Community. The combination of markets crashing, mainline banks failing with the inevitable consequence of bringing massive unemployment in its wake, will for sure bring substantial upheaval and social unrest leading to civil disorder throughout Europe. It almost seems that those sinister shadowy figures behind the EU project have planned the collapse of their (*deliberately?*) flawed monetary system all along, as they wish to create a replay of the 1930's. The 19th century German Philosopher Friedrich Wilhelm Nietzsche, the author of the *"God is dead"* concept, in commenting on German character stated: *"The German is acquainted with the hidden paths to chaos!"*

The political analyst and historian, Dr Tony Corn states: "If Clausewitz is right that *"war is the continuation of policy by other means,"* then Germany is again at war with Europe, at least in the sense that German policy is trying to achieve in Europe the characteristic objectives of war: the redrawing of international boundaries and the subjugation of foreign peoples.... Germany is planning to use its financial domination of Europe to remake the EU into an extension of German power—more or less the way that Prussia used the "zollverein," (a Customs Union of German States), to bring northern Germany under its control and then dominated the Bismarckian Reich through a rigged constitutional system. A constitutionalization of the EU treaties, would irreversibly institutionalize the current "correlation of forces," and allow German hegemony in the 27-member European Union to approximate Prussian hegemony in the 27-member Bismarckian Reich. Once that is in place, the Germans will continue their policy of deepening relations with Russia at the expense of NATO and transatlantic ties, and end Europe's embargo of arms sales to China."*[1]

It was in 1930s Germany where civil disorder and absolute mayhem were the order of the day, caused by the staggering failure of the German currency, which in turn led to the cry for a strongman to bring order out of the chaos. As history is our witness, Adolph Hitler seized his chance to take power then and this subsequently led to the disaster of World War II. With the (*planned?*) collapse of the Euro, all of Europe will be in uproar and the whole European Union project will look set to fall apart with untold consequences for the nations that have so willingly surrendered their national sovereignty to the dream of a United Europe. Even without this collapse, social and political conditions in Europe today are beginning in quite an ominous way to resemble conditions that existed just before the outbreak of the last world war. The coming collapse will lead to a huge vacuum and this kind of scenario always cries out for leadership. The future leader likely to emerge will be seen to be extremely plausible and charismatic. He will present a new vision that will capture the imagination of the majority of EU citizens. He will have the total and unqualified support of the controlled Media and will both inspire and command a New globally assertive EU to rise like a phoenix from its ashes. This great demagogue leader will then galvanise this EU MARK II, much like Hitler before him into a mighty war machine once again!

The French have a beautiful saying which describes a situation like this very well, it goes: *"L'histoire ce répète!"* History does indeed repeat itself and history proves the fact that mankind seldom learns the lessons of history. Of course King Solomon has said it all before, when he said: *"That which has been is what will be, that which is done is what will be done, and there is nothing new under the sun."* (Ecclesiastes 1:9)

Leopards Do not Change Their Spots!

A most important principle in human nature is that it is very difficult for anyone to change the inherent ancestral character they have inherited at birth. As it is with the individual so it is also with the nation! The pattern of behavior that nations have exhibited over past centuries is a sure guide to their future actions!

At the end of the Second World War, Winston Churchill wrote a six-volume history of the war, in which he included the events that led up to the outbreak of the conflict. He wrote: *"It is my earnest hope that pondering upon the past may give guidance in days to come... [to] a new generation."* Churchill was supremely qualified to talk about this, as five years before the outbreak of World War II he had warned his own generation that; *"none of the lessons of the past had been learned, not one of them has been applied, and the situation is incomparably more dangerous."* [*2]

In view of Germany's record of having started two World Wars in the last century, the one lesson of history mankind needs to learn is that we need to take careful notice of what leading Germans are saying. One of these men is the former Defense Minister Franz Joseph Strauss, who was commonly referred to as "The Strong Man of Europe!" Strauss writes: *"Germany needs*

Europe more than any country.... It has seen in the European idea not only a way of compensating for the immediate past [such as starting two World Wars] but an honorable outlet for its formidable energies. In contributing to the formation of a European federation, Germany herself would find a NEW IDENTITY!"*3 Straus saw that by creating a United States of Europe, *"Europe could again fulfill the historical role which it began to lose at the end of the First World War...When we look back at the European continent of 1914, we need to remember it was the very fulcrum of the world the summit of splendor on this earth!"* *4

German leaders recognize that the path to European unity is also a path to power and glory and this is the goal Germany has aspired to for centuries. Since the reunification of East and West Germany in 1989, Germany has today not only become the most populous nation in Europe, but also the richest, strongest, the most efficient, disciplined, and productive, as well as scientifically and technologically advanced. Franz Joseph Strauss stated that since Germany is the third largest economic power in the world, *"the time must come when that economic power seeks political expression on the world scene."**5 He openly stated that it would be, *"much easier for Germany to make a "comeback" as a member of an international family, as a member of a European Federation, than as a German Reich"* and that, *"our European attitude was the only escape hatch we had."* *6

Former U.S. National Security Advisor Zbigniew Brezinski comments that, *"By redeeming itself through Europe, Germany is restoring its own greatness while gaining a mission that will not automatically mobilize European resentment and fears against Germany"* *7 However he warns that if the drive to unite Europe falters, *"Germany would probably become more assertive and explicit in the definition of its national interests and attempt to reassert its historical role of "creating order" in Europe.'"* *8

Brezinski foresees the emergence of *Mitteleuropa* under the influence, as was the case in the Middle Ages during the Holy Roman Empire of the German nation. A policy paper released by Germany's ruling political parties reached essentially the same conclusion: *"If European integration were not to progress, Germany might be called upon, or be tempted by its own security restraints, to try to effect the stabilization of Eastern Europe on its own and in the traditional way!"* *9 For most of the world, Germany's *"traditional ways"* have brought the most painful and unfortunate memories.

The Islamic Death Pact With Nazi Germany

The Death Pact tells the story about how National Socialism and Islamism formed an alliance in Germany with the specific purpose of plotting the Holocaust together. This account is written after the most thorough research by Rosamund Stresemann, and published on behalf of "Christen an der Seite Israels," - (Christian Friends of Israel, Germany).

Synopsis

The action plan for the Holocaust, which was presented at the Wannsee Conference on January 20th 1942, already included Jews who were in areas that were not under German control. In a pact between Hitler and the Grand Mufti of Jerusalem made in 1941 in Berlin, there were already plans to annihilate Jews in Palestine and in the entire Arab region. There is in fact a link between Germany and radical Islam that actually began long before Hitler under the German Kaiser Wilhelm II and the German Foreign Office, which has continued to have an influence, often hidden, to this day.

Rosamund Stresemann, one of the leaders in the "Call of the Watchman" prayer network in Germany, reveals in this booklet the consequences of this link in such a way as to be a helpful guide to intercessors as they prayerfully come to terms with these facts in the spiritual realm. Rosamund has given me special permission to reproduce her entire article in this book, and our plans are to publish this, "The Covenant With Death" version also in the German language, as a witness for the benefit of the German people.

Foreword by Rosamund Stresemann

In the summer of this year [2012], on a DVD from "Spiegel TV" about the history of the Middle East, I watched the following scene: a high ranking officer of the SS knelt on the ground together with Muslim SS soldiers and prayed with them to Allah. This immediately alerted me and made me clearly aware that there is a connection between Germany and Islam, which has been hidden from the eyes of intercessors until now. I felt compelled to research the historical basis for this connection.

The purpose of this booklet is to reveal to intercessors the guilt that lies in this hidden connection, which in the spiritual realm is burdening the relationship between Germany and Israel. In my research of the historical background I asked myself the question: *"What information is important for intercessors to be aware of, so that the Spirit of God may guide each one of them exactly how they should pray?"* The reader can check the historical facts for himself/herself from the sources that I have given in the footnotes. There are two recent films (in German) that offer a very good introduction to this subject. One is from the program series of ZDF "Der Heilige Krieg" (The Holy War) entitled "Dschihad für den Kaiser" , (Jihad for the Kaiser) and is available in the ZDF media library at: http://www.zdf.de/ZDFmediathek/hauptnavigation/startseite/#/beitrag/video/1416738/Dschihadf

The other is from ARTE with the title: "Turban und Hakenkreuz -der Großmufti und die Nazis" (Turban and Swastika—the Grand Mufti and the Nazis) available at: http://www.youtube.com/watch?v=lrSvzx6FsKI

Another documentary film (in part English, and part German with English subtitles), that gives an interesting summary of this subject is: "Mohammed Amin al-Husseini and Adolf Hitler" which can be seen on YouTube at: http://www.youtube.com/watch?v=5b-IzblQPkI

A recording of a lecture (in English) by Jeffrey Herf at the Hebrew University concerning the link between the anti-Semitic radio propaganda of the Grand Mufti during the Nazi period and the current anti-Semitism of Hamas and in the Arab world in general can be seen at: http://www.youtube.com/watch?v=y5HtppgS42Q

The Death Pact (Foreword by Harald Eckert)

Rosamund Stresemann is one of the leaders in the "Call of the Watchman" prayer movement in Germany and in the network organization, "Together for Berlin" and, as an intercessor from the city of

Berlin, she has stumbled upon an important chapter in German history: the alliance between Hitler and the Grand Mufti of Jerusalem during World War II and the consequential alliance between Germany and radical Islam. This is an alliance which actually began before Hitler during the time of Kaiser Wilhelm II and which has continued to have an influence, often hidden, to this day. There is certainly still more to discover and learn concerning exactly how this is impacting our world today.

In my view it is very significant that we are now being made aware of this inter-relationship, since we just had the 70th anniversary of the Wannsee conference, which took place on January 20th 1942. On this historic occasion the coordination and escalation of the demonic "master plan" of the Nazi rulers was for the first time merged and bound with the state controlled industrialized murder of 6 million European Jews—the so-called "final solution." If Hitler had won World War II and the plan of this deathly alliance had become a reality, this would only have been "Phase 1." "Phase 2" would then have been the murder of all Jews in Palestine and the entire Arab-Muslim world. "Phase 3" would have been global annihilation. The disturbing fact for us today is that "Phase 2" is actually continuing on the side of the Arabs and Muslims. The Grand Mufti was one of the founders and leaders of the Muslim Brotherhood in the years before World War II. This spirit has not been broken and is still active today in Hamas and in the numerous terror groups in the Middle East and world-wide. It is also active in other groups of different persuasions who nevertheless agree with Hitler, the Grand Mufti and all of his present-day followers and protégés on this one point: they want to annihilate the Jews world-wide. And today this also means they want to wipe out Israel.

This publication is written primarily for intercessors in Germany who not only have Israel on their hearts but also the future and fate of the German nation. The Spirit of God has been leading us for years step by step to break through the "veil of silence." This contribution by Rosemund Stresemann shows us something more--that we just cannot allow ourselves to set a "closing date" for this process, but rather we should always be open to be led by the Spirit of HaShem when He is there to shed His light into another dark corner of our history. He does this because He has good thoughts and far-reaching redemptive plans—for Israel, for the Jewish people and for the German people.

With this in mind I commend this reading material to all of us as a praying community in Germany.

Harald Eckert, Chairman,

Christen an der Seite Israels

On January 20th, 2012 it was exactly 70 years since the plan for the total annihilation of the Jews in Europe was laid out in a systematic way at the Wannsee Conference in Berlin under the leadership of SS Senior Group Leader Reinhard Heydrich.

As Christians in Germany, we already began in 1980 to openly face up to our guilt. In large gatherings, for example in 1985 in Nuremberg (50th anniversary of the Race Laws), and in 1988 in Berlin (50th anniversary of the Evian Conference in France), we came before God together with Messianic brothers and sisters to confess our guilt and ask for his mercy. But this process of repentance is by no means complete!

Since then we have experienced so much of God's mercy—the reunification of our land has surely been a clear sign for us of the grace and forgiveness of God! The prophetic promises of God for our land and its calling to stand as a friend on the side of Israel have been clearly fulfilled in the past 20 years. Politically speaking, Germany is now considered as a very close friend of Israel by Israel itself. This friendship is however being challenged—in that it still needs a release from old historical ties in the spiritual realm—something that we were not aware of until now.

Fatah and Hamas are winning more followers day by day with anti-Semitic propaganda, which leans heavily on sketches of role models from the Nazi newspaper "Der Stürmer." Time and time again statements in their propaganda seem to emerge word for word out of Nazi propaganda.

This is not however a fallback to the old propaganda methods of the Nazis—it is much more a continuity of anti-Semitic propaganda for which we as Germans carry a great responsibility. It finds its roots in a "pact" or "alliance" that Hitler entered into with the Grand Mufti of Jerusalem in November 1941 in Berlin. The Grand Mufti was one of the most influential and powerful political and religious leaders within Islam and the Islamic world. This is based on the belief that Jerusalem is a "holy Islamic city"—the third most holy after Mecca and Medina.

The purpose of the pact was clearly defined:

- Prevention of the establishment of a national homeland for the Jews in Palestine.

- Annihilation of the Jews not only in Europe, but also in the whole Arab region– especially Palestine.

In plain language, this agreement not only signified a pact with an Arab leader, but it was an alliance of spirit powers. It was in Germany (actually in Berlin) that two ideologies, both hostile to Jews, were banded together: Fascism and Islam/Islamism, with wide-reaching consequences for the future.

This "death pact" continues to influence the entire Islamic world even today. But we Germans are not aware that we laid the foundations for the success of organizations such as Fatah and Hamas. We must think and pray about these inter-relationships and repent before God for what was precipitated out of our country. To fully understand this, we need to look deeper into the background.

For confirmation please check the following:

http://www.youtube.com/watch?v=0ThxFEz3co0&feature=related as well as http://www.wikiislam.net/wiki/Images:Antisemitic_Cartoons

A Death Pact to Bring About a Final Annihilation of the Jews!

Both Fascism and Islamism embrace the concept of annihilating the Jews: German Fascism with a systematic holocaust and Islamism with its concept of "jihad" (holy war against unbelievers).

Germany as a nation was used by the powers of darkness to carry out a plan to annihilate the Jews and to thus ensure that there would never be a new state of Israel. This required a dual strategy: Germany not only had to be bound to the Nazi creed of National Socialism but also needed at the same time to support the annihilation of the Jews through an alliance with Islam (in the form of the ideology of Islamism). <u>By getting Germany to</u>

finance the murderous intentions of Islamism, as well as lending support both materially and ideologically, the plan of the powers of darkness was safeguarded on two fronts. If one ideology did not prove to be effective, there was in this way through Islamism a "fallback" strategy.

Islamism

At the same time as National Socialism as an ideology and political force was emerging in Germany, the strengthening of which from 1933 on directly led to the Holocaust, another movement came into being in the Arab world in Egypt: The Muslim Brotherhood, which launched Islamism as a political ideology.

The Muslim Brotherhood was founded in 1928 by Hassan al-Banna in Egypt and to this day is the ideological platform for all Islamists including al-Qaeda. It was developed according to the "Führerprinzip," (leadership principle), it had paramilitary units at its disposal and wanted a system of government on the basis of Sharia law and a Caliphate. The Quran was interpreted in a new way by leading Muslim brothers. They placed at its center the concept of "jihad"—with the ardent desire to die as martyrs in the war against infidels. Their motto: "Allah is our desire, the Prophet is our leader, the Quran is our constitution, Jihad is our way, and martyrdom for the sake of Allah is our highest goal." *10

"The Death Industry"

In 1938 an editorial by Hassan al-Banna was published with the title "The Death Industry:" *"To the one nation that brings the industry of death to perfection and understands how one dies a noble death, Allah gives a life of pride in this world and eternal favor in the life to come."*

Al-Banna promoted a new interpretation of the Quran: *"The Quran has set a duty before believers to love death more than life. Only the one who masters the "art of death" can be victorious."* *11

The anti-Semitism of Hitler and the Nazi regime was a source of inspiration for the Muslim Brotherhood. For example, already in 1926 there was a foreign branch of the Nazi party (NSDAP/AO) in Egypt that was formed by Alfred Hess, the brother of Hitler's later deputy Rudolf Hess. German anti-Jewish propaganda was disseminated in Egypt by this organization using leaflets. As the Muslim Brotherhood grew stronger, Nazi Germany gained an increasing influence in Egypt and was admired. Pro-fascist paramilitary youth organizations were formed and the Muslim Brotherhood was inspired by the anti-Semitic propaganda. In Egypt, al-Banna worked undercover together with agents of the German Reich to incite an anti-British insurgency in Egypt.

How Nazi Propaganda Changed Islam's Perspective on Jews

Even though the Jews were degraded in the Quran, the Islamic world was not aware of the Fascist view and belief that "world-wide Jewry" was a threat and the enemy of all mankind. They did however gain this completely new perspective on the Jews from the Nazis. Core issue of the Nazi propaganda: the danger of world-wide Jewry. The starting point in Nazi propaganda was always to portray the "danger of Jewry." In Hitler's world view, there was a "world-wide Jewish conspiracy." Everything that happened in world history was attributed to a Jewish plot. Behind communism, capitalism, materialism—and later behind the warring allied powers of America, Russia and Great Britain—always stood the real enemy, who was clearly named by the Nazis as the Jew. As documentary evidence, Hitler used a book that contained the so-called "Protocols of the Elders of Zion." The book was a complete fabrication from beginning to end. It supposedly contained 24 protocols of a secret global Jewish conspiracy. These imaginary protocols described how the alleged world-wide Jewry was planning to take over the governments of various countries and thereby rule the world, and were presented as pure tyranny and all-embracing terror.

Just like Hitler's book "Mein Kampf" ("My Struggle"), the infamous book "Protocols of the Elders of Zion" was disseminated in the Islamic world in the Arabic language. The Muslim Brotherhood was inspired by this anti-Semitism. In 1938, they allowed both books as well as anti-Semitic tracts to be distributed at an "Islamic Parliamentary Conference in support of Palestine." They also copied Germany in boycotting Jewish products and businesses. During the Arab uprising against the British in

Palestine between 1936 and 1939, the Muslim Brotherhood organized large, violent anti-Jewish protests in Egypt under the rallying cries "Down with the Jews" and "Jews get out of Egypt." Thus the Muslim Brotherhood supported the Arabs in Palestine—inspired by the German example. *12

Islamist from the Outset - the Grand Mufti of Jerusalem

A Mufti was the highest religious-judicial authority in Islamic matters within a political region of the old Ottoman Empire. His interpretation of the Quran was legally binding. In 1921 the British had appointed the son of the very influential Arab family clan of the Husseinis, whose ancestry could be traced back to Mohammed, to "Grand Mufti of Jerusalem" in the area of the Mandate for Palestine. They gave the honorary title of "Grand Mufti" to the very young 28 year old Haj Amin al-Husseini (1893-1974) and thereby strengthened his standing in the Arab world. They also made him leader of the "Supreme Muslim Council" and so gave him control over the finances and the personnel of all religious institutions in Palestine.

Single-mindedly, the Grand Mufti enlarged his power base, formed a "Palestine Arab Party," founded the first "Islamic World Congress," which met in Jerusalem in 1931, and in 1936 was chairman of the "Arab Higher Committee," the political representative of the Arabs in Palestine made up of many Palestinian parties.*13 His religious views were formed, together with the founder of the Muslim Brotherhood, Hassan al-Banna, by a common religion teacher who was a follower of the Saudi Wahabi sect. He was the Syrian Rashid Rida. The leader of the Muslim Brotherhood, Hassan al-Banna, and the Grand Mufti encouraged one another. There had to be no place for Jews in an Islamic Palestine. The Islamization of the Palestinian cause brought in such a huge flow of support for the Muslim Brotherhood in Egypt that they grew into a large political force.*14

Al-Banna advocated, just like the Grand Mufti, aggressive armed jihad against non-Muslims, especially Jews and those who helped them. The Muslims had to defend the al-Aqsa Mosque in Jerusalem through jihad. From 1936 there was an official relationship between the Muslim Brotherhood and the Arab Higher Committee under the leadership of the Grand Mufti.

The Link With National Socialism

Although the Muslim Brotherhood was influenced by the ideology of the Nazis and its hostility towards Jews, the Grand Mufti's hate for Jews came from his father. He grew up as a child with a hate for Jews from his father who was also a mufti and had fought against Jewish immigrants into Ottoman Palestine. From 1920 onwards, his son Amin al-Husseini was behind every anti-Jewish riot. But the British still made him Grand Mufti anyway.

In 1929 he sparked off a pogrom in Jerusalem and allowed the distribution of flyers in Jerusalem with the words: *"Oh Arabs! Do not forget that the Jew is your worst enemy and from time immemorial was the enemy of your forefathers."* *15

Going back to the origins of Islam, the Grand Mufti found enough evidence in the Quran to feed his hate for Jews and to give him the possibility right from the beginning to propagate the fight against Zionism as a religious war for Islamic territory.

- "those who incurred the curse of Allah and His wrath, those of whom some [the Jews] He transformed into apes and swine ..." Sura 5/60

- "Every time they kindle the fire of war, Allah doth extinguish it; but they [the Jews] always strive to do mischief on earth." Sura 5/64.

- "Strongest among men in enmity to the believers wilt thou find the Jews ..." Sura 5/82. *16

- The unbelievers are to be killed. "And slay them wherever ye catch them, and turn them out from where they have turned you out;" Sura 2/191. *17

The Grand Mufti's hate for Jews made him into an ardent follower of National Socialism. The youth organization of his Palestine Arab Party carried the name "Nazi-Scouts." Nazi slogans were printed on flyers and swastikas were used as symbols. Hitler received telegrams with good wishes from Palestine, as he was announcing the Nuremberg Race Laws in 1935.

The most important common precepts of the Islamic and Nazi world views were summarized later by the Grand Mufti as follows:

1. Monotheism—unity in leadership, leadership principle (Führerprinzip).

2. Appreciation of obedience and discipline.

3. War and the honor of falling in battle.

4. Community spirit according to the motto: common interest before self-interest.

5. High regard for motherhood and prohibition of abortion.

6. Relationship to Jews -"in the fight against Jews, Islam and National Socialism come very close to one another."

7. Glorification of work and production: "Islam protects and honors work, whatever it may be." [*18]

Since the Grand Mufti was waging a gruesome war against all Arabs who did not share his anti-Jewish policy, the swastika was used as an identification symbol to show which ones were on his side. With a swastika on your car you were protected. In fact many of the so-called "collaborators" were cruelly executed by the Grand Mufti's followers: "This is how we deal with traitors to the national cause!" was written on labels pinned to the murdered Arabs, where the heart had been cut out of the body or the tongue pulled out through the throat.[*19]

The dream of a "Greater Arabia"

Soon after the seizure of power in 1933, the Grand Mufti made contact with German government agencies—he had direct contact with Adolf Eichmann and with the SS, (Hitler's protection squadron). He was looking for a coalition with Hitler in order to achieve his claims for power over a Greater Arabia. The Grand Mufti was not only an Islamist, but also a proponent of Arab nationalism. He dreamed of a "Greater Arabia" in which all Arabs from the Atlantic to the Persian Gulf would be united under his leadership. The Nazis did not hide their support for the Grand

Mufti, but they were not too open about it at first because of how Great Britain might react.

The Death Pact was Beginning to Take Shape

In 1937 the British Peel Commission made a proposal to divide the area of the Mandate for Palestine into a small Jewish state and a larger Muslim Arab state. In this way they hoped to calm the Arabs and establish peace in Palestine. This alarmed the Nazis and they decided to support the Arabs in order to prevent the formation of a "Jewish state." The "Arab Club" was established in Berlin, as a center for Palestinian agitation with an Arabic radio station. Eichmann, Baldur von Schirach, military intelligence chief Canaris and the leader of the Oriental Department in the Foreign Office, Werner Otto von Hentig, explored the possibility of getting the Arabs on their side. As a result, the Grand Mufti became the central figure.

The Oriental Department of the German Foreign Office

The Oriental Department of the Foreign Office had been created at the beginning of World War I at the time of the German Kaiser. The political and spiritual fertile ground for a "death pact" with Islam was being made ready at this time by employees in this department. [*20]

Long before there was a discussion about the presence of Islam in Germany, long before our current president said: "Islam belongs in Germany," the German Kaiser had already decided that Germany and Islam should form an alliance. Kaiser Wilhelm II declared himself to be the "Protector of 300 million Muslims" in an after-dinner speech in Damascus during his trip to the Middle East in 1898. He concluded a friendship, trade and shipping contract with the Ottoman Sultan. Only a short time before this, Theodor Herzl had sought out the Kaiser during his trip to the Middle East and proposed to him his idea of an autonomous Jewish state under a German protectorate within the Ottoman Empire. The Kaiser did not however want to support a Jewish state at the expense of friendship with Islamic states. He did not want to displease the Ottoman Sultan but rather gain him as a friend in order to enforce his own power politics against Great Britain. In fact long before the Nazis considered the idea, he advocated the gassing of Jews like mosquitoes!

Kaiser Wilhelm II's First German "Jihad" Plan

The German diplomat and specialist in Middle Eastern affairs, Baron Max von Oppenheim (1860-1946), had developed a "jihad concept" at the beginning of World War I with the intent of destabilizing British power in the area. He presented it to the Kaiser. It carried the title: "Revolutionizing the Islamic territories of our enemies." The tactic of this plan was to use the Islamic teaching of jihad as a means of war against Germany's enemies (Great Britain, France and Russia). In this way a third front would be opened against Great Britain and France in the war by creating insurgency in the Islamic world.

Max von Oppenheim was an Islam expert. He knew that militant Islamic jihad was in fact intended to be used to create an Islamic state—an Islamic caliphate—in the war against unbelievers. He now developed a completely new concept of jihad:

The Kaiser, who was regarded as a representative of Christian power, should incite Islamic jihad to attain his own ("Christian") power ambitions/goals and then exploit it for German war purposes. Thus a politically construed version of Islamic jihad was born—out of a German strategy!

The plan of Oppenheim was all about the destabilization of the "Islamic territories of our enemies" by calling for jihad along with Islamic insurrection and acts of terrorism. The plan was accepted by the Kaiser just two months after the start of the war and was set in motion. Accordingly a new department was opened in the Foreign Office in Berlin: the Intelligence Bureau for the Middle East—the Oriental Department. The Muslim nations would now be spurred on to insurrection from this planning department.*[21]

In 1925 there were already more than 60 people working in this department. Leaflets in Arabic and Persian were printed and the intelligence bureau even produced a propaganda sheet in Arabic called, "Al-Jihad." The organizations mission was to influence all Muslim prisoners of war in order to win their support for German policy against the British. Thus those Muslim prisoners of war were given their own mosque and were trained for jihad by special imams. They were housed in specially constructed camps (so-called "crescent moon camps") in Wünsdorf and Zossen, (south of Berlin). On July 13th 1915, the first mosque on German soil with a 23 meter high minaret was dedicated.*22

Furthermore, a large monument with the Islamic confession of faith was erected in the Muslim section of the Zehrensdorf war cemetery which is near Wünsdorf. *23

In fact "jihad" was called for by the Sultan in Constantinople, (now Istanbul) by way of a "Fatwa," (an Islamic legal ruling), in the middle of November 1914 after the Ottomans joined the war on the German side. The Tunisian Sheikh Salih, a descendent of Mohammed, further explained the call for jihad. He stated: "The Ottoman Sultan-Caliph is leading this small jihad with his allies, mainly the Germans, against the enemies of Islam, the British, French and Russians." *24

In the Sultan's legal ruling, "jihad" was now redefined from a "general Islamic duty" into an "individual duty to rebel against occupying forces." The British suffered so many problems with Arab terrorist organizations which were being stirred up by Germany that they tried by all the means at their disposal to draw the Sheikh of Mecca onto their side before Germany could get to him. The Germans wanted him, as the head man in Mecca, to also call for jihad from there. The British drew him to their side with much gold plus the promise of his own Arab kingdom as a reward for an uprising against the Ottoman Empire. With this promise, a political weakness was exposed which has a bearing even today on the unresolved Palestinian conflict. *25

"The Jihad Genie is Out of the Bottle"

The idea propagated by the Germans to drive out foreign occupying forces by the use of jihad proved itself to be an idea that, once set in motion, could no longer be stopped. After World War I the idea was taken up in the Arab world by the Muslim Brotherhood, further "refined," and incorporated into their concept of Islamic jihad, which to this day stands behind all terrorist attacks. <u>To think that a German Baron initiated all this —a non-Muslim who called the "jihad genie" to come out of its bottle to aid Germany's political interests. Since 1914 this genie has been gaining steam.</u> When Hitler came to power, Baron Max von Oppenheim was no longer in the service of the Foreign Office. However in 1940 the Baron felt compelled to again lay out his old ideas in Berlin in order to support the German advance in North Africa. Although Sultan-Caliph and the Ottoman Empire were long gone, nevertheless, Oppenheim's idea to destabilize British and French rule in the Muslim Arab regions through jihad and insurrection could still work to Germany's advantage. Following Oppenheim's suggestions, the Foreign Office developed a complete set of actions to initiate insurrection among the Arabs. The experience of the Oriental Department from World War I was of great help. Many of the employees from the time of the Kaiser were still employed in the same department!

The Reich's Foreign Office now proposed extending propaganda to the Muslim world and it empowered Wilhelm Canaris, the Nazi intelligence chief, to start uprisings in Palestine and Jordan. The programs included the supply of weapons, as well as training in the handling of explosives. An alliance was made with the Grand Mufti of Jerusalem, who was generously funded by the German Reich. *26

German Support for the Arab Uprising in Palestine

Starting in 1937, the German Nazis were training the recruits in the revolutionary movement of the Grand Mufti. The whole region was covered with Canaris' spy network. The SS trained more terrorists in the coming years, including the formidable bomb maker Fawzi Al Kutub. *27

"Kutub had not only blown up the Jewish Agency building in Jerusalem on March 11th, 1948, but had also prepared the explosives for the attacks on the building of the Jerusalem Post, (then named the Palestine Post), on February 1st, 1948. He also blew up a hotel in Ben Yehuda Street in the heart of Jerusalem on February 28th, 1948, causing 46 deaths and leaving 130 injured. In May 1948 it was Kutub who blew up both of the two large synagogues, Tifereth Israel and the Hurva, at the

The Covenant With Death

request of Abdullah el-Tell of the Jordanian Legion. This expedited the fall of the hard fought-over Jewish Quarter in the Old City of Jerusalem." *28

The Arab insurgency in Palestine from 1936 to 1939, which had such a disastrous impact upon the Jewish population, could only be sustained thanks to the guaranteed financial support from Germany according to later statements of the Grand Mufti!

The Arab insurgency against the Zionist movement was actually financed with German money and strengthened by the delivery of weapons. This had far reaching consequences: "The ferociousness of the insurgency forced Great Britain to offer major concessions to the Arabs in 1939. The British abandoned the idea of establishing a Jewish state in Palestine and limited Jewish immigration for the next five years to 75,000 people in total. After this, immigration was made contingent on Arab consent. However Al-Husseini did not think that these concessions went far enough and rejected this new policy." *29

Although the British knew that the Grand Mufti was the driving force behind the Arab insurgencies, they let him stay in office for a long time. Only at the end of 1937 were the members of the Arab Higher Committee arrested. But the Grand Mufti was able to flee to Syria, and from there he went to Iraq.

Between 1939 and 1941, with the help of Germany, the Grand Mufti organized a revolution against the British in Iraq. The Germans had promised military support, but then were not able to provide it. The revolution collapsed and the Grand Mufti had to flee once again. On November 6th, 1941 he finally arrived in Berlin. He lived in Schloss Bellevue at first, then he was given the expropriated residence of the "Jewish Institute," which later became the seat of the "Central Institute for Islam" and an apartment block in the vicinity was also made available to him.

Cognizance of the Plans to Kill

He met with Himmler and Eichmann in Berlin. Eichmann gave him a detailed presentation on the "Solution to the Jewish question in Europe." The Grand Mufti was fully in the picture about the methods for the annihilation of the Jews because he was also taken by Eichmann to Auschwitz concentration camp, and even visited other extermination camps as well. He surpassed even Eichmann in how radical he was in his determination to annihilate the Jews, as we will see later. Dieter Wisliczeny, one of Eichmann's assistants, attested to the fact that the Grand Mufti had asked Himmler in one meeting to send one of his assistants to Jerusalem after the war in order to help the Grand Mufti with the "Solution to the Jewish question in the Middle East." *30

Already in 1940 the Grand Mufti formulated the following draft of a German-Italian declaration of intent of an alliance that he wanted to create: *"Germany and Italy recognize the right of Arab countries to resolve the question of the Jewish elements in Palestine and other Arab lands in the national and racial interests of Arabs, and in the same way as the Jewish question has been resolved in the countries of Germany and Italy."* *31

The Death Pact with Hitler

Having only just arrived in Berlin, on November 28th, 1941, the Grand Mufti was welcomed by Hitler. This meeting resulted in the alliance that the Grand Mufti was looking for. Thanks to the envoy Schmidt, who was present when this discussion took place and who kept a record, we know the content of this alliance. The most important extracts from the record are as follows:

The Grand Mufti made clear ... *"The Arabs are the natural friends of Germany because they have the same enemies as Germany, namely the British, Jews and the communists. They are therefore also ready to work enthusiastically with Germany and are available to participate in the war, not only in a negative way through the perpetration of acts of sabotage and the incitement of revolution, but also in a positive way by the creation of an Arab Legion."*

Hitler replied: *"At present, Germany is in a struggle of life and death with two power bases of Jewry: Great Britain and Soviet Russia....Of course Germany would welcome positive and practical help from the Arab people who are in the same struggle, because, in a fight for very existence, superficial promises are useless, especially where Jewry might be able to use British power resources to achieve their own ends."* [...] The Führer (Hitler) then delivered the following statements to the Grand Mufti and asked him guard them deep within his heart:

1. *He (Hitler) will continue the fight until the European Jewish-communist Empire is completely destroyed.*

2. *In the course of this fight the German army will reach the southern end of the Caucasus region at a point in time which today cannot be defined exactly but is not too far in the future.*

3. *As soon as this point in time is reached, the Führer (Hitler) will personally deliver to the Arab world the assurance that the hour of deliverance has arrived. The goal of Germany would then simply be to annihilate all the Jews who are living in Arab areas under the protection of the British Mandate. At this moment the Grand Mufti would then be the most qualified leader for the Arab world."*[*32] In plain language this agreement not only signified a pact with an Arab leader, but it was also an alliance between spirit powers, and as a result, two Jew-hating ideologies joined forces in Germany:

Fascism and Islam/Islamism.

The goal of this pact was clear: the wiping out of Jewry, not only in Europe, but also in the entire Arab region. "These agreements on war aims and the annihilation of Jews were the Middle Eastern equivalent of the Wannsee Conference in 1942." [*33]

On April 28th, 1942, the Reich's Foreign Minister Von Ribbentrop, wrote a letter to the Grand Mufti in which he not only promised support for the Arab fight for freedom, but also specifically promised support for the "elimination of a Jewish national homeland in Palestine." [*34]

In 1943 the Grand Mufti declared in a speech in the German Air Force building, [today the home of the Berlin City Parliament], the firm and lasting basis of the pact: *"... the Germans have never done anything to harm a Muslim. They fight against our common enemy who persecute the Arabs and Muslims. But above all they have in any event solved the problem of the Jews. These concerns which we share, especially the last, make our friendship with Germany not just temporary, and dependent on certain conditions, but a permanent and lasting friendship based on common interests."*

The Final Solution to the Jewish Question was the Basis of the Lasting Friendship.

The consequences of this pact was that the Grand Mufti now got every imaginable support in Berlin for the *"Arab fight for freedom,"* including his plans to annihilate the Jews.

His comprehensive activities included:

1. Radio propaganda to the entire Arab-speaking and Persian region with programs packed with a mixture of anti-Semitic agitation and interpretations of the Quran. The seeds of hate were sown by the ultimate propaganda weapon of "Radio Zeesen," the most powerful radio transmitter in the world.

2. Preventing the emigration of European Jews so that they would be murdered in the concentration camps instead.

3. Espionage in the Middle East.

4. The organization of Muslims into military units (particularly SS units) in the lands occupied by the Axis powers, as well as in North Africa and Russia, which brought death and destruction in the name of Hitler and Islam.

5. Formation of the Arab Legion and the Arab Brigade that were trained by the German military and were later used against Israel in the first War of Independence in 1948.

From 1941 onwards the Grand Mufti was the director of the Islamist world headquarters for the annihilation of the Jews in the Arab speaking world. From here he broadcast "jihad" against the Jews over the most powerful short wave transmitter in the world that was located in Zeesen, south of Berlin. Someone at the time summed up the continuously repeated message from "Radio Zeesen" as follows: *"The Jew has been the eternal* *enemy of Muslims since the time of Mohammed. Killing him pleases Allah."* *35

The radio transmissions of the Grand Mufti reached the entire Arab-speaking world in the Middle East as well as Persia (now Iran) and reached as far as India and present day Pakistan and Bangladesh. The programs were translated into Turkish, Persian and Hindi. Shortly after his arrival in Berlin, the Grand Mufti became one of the directors of the "Arabian Office" in Berlin, which carried the responsibility for the preparation and transmission of programs in Arabic under the supervision of Goebbels Ministry of Propaganda. Come 1943, Josef Goebbels estimated that the number of anti-Jewish programs had reached 70 to 80 percent of all vocal transmissions from Radio Zeesen.*36

One can only appreciate the impact of this anti-Semitic radio propaganda into the Arab world when we bear in mind that at this time at least 80% of the population was illiterate. Radio programs were therefore the most important tool in influencing public opinion. Between 1939 and 1945 there was no other station that had anywhere near as many listeners in all public places throughout the Arab world, as this Nazi station! It made the Grand Mufti known throughout the Arab world, as well as in Persia and India and it gave him a prestige and position of influence that far exceeded his former status. The impact of the propaganda from Radio Zeesen was thoroughly researched by Matthias Kuentzel, who describes the impact of the programming as follows:

"First of all the programs were well made: items of propaganda with quotes from the Quran were mixed with music of the region. Secondly the talks were aimed not at the intellect but at the emotions of the masses." *37

Kuentzel describes the station as: *the "instrument that transposed an anti-Semitic world view into the Arab world and bound early Arab Islamism with later National Socialism."* *38

Goebbels' "Long Distance Weapon Over the Air Waves"

The Nazis had endeavored ever since 1939 to take anti-Semitic propaganda into the Arab world and beyond. As already mentioned they had some success in Egypt especially in giving ideas to the Muslim

Brotherhood. From the outset the tactic was to establish a connection between the verses in the Quran that were hostile to the Jews and Hitler's anti-Semitic ideology. Until the Grand Mufti arrived they had only limited success in other Arab states. As soon as the Grand Mufti took over the production of the radio programs, this propaganda developed into seeds of hate, which fell onto the fertile soil of receptive hearts through the person of the Grand Mufti and his significance in the Islamic world. Goebbels called the Arab programming *"our long distance weapon over the air waves."* The Grand Mufti could now stir up the Arabs against the Jews unhindered over four years. Any Arabs that wanted just to negotiate with Zionists, like the Jordanian King Amir Abdallah, were ridiculed in the transmissions. "World-wide Jewry," according to the propaganda, stood behind all the enemies of the Arabs—but Hitler was their true friend who would bring them freedom. Great Britain and the USA were henchmen for the Jews. The fight of the Arabs against the Zionist movement in Palestine was no longer a local political issue, but, with the help of the Grand Mufti's propaganda, it was declared to be a fight against the "Zionist world-wide conspiracy" from which Adolf Hitler wanted to deliver them. This misrepresentation of a local political conflict between the Arabs and the Zionist movement in Palestine took a firm hold in hearts and minds in the Arab world and it is still alive and well to this day! A fear of *"world-wide Jewry"* and its designs for conspiracy, which did not exist in the Islamic world until then, was stirred up during these years. The fear of Jews was just not there before then, since Mohammed and his Arab followers had actually defeated the Jews. Many Islamists adopted this model of interpretation, and one of them was the Ayatollah Khomeini who was an enthusiastic listener of the Grand Mufti's Programs in Iran.

The Call to Kill the Jews

On July 7th, 1942 the following "call to kill" was broadcast over the radio by the Grand Mufti: *"In the face of the barbaric plan of action of the British, we think it best, if the Egyptian nation is to be saved, for Egyptians to rise up and kill as many Jews as they can before the Jews get any chance to betray the Egyptians. It is the bound duty of every Egyptian to annihilate the Jews and destroy their property ... you must kill the Jews before they open fire on you. Kill the Jews who have stolen your wealth* *and forged secret plans to undermine your security. Arabs from Syria, Iraq and Palestine, what are you waiting for? The Jews are planning to rape your women, kill your children and wipe you out. According to the Muslim religion the defense of life is a duty that can only be fulfilled if the Jews are killed. This is your best chance to take care of this filthy race that has stolen your rights and brought you disaster and destruction in your own lands. Kill the Jews, burn their property, destroy their businesses, and eradicate this base of support for the British imperialists. Your only hope of salvation lies in the annihilation of the Jews before they annihilate you."* *39

The hate propaganda of the Grand Mufti was not only spread by radio, but also by tons of small leaflets that were adorned with verses from the Quran and called for attacks on the Jews in North African countries.

Preventing the Emigration of European Jews—an Effective Step Towards Annihilation

Is it by accident or does it rather fit into the plan of HaSatan that the arrival of the Grand Mufti Coincided with the Wannsee Conference in 1942 and the plan for the total systematic Annihilation of the Jews in Europe? Until the middle of 1941 the official policy of Germany concerning the Jews was geared towards driving them out and enforced deportation. Eichmann actually worked with Zionist leaders for this. From the very beginning the Grand Mufti had despised the fact that European Jews were immigrating into Israel and through the use of terrorist attacks in Palestine ensured that the British only allowed minimal immigration from 1939 onwards. Having only just arrived in Germany, he had the opportunity to meet Eichmann and to make clear to him that Germany should in no way allow European Jews to emigrate. From October 1941 Himmler placed a ban on Jews leaving Germany. We cannot estimate the effect of the Grand Mufti's campaign but his protests certainly influenced the plans for a "final solution?"

Jews could still emigrate after 1941 from the occupied countries in the Balkans. Even Himmler still wanted to "sell" Jews for foreign exchange after 1941. The Grand Mufti was against any possible kind of emigration with all his might, not only in his dealings with Eichmann. Even in 1943 he wrote letters to the Romanian, Bulgarian and Hungarian governments insisting that Jews in the Balkans should in no way be allowed to leave. The Grand Mufti often argued his case that allowing them to leave "would by no means solve the Jewish problem." *40

"A rough survey shows that Haj Amin (Grand Mufti) directly prevented the escape from the gas chambers of up to 100,000 Slovakian, Romanian, Bulgarian and especially Hungarian Jews, who could have perhaps still emigrated to Palestine, Sweden, Turkey or South America. Jewish children from France and Belgium were also included. The actual total must be much higher. Just in one single round of applications between July 14th and 23rd 1944 there was talk of some 40,000 people plus 1,000 children under ten years old where the refusal of permission to emigrate was, in the final analysis, based on "consideration for the Arab issue." For "Arab issue" read Haj Amin Husseini, the Grand Mufti of Jerusalem. *41

Dieter Wisliceny, Adolf Eichmann's deputy, expressed his conviction at the Nuremberg War Criminal Trials, that the Grand Mufti had played a decisive role in the murder of European Jews. Husseini had recommended their eradication to many of the Nazi leaders including Hitler, Von Ribbentrop and Himmler. He testified that the Grand Mufti had been a good friend of Himmler.

The Grand Mufti called for a "final solution" in Palestine, and a concentration camp in Jenin was planned.

The Grand Mufti had asked Eichmann for concrete support for the murder of Jews in Palestine if the Axis forces were victorious. He vehemently demanded a "final solution" for Palestine and all the Arab areas. In 1942 the elimination of the national Jewish homeland in Palestine was planned in detail by the SS Task Force "Egypt" under the leadership of Walter Rauft in cooperation with Rommel's Tank Division. A concentration camp was to be built in Jenin. This was only prevented by the British victory over Rommel at El Alamein!

For the Grand Mufti there was no question of an alternative to completely wiping-out all of the Jewish presence in Palestine. He wanted to establish a pure Islamic state—a parallel to Hitler's "racially pure" Aryan state.

Attempt to Poison the Population of Tel Aviv—"Operation Atlas"

"Operation Atlas" was another devilish plan of the Grand Mufti. The plan was to poison the source of drinking water for Tel Aviv at Rosh Ha-Ayin (Ras el Ein) in order to kill the 160,000 Jewish inhabitants of the city. In October 1944 "Operation Atlas" with German SS personnel and Palestinian terrorists was set in motion and executed. By God's mercy the plan failed, Baruch HaShem! Bedouins found the hidden cashes of poison along with other items after they had seen the attackers arrive by parachute and informed the British Mandatory authorities.

Grand Mufti's Islamic SS Divisions

The Grand Mufti made contact with Himmler soon after his arrival in Berlin in 1941. He made a proposal to use his influence in the Islamic world to recruit Muslims in the areas that Hitler had conquered and occupied for the fight against the common enemy. As the Nazis needed more and more fighters for their forces as the war went on, Himmler, who was enthusiastic about this plan, in May 1943 made the Grand Mufti part of his SS apparatus with an office in the main security agency for Germany, in the office for terrorism. It was agreed that he would recruit volunteers first of all in Bosnia for the formation of armed SS units.

At a first glance, the formation of Muslim SS units did not appear to be at all consistent with the Nazi ideology. Until then only "racially pure Arians" were admitted into the SS. Himmler defended this decision before Goebbels and explained that he "could not hold anything against Islam, because Islam was raising up men for him in the SS division and promised them a place in heaven if they fight and fall in battle—a very practical and attractive religion for soldiers!" The Muslim Bosnians were called "Muselgermanen" for short.

With the help of the Grand Mufti and his "jihad call" to holy war against the common enemy—the Jews, the Bolsheviks and the nations allied with them—starting in 1943, tens of thousands of Muslim soldiers were recruited, especially from the Balkans. Himmler allowed the Grand Mufti to train imams to look after the soldiers and appointed him to the position of SS Group Leader. In this way two Islamic mullah schools were founded by the Grand Mufti in Germany: one in Potsdam and one in Dresden. The training for the imams included a mixture of Islamism and Nazi hate for Jews, and was set up by the Grand Mufti.*42

In a speech to the imams of the Bosnian Muslim SS Division "Handschar," (named after the Bosnian word for an Arabian sword), the Grand Mufti declared: *"You my dear Bosnian Muslims are the first Islamic division and serve as an example of real cooperation between Germany and Muslims. I wish you every success in your holy mission."* This "holy mission" comprised the active pursuit of the extermination of the Jews and the fight against the Partisan army of Tito. All these troops were feared for the great cruelty with which they perpetrated numerous war crimes. In the records of the Nuremberg war crime trials from August 1946 it states: *"Wherever they went in Serbia, Bosnia and Herzegovina, overall they left behind ashes and desolation, bodies of innocent men, women and children who were burnt in their own homes."*

Besides the Bosnian SS divisions there were still some other SS divisions with a Muslim majority. In many cases Muslims were also integrated into existing German army units. Parts of the Bosnian SS Division "Handschar" later fought on the eastern front and then in the final battle for Berlin in 1945.

Islamic Terrorists were Trained by Hitler's SS

The Grand Mufti also recruited as his henchmen Arabs from Palestine who in 1943 were trained as terrorists in the SS General School for Espionage at Sorghvliet Park in The Hague. The men received courses in sabotage and were instructed in the use of radio transmitters and automatic weapons. They were also trained in the use of explosives. These terrorists were then again active in Palestine in 1945.

The Seeds Sown Begin to Sprout—the Impact of the Grand Mufti and his Propaganda After 1945

Although the Grand Mufti was on the list of war criminals because he was responsible for the atrocities of the Muslim SS Division in Bosnia, as well as for the killing of thousands of Jewish children in the Holocaust, the USA and Great Britain eventually gave up on any criminal proceedings against him. The prestige that the Grand Mufti had gained with the help of the German propaganda transmissions over Radio Zeesen was so great that the western powers did not want to fall out with the Arab world. In 1945 France was holding him under light surveillance and allowed him to "escape." *43

The Consequences:

- The anti-Semitism that the Nazis fanned into flame in the Arab world was for all intents and purposes exempted from any punishment, because the Grand Mufti was never brought before an international court. The link between Islamism and National Socialism remained unbroken and was further used as a weapon against the Jews. Both Hitler's book "Mein Kampf" and the "Protocols of the Elders of Zion" continued to be published and to this day have large sales and enthusiastic readers in the Arab world.

- Since the Grand Mufti could not return to Palestine, which was still ruled by the British, he settled in Cairo and from there again built up his power base. Al-Banna, the head of the Muslim Brotherhood, gave him the responsibility, as his deputy leader, for the Muslim Brotherhood in Palestine. In the Muslim Brotherhood, Hitler was now glorified as "Allah's chosen tool" for the punishment of the Jews.

- Further consequences of the propaganda link between Islamism and National Socialism have been the acts of terrorism by Al Qaeda, the mastermind of which was Sayyid Qutb of the Muslim Brotherhood.

The good connections of the Grand Mufti within the Nazi regime were now very useful to the survivors of the regime. Many Nazi supporters fled to Egypt. Many German officers were smuggled out of prisoner of war camps with bribes of money so that they could be used to train the Arab resistance movement. The Arab League supported the Grand Mufti with a large amount of money as Hitler had done in the past. He obtained weapons so that he could build up the Palestinian Liberation Organization (PLO) and amongst other things had his fighters trained by former Nazi officers in the conduct of terrorist activities. The Grand Mufti employed his forces not only to drive the British out of Palestine, but also to have everyone killed that stood in the way of his radical Islamist ideas and plans for Palestine.*44

Ramifications for Germany

After the war some of the Muslim SS soldiers remained in the west zone, especially in the area of Munich. Although the traces of many were lost, in 1958 the chief imam of one of these Muslim SS units turned up as a founder member of the "Munich Mosque Building Project." The "Munich Mosque Building Association" was now a meeting place for members of the Muslim Brotherhood. The chairman said Ramadan was the son-in-law of Hassan al-Banna, the already mentioned founder of the Muslim Brotherhood in Egypt. The mosque, which in the end was financed by Muammar Gaddafi of Libya, developed into a Coordination Center for the Muslim Brotherhood according to author Ian Johnson.*45

In 1998 the Al Qaeda financier Mamduh Mahmud Salim was arrested in Munich and Extradited to the USA. As we have learnt in the meantime, Germany became a "deep cover agent haven" for the terrorists who carried out the 9.11 attacks in the USA in 2001. The death pact with Islam gave the powers of darkness enough right to act unhindered out of Germany.

After 1945 a new "Middle and Near East Department" was formed in the West German Foreign Office with mostly the same personnel as the old Oriental Department. Only recently was the role of the Foreign Office and its involvement in the genocide of the Jews subjected to a historical investigation. During this investigation it was also discovered that the staff actually tried to block the Reparations Agreement between Israel and West

The Covenant With Death

Germany, (Luxembourg Agreement), and to this end restored contact with the former Grand Mufti of Jerusalem, (whom they still knew very well from the time of Hitler). *46

Consequences of the Death Pact for the Conflict Between the Palestinians and Israel

The Grand Mufti was never interested in peace with Israel. He always propagated "jihad." Palestine could not be ruled by unbelievers because areas that have once been conquered by Islam could never be given back to "unbelievers." *47

He was the first political and religious representative of Palestine in an unbroken line of Palestinian leaders who, without compromise, wanted to see Palestine as a pure Islamic country without Jews. The Grand Mufti was the one who violently opposed the UN Partition Plan in 1947 and called the Arab states to war. Although not all the Arab leaders were against a Jewish settlement called "Israel" in Palestine, the Grand Mufti had gained such a power base in the Arab world by the devious route of an alliance with Hitler, that nobody dared to stand in his way. It was the Grand Mufti who created the "Palestinian" myth whereby all Arabs who were resident in Palestine were given a new identity that was later incorporated into Article 4 of the PLO Charter.*48

The PLO leader Yasser Arafat came from the line of the Husseini clan. He stayed for a long time with his uncle the Grand Mufti in Cairo. He was trained there with others for the Palestine freedom fight by a German officer. Arafat was strongly supported financially by the Grand Mufti, especially during the initial phase of the formation of the Fatah movement. *49

The Cancer of Hate Propaganda

Through Nazi propaganda the following main anti-Semitic theories bonded themselves to Islam:

1. The Jews are the enemy of all mankind.

2. There is a world-wide Jewish conspiracy to establish Jewish domination over the whole world—Zionism is one manifestation of this conspiracy.

3. "World-wide Jewry" must therefore be fought with all possible means before it is too late.

These theories were repeated constantly in the propaganda of the Grand Mufti and the Muslim Brotherhood and linked to the Palestinian problem. In this way the fight for Palestine was made into a fight against "world-wide Jewry." Zionism was redefined as having the same meaning as the term "world-wide Jewry." In this way it was propagated as reputedly a major threat to the whole of mankind. This is also how the leader of the pilots in the suicide attacks on September 11th 2001, Mohammed Atta, saw it. For him New York was the center of world-wide Jewry. Therefore the war for deliverance had to begin in New York.*50

The clear aim of Bin Laden was as follows: America should be compelled to end its support for Israel. In 2003, the Arab satellite TV station Al-Manna transmitted for the first time a 29 part series with the title "Al-Shatat," (The Diaspora), which was shown all over the Arab world. This notorious series was even shown on German television. In this way Hitler's propaganda was coming back into Germany. As a consequence, the fantasy of a Jewish world-wide conspiracy was now being burnt into the minds and hearts of Islamic viewers through cinema pictures. The viewers learned that Jews had brought only death and destruction to mankind. They were the cause of both world wars. They used the blood of Christian children to make their matzo (unleavened bread). In the film a rabbi cut the throat of a frightened boy to get his blood.

Hamas

Hamas considers itself to be the Palestinian wing of the Muslim Brotherhood. The entire anti-Semitic conspiracy theory is reiterated in its charter. There the talk is of "world Zionism." The struggle by means of terrorism is justified in a literal way by the "Protocols of the Elders of Zion." Article 32 of the Hamas Charter reads:

"Today it is Palestine and tomorrow it will be other countries. Zionist scheming has no end, and after Palestine they will covetously expand from the Nile to the Euphrates. Only when they have completely consumed the areas on which they have laid their hands, will they proceed with more expansion, and go even further. Their scheme has been laid out in the Protocols of the Elders of Zion, and their present conduct is the best proof of what is said there." *51

Iran

The Ayatollah Khomeini was already an enthusiastic listener to the Grand Mufti and received inspiration from him. The Iranian President Mahmud Ahmadinejad has repeatedly called the Holocaust a "big lie." Again and again he announces that Iran is committed to "wiping out" Israel and refers to the State of Israel as a "cancer cell." *52

The Veil of Silence Must be Lifted in the Spiritual Realm

Today the mood of the people in our land [Germany] and in other western nations is generally anti-Israel. Israel is seen as being responsible for the entire Palestinian conflict. The Palestinians are presented as the victims even in German school textbooks. The anti-Semitism of the Arabs is either never mentioned or played down as a *"natural consequence"* of the Middle East conflict. The roots of anti-Semitism in National Socialism are not openly talked about. The hate for Israel and the threats of murder and eradication from the Iranian President are not taken seriously. The central role of the Grand Mufti and the support of Hitler's Germany and their consequences are covered with a veil of silence. The few historians who have worked on this subject have found no real reaction or interest in their theses, neither in the media nor in the political sphere. Only after the year 2000 was the connection between the propaganda of Radio Zeesen and the current anti-Semitism in the Islamic world openly reported by historians in their publications. It seems it is simply not "politically correct" to establish a link between the anti-Semitism of the Nazi regime and the anti-Semitism of the Palestinians. If this fact was to be clearly established and placed in the public domain, the support of the Palestinians as well as Iran would no longer be a given!

Much more could be said on this subject, but this would however go beyond the scope of this paper. We pray that the veil of silence that surrounds the links which have been presented here will be lifted and that Germany accepts its responsibility towards Israel in a much more tangible way.

Prayer Points for Intercessors

Let us pray and repent on behalf of our nation, Germany, for the following:

- The friendship contract of the Kaiser with the Sultan/the Islamic world instead of supporting the establishment of a Jewish state.

- The development of a "jihad strategy" to further German ambitions for greater world power.

- For facilitating concepts of terrorism and jihad that have no respect even for civilians.

- Implanting of the concept of "jihad" as a means of insurgency against occupying forces.

- Sowing the seed of hate for Jews that has since arisen across the entire world.

- For the "lasting friendship with the enemy of God," (like the peace treaty with the enemy that the Israelites were commanded not to make), that began under the Kaiser and was continued and strengthened through the explicit Death Pact between Hitler and the Grand Mufti.

- That Germany did not want to trust in God but rather looked for its strength in an alliance with Islam.

- For inviting Islamic/Islamist teaching into our land and the building of training centers and mosques at the cost of the German state under the Kaiser and later under Hitler.

- The setting up of Islamic military SS divisions.

- For a death pact that involved the annihilation of all Jews including in Palestine.

- The propaganda from Radio Zeesen and the continuing influence of the media to set our land against Israel.

- The role of the Foreign Office and the continuity in the appointment of personnel to this office who were anti-Jewish and anti-Israeli and remained so today.

- Confession of our share of responsibility and guilt for the ongoing Palestinian-Israeli conflict because of the financial, material and military support of Arab uprisings and the spread of the concept of jihad in our past. All these alliances must be broken! The veil of silence must be torn away! The influence that this death pact is having on current German policy towards Israel must be brought into the light and put to an end. Germany is still hiding behind its past and not facing up to it. Through heartfelt repentance and the power of God's forgiveness, we pray that Germany will be set free from Islamism and all that remains hidden in our land.

Special prayers are needed for the German Foreign Office! Here is some further information: Werner Otto von Hentig directed the Oriental Department of the Foreign Office in Berlin from 1937 to 1939. One of his duties was to take care of Amin al-Husseini, the Grand Mufti of Jerusalem, whom he accompanied from Berlin to Gustav Scheel in Salzburg on April 6th 1945 to help him successfully flee from besieged Germany. From 1952 to 1953, von Hentig was the German Ambassador to Indonesia and after retirement from the Foreign Office he served for two years as advisor to the Saudi royal family.

During his time in Indonesia, he repeatedly stopped over in Egypt to organize resistance to the Luxembourg Agreement, (Reparations Agreement between Israel and West Germany), which was then under negotiations, together with the Grand Mufti and the numerous German National Socialists [former Nazi's] who were there. In breach of his official duties he opposed the signing of the agreement and gave internal information from the German Foreign Office to the Arab anti-Semitic faction. Hentig was decisively one of the reasons that the Foreign Office served as a shelter for National Socialists into the late '60s. When the first information about Adolf Eichmann living in Argentina started to trickle through, Simon Wiesenthal, (Holocaust survivor and Nazi war crime researcher), and Georg August Zinn, (one of the fathers of the German constitution), took great care that the Foreign Office, which was actually responsible for further investigation and an extradition order, was not informed.*53

Naziism Did Not Die After World War II

As has been so powerfully illustrated in the Rosamund Stresemann article quoted above, Naziism lives on today in a new guise, as it has metamorphosed in the world of Islam! Islamists the world over now carry Hitler's baton of Nazi terror. The whole world it seems is cowed in fear before this brutal Islamist beast that threatens to devour all who would oppose its onward march towards world conquest and domination. The dreaded fear of them has paralyzed the hearts of the nation's leaders into a state of abject appeasement of this Jihadic monster, whilst totally unaware its origins go back to Kaiser Wilhelm II, and Adolph Hitler's Germany. They do not realize that modern-day Islamism is a Nazi construct and that The Muslim Brotherhood, Fatah, Hamas, the P.L.O., Hesbollah and Al Qaedah all obtained their doctrine of hatred from Nazi Germany.

Naziism did not die in Germany either, as it would be most unrealistic to think that an ideology, which had so totally brainwashed and indoctrinated the German people for some fifteen plus years, could possibly evaporate without leaving some trace behind.

President Franklin Roosevelt and Prime Minister Winston Churchill, in February 1945 signed an official document about American-British policy in Germany, in which they stated: *"It is our inflexible purpose to DESTROY German militarism and Naziism and to ENSURE Germany will NEVER AGAIN be able to disturb the peace of the world. We are determined to disarm and to disband all German Armed forces, break up FOR ALL TIME the German General Staff that has repeatedly contrived the resurgence of German militarism, remove or destroy all German military equipment, eliminate or control all German Industry that could be used for military production. It is not our purpose to destroy the people of Germany, but ONLY WHEN NAZIISM AND MILITARISM HAVE BEEN EXTIRPATED, will there be hope for a decent life for Germans and a place for them in the community of nations."*

It was a good idea back then, but sadly it was not carried out, as Brian Connel points out in his book, "A Watcher on the Rhine: "The vexing problem of denazification which had been handled up to that time [the spring of 1947] by the Allied authorities WAS HANDED OVER TO THE GERMANS." Arthur Spiegelman of Reuter's said on May 10, 1996, "Realizing they were losing the war in 1944, Nazi leaders met top German industrialists to plan a secret post-war international network to restore them to power, according to a newly declassified U.S. intelligence document." *54

Beyond these disturbing reports that Naziism did not die after World War II, one only needs to look at the resurgence of German might today. It surely is one of the modern world's greatest ironies that Germany today finds itself right back where it wasn't supposed to be: dominating Europe! She is the region's richest, most populous nation, with control over the EU purse strings and has become the unquestioned boss amid Europe's stubborn debt crisis. She has become the third largest arms exporter in the world and boasts the seventh most powerful armed forces. Her industry has become the envy of the world and she has become the undisputed engine, paymaster, and leader of the European Union. Thus, Franz Joseph Strauss' "Grand Design," dream of Germany becoming the third largest economic power in the world, *"the time must come when that economic power seeks political expression on the world scene,"* has today become reality. Or, as Joseph Joffe, editor of Die Zeit, newspaper so succinctly expressed it in a recent article: *"Gone are the days when Germany was considered an economic giant but a political dwarf, as the cliché had it, in an age where economic power suddenly moves to the fore, as it has in the last eighteen months, the economic giant also becomes a political giant."*

Margaret Thatcher, the former Prime Minister of Great Britain, said in a speech given in Colorado on October 9, 1995, that German reunification was a BIG MISTAKE for which all of Europe is now paying. "Germany is very powerful now—her national character is to DOMINATE," she said.

In her book, "The Downing Street Years," Thatcher stated: *"I do not believe in collective guilt; it is the individuals who are morally accountable for their actions. But I do believe in national character. People are responsible for their own actions. And the reason we are heading for a worldwide, cataclysmic disaster is because of the inherent human nature within all mankind. But nevertheless, nations are simply families grown large. There are certain family traits, or a national character, among different peoples. And the German character, as thousands of years of history proves, is to dominate! You have not anchored Germany to Europe, you have anchored Europe to a newly dominant, unified Germany. In the end, my friends, you'll find IT WILL NOT WORK!"* [*55]

More recently a further cautionary note was expressed by Ulrike Guerot, senior research fellow of the European Council of Foreign Relations in Berlin: *"Germany has an ambivalent relationship with power, we have never gotten it right!"* [*56]

CHAPTER NINE

―――・❖・―――

Is the EU the Mortal Enemy of America?

The author is pro unity and brotherhood. However, he believes that there are nefarious forces that are merely using such terms to gain for their own self-interest incredible wealth and power. Free peoples of Europe have surrendered their hard won freedoms to unelected appointees that exercise control over the European Union! Our urgent prayer ought to be that the State of Israel does not step into the same trap!

A retired former British ambassador to Washington summed up Britain's situation perfectly, as he explained his implacable opposition to Britain joining the Euro—the European currency: *"I want to be sure that my grandchildren will be fighting on the right side when it comes to the inevitable war between America and Europe."*

Some forty years ago General Charles de Gaulle, the former President of France, prophesied that war between Europe and America was inevitable. In a BBC program called "Allies at War" De Gaulle was reported as saying: *"The real enemy is America! France would reconcile with Germany and the real ultimate war would be between Europe and America."*

Professor Mary Kaldor, Director of the Center for the Study of Global Governance at the London School of Economics and Political Science, in her book, "The Disintegrating West," predicted: *"All out war between Europe and America."* [*1]

The reality of today is that the early skirmishes have already started as Europe is set on a collision course with the United States of America on many different fronts. The hidden agenda behind the formation of the European Union is to wrest the "birthright" crown of global hegemony from the head of the United States. Their grand vision of a new European World Order drives all European initiatives.

The medium goal of the shadowy unelected figures behind the EU is to drive a wedge between Great Britain and America. Their purpose is to split up these two sons of Joseph in order to more easily overcome and destroy them.

The Anglo-Saxon world, in its ignorance and naivety, seems blissfully unaware that the German-dominated European Union is the current method being used to create a "Fourth Reich" in which Europe becomes the dictator of the whole world! It must be said that this is true also for the vast majority of the citizens of the European Union, as most of them are sincere good natured people who are completely oblivious to the hidden agenda behind the EU project. They have never been told about the secret Eurabia Covenant that was made between the EU and the Arab League in the aftermath of the 1973 Yom Kipur War and the resultant OPEC Oil Embargo. They have no idea of the consequences of the hidden clauses in that secret covenant, as they never had the chance to discuss the matter, let alone vote on it. None of them had bargained for the influx of multiple tens of millions of Muslims into their society, which was justified by their rulers under the oft repeated mantra of creating a multi- cultural society. They have no idea that the EU is a concept that was birthed in Nazi Germany! Its army of decent citizens would be absolutely horrified to realize the sinister intent of those shadowy placed men behind the scenes who are directing the policy of the union. Many EU citizens like the idea that they belong to a large entity forged through cooperation with the other nations around them. Many of them have simply swallowed the propaganda that it is not possible in our global economy for nation states to stand on their own feet anymore and thus for them the EU makes economic sense. They have been told that the sublime purpose of the union is the prevention of war and that it is about preserving peace. They do not need to be reminded of Europe's former record, and as evidence for the success of the EU, they are regularly reminded that the union to date has brought some 66 years of peace. At least this is true if one conveniently forgets the Balkans wars in Bosnia, Kosovo and Serbia. They are simply naïve and they have been hoodwinked and manipulated by the media and their politicians, who in turn are being controlled and manipulated by the wicked powers behind this New World Order project.

The EU is a Concept Birthed in Nazi Germany!

It seems very few are aware of the fact that the idea of a European Union, to rival and overcome Anglo-Saxon power, has sprung from the breast of Adolph Hitler and the German Reich. According to Rodney Atkinson in his well researched book, "EUROPE'S FULL CIRCLE— *Corporate Elites and the New Fascism"* the idea for the European Union was spawned by Walther Funk, Minister for Economics in Nazi Germany. He also claims that Professor Heinrich Hunke, a leading Nazi academic, and Dr Bernard Benning, the Director of Hitler's Reichs-Kredit-Gesellschaft in Berlin, played a leading role in promoting the idea of constructing a supra-national European block as a counter to the Anglo-Saxon trading system. Their ideas involved the suppression of the nation state. Atkinson claims that the principal organization promoting the "European Union" was founded by a former Nazi party member and SS intelligence officer. He argues with devastating clarity that the model upon which today's Europe is unequivocally built is Hitler's 1942 plan for a "European Economic Community:"

Furthermore the methods used by the unelected European Commission in Brussels to bring about this destruction of European nations are identical to Hitler's use of "Notstandsgesetze," (emergency laws), to bypass the German parliament and people. Rodney Atkinson also reports that further details of the new Europe under German control were contained in a 1941 report prepared for Secretary of State von Weizsacker by Albrecht Haushofer, a Rudolf Hess adviser. The principal theme of the proposals was a federal structure for continental Europe centered on the German Reich of 1914 with varying degrees of association for different countries. The Nazis" idea of sovereignty was that the nations should be ruled by German puppets or by kindred regimes, as in Mussolini's Italy and Franco's Spain.

Hitler's Europe	Today's Europe
"Europaissche Wirtschafts Gemeinschaft"	European Economic Community
Lebensraum (living space)	European Space
Collective access to basic commodities	Common energy, fishing and agricultural policies
European Currency System	The Euro & the European Exchange Mechanism
Europabank (Berlin)	European Central Bank (Frankfurt)
European Regional Principle	Committee of the Regions
Common Labor Policy	Social Chapter
Economic and Trading	Single Market Agreements
European Industrial Economy	Common Industrial Policy
Replacing capital with European Works	Councils Organized labor

Furthermore, there is an ominous irony in the fact that the European Central Bank is located in the former headquarters of I.G. Farben, the Nazi conglomerate responsible for producing the Sarin gas used for the systematic extermination of the Jews.*2

The EU May Represent the Final Resurrection of the Holy Roman Empire

It is clear that Europe's covetous eyes are firmly focused on America's "birthright" of global leadership. Charles de Gaulle was entirely correct in his assessment that: "War between Europe and America is inevitable!" The Franco-German axis driving this emerging European superpower is following de Gaulle's prescription to the letter. For the past thirty years they have sucked up to the Muslim world and made them their ally in crime and are making powerful alliances with Russia, China and India as well as the major nations of South America and Africa. There is every possibility that eventually even Turkey, with its population of some seventy five million Muslims, will become a fully-fledged member of the EU. With the so-called Barcelona Process of, "Euro-Mediterranean dialog," the southern Mediterranean, mainly Muslim nations of Morocco, Algeria, Tunisia, Egypt, Libya, Jordan, Lebanon, Syria and the Palestinian Authority are being brought into the European economic sphere. Israel too is included in this, "Euro-Mediterranean dialog," with the intent of her joining this global colossus in the making. This political process has the eager support of the Israeli government even to the point where for the past three years Israel has held joint cabinet meetings with Germany, the undisputed leader of the European Union. The problem with our modern society today is that people are so focused on living in the present that they forget that history tends to repeat itself. King Solomon spoke a great truth when he said: *"That which has been is what will be, that which is done is what will be done, and there is nothing new under the sun."* (Ecclesiastes 1:9). Thus, once the Barcelona process has achieved its objective, the world will see a replay of the Roman Empire, as, just as in the days of the Roman Empire, the whole of the Mediterranean Sea will become a European domain.

Once the present embryonic relationship envisaged by the Barcelona Process between the Mediterranean nations and the EU comes to its intended maturity, and with Turkey's proposed formal accession, it will add a further 276 million Muslims to the EU, bringing the total Muslim population to some 330 million souls out of a total projected EU population of 726 million. This will have the immediate effect of increasing its Islamic population to 45% of the total. This will give the Muslim vote overwhelming power in any EU national or supra-national election. It is a well-established fact that many of the northern EU states suffer from negative population growth, whereas the Muslim birth-rate is very much higher. It will not take many years therefore before Muslims will become the majority population of the EU. Thus this German-led Eurabian Beast-power will have an Islamic face and orientation, which portends exceedingly bad news for the free world. It will be especially bad news for the State of Israel, as well as for the other Hebrew nations, such as the United States and the United Kingdom, including the other Anglo-Saxon nations such as Canada, Australia, and New Zealand. Some few discerning students of history can already see the handwriting on the wall. This Nazi-inspired European monolith is destined in the near future to unite with the Islamic world in a "Common Purpose," to destroy and annihilate the Anglo-Saxon and Jewish, (e.g. Israelite) world order.

Past historic precedents suggest that one day even Russia itself will join this Eurabian Club, placing her awesome nuclear arsenals under the Eurabian umbrella. The fact is that the EU has already forged a formal "strategic partnership" with Russia. This arrangement was greatly strengthened in May 2010, when Angela Merkel, the German Chancellor, initiated the 'Meselberg Process,' (without prior consultation with either the EU or NATO). Once you read the fine print of this treaty, you discover that the Meselberg Memorandum calls for an EU-Russia Committee which would have greater powers than the present NATO-Russia Council, as it would give Russia access to the EU decision-making process and, ultimately make NATO altogether irrelevant."[3] Thus, judging by the geo-political moves this Franco-German Euro Beast is making all around the world, we are in effect witnessing a new empire in the making.

Author's Disclaimer Re: The Catholic Church and Ancient Religious Orders

Before introducing this next section, the author desires to clarify his position with regard to ancient versus the modern-day Catholic Church and its adherents versus the historical Roman Catholic Empire its origins, incursions and sins over the past 14 centuries. Comments about "The Church" its origins and historical vagaries, are in no way intended to reflect negatively upon the much good that the Church and its sincere adherents have done over many years (and continues to do). There are, however, undeniable, historically established facts surrounding its founding and non-biblical (unChristian) assertions of power and unrighteous dominion in times past that simply cannot be swept under the rug or passed lightly over.

We observe in the annals of history that nearly all organizations—after they rise in prominence, influence and/or political power—tend to fall victim to the adversary as he seeks to infiltrate and usurp legitimate power and authority replacing it with counterfeit authority that then thrives upon the blatant abuse and misuse of that power. This work of corruption is initiated by servants of the dark who enter in as "wolves dressed in sheep's clothing." Indeed, as Luke predicted "…that after my departing shall grievous wolves enter in among you, not sparing the flock." (Acts 20:29) Such is the path of the "natural man" in this world, as we examine the course of history over the centuries.

Notwithstanding the emergence of a wolf (or many wolves) into the flock, that alone does not transform all of the sheep suddenly into wolves. There have always been pure sheep (true humble disciples) who, will always stay true to the Good Shepherd.

Fortunately, Hashem, in His wisdom, has repeatedly raised up—in times past, and will doubtless do so in the future—those righteous men and women destined to leaven the lump and salt the earth with His goodness, wisdom, guidance and discipleship. These true "sheep" will always seek the guidance of the Holy Spirit to direct them on the right path.

To reiterate, by no means does the author harbor any ill will or enmity toward adherents of the Catholic Church or any other Christian religious tradition (so long as that tradition humbly seeks the Kingdom of God on earth and whose fruits are made manifest through acts of genuine love and service toward their fellow man). The author has no tolerance, however, for those "ravening wolves" who "enter in" seeking to thwart the work of God and His righteousness by replacing it with kingdoms of men which seek to *merge the spiritual authority of the church with the corporal enforcement power of the state* and thus becoming part of that nefarious cabal that conspires to become the "great whore who sitteth upon the many waters" (Rev 17) which seeks dominion and control over the children of men.

A United Europe is a "Catholic" Concept

The vision of a global European Empire was enshrined and inaugurated by the Treaty of Rome in 1957. What we may be witnessing is in effect the final resurrection of the Roman Empire spoken of by Daniel the prophet in Daniel 2:31-34 & 36-43.

Even the press has described *"the idea of a united Europe as essentially a Catholic concept,"*[*4] The papacy recognized the possibilities of a United Europe where in many countries Roman Catholics comprise 80 to 90 percent of the population. Fifty years ago Pope John XXIII urged Roman Catholics to be, *"in the front ranks of the effort to unify Europe!"* The pope predicted that *"the new Europe would become "the Greatest Catholic Super State the world has ever known"* and *"the greatest single human force ever seen by man!"* Many of the "founding fathers" of the new Europe were devout Catholics, as are many of its leading proponents today. It was no coincidence that Tony Blair converted to Roman Catholicism as soon as he left office as Prime Minister of Great Britain, as he had put himself forward as a future president of the union. The unspoken rule is that any President of Europe must be a Catholic. The former Pope John Paul II has especially promoted the key Vatican agenda for a united Europe. During his reign of over a quarter of a century, he has given nearly *700 speeches concerning Europe,* in which he repeatedly urged Europeans to *"discover their roots,"* as they build their *"common European house!"* Those roots go back to the illegitimate alliance between the Catholic Church and the Holy Roman Empire of the German nation that ruled Europe with an iron fist for more than a thousand years. For over four hundred years of that rule, the ghastly terrors of the inquisition cast its cruel black shadow over all of its territory including its Catholic colonies in South America and the rest of the world. Pope John Paul II has warned that dark clouds hover over a continent that yields to unbridled secularism, that Europe could *"lose its identity"* and that its unity could *"collapse within a decade, if it fails to acknowledge its Catholic Christian heritage."* [*5]

Some may be shocked to find that Hitler was trying to create a United Europe and that he fashioned his SS to be an exact model of the Jesuit order, which he admired greatly. The belt buckles of his Gestapo SS soldiers were inscribed with the quazie religious motto; *"Got mit uns,"* ["God with us!"]. Cardinal Pacelli acting for the Vatican and Franz von Papen, Foreign Minister for the German Reich signed a Concordat in 1933, after which the Jesuit Skull and Bones symbol was incorporated by Reichsfuhrer Himmler into the military insignia of the SS. Prior to its use by Himmler, the designation SS was the official abbreviation of "Sedes Sacrorum" or the "Holy Seat," better known as the "Holy See," which is the legal name of the Vatican! It is an extraordinary coincidence that Himmler and his elite began wearing the SS designation, meaning "Holy See," immediately after the signing of the Reich Concordat with the Vatican, [Sedes Sacrorum i.e. the Holy See]. When we consider that Nazi SS translates most perfectly into meaning "Knights of the Holy See," one can understand the rumor that Heinrich Himmler was suspected of being a Jesuit priest. If the SS were considered to be the "knights" of the Holy See, that would make Reichsfuhrer Himmler its "Grand Inquisitor!" Hitler was in fact a Roman Catholic and Heinrich Himmler too was the son of a devout and well respected Catholic family. Pope Pius XII, who as Papal Nuncio Pacelli, spent his early career in Germany from April 1917 to February 1930. Significantly, those were the years when he witnessed the social revolution which led to Hitler's rise to power and the formation of the NDSAP, [Nazi Party].

Pope Benedict XVI, is the eighth German national to become Pope, and he was once dubbed as *"God's Rottweiler!"* As Cardinal Ratzinger, he spent 24 years at the head of the Congregation for the Doctrine of the Faith. He continued to emphasize the importance of Europe to the Catholic Church. On an official visit to Prague in the Czech Republic in 2009, he stated that: *"Europe is more than a continent. It is a house, a spiritual homeland, the hallmarks of which are freedom and Christian [i.e., Roman Catholic] values."*

What is not generally appreciated is that the pagan origins of the Catholic Church go way back to Babylon, as Roman Catholicism is largely the modern manifestation of the ancient Babylonian mystery religion. The idea of the Sovereign Pontiff, the celibacy of the Priests, Monks and Nuns, the Idol Processions, Relic worship, the Clothing and Crowning of Images, the Rosary and even the Sign of the Cross are all Babylonian in origin. The Doctrine of the Trinity, the veneration of the Virgin Mother and Child, as well as the celebration of Christmas, Easter, and the Sacrifice of the Mass all originate in Babylon.*7

Martin Luther, the Protestant reformer, in a letter to his friend Herman Tulichius wrote: *"I now know that the Papacy is the kingdom of Babylon, and the power of Nimrod the mighty hunter."* *8

Nimrod, the grandson of Ham and the great-grandson of Noah was the founder of Babylon. (Genesis 10:10). The name Nimrod comes from the Hebrew verb *"marad"* which means; "The rebel!" Thus Nimrod may not be the character's name at all. It is more likely a derisive name identifying a person or system that epitomized rebellion against the Creator, the one and only true God. Flavius Josephus says of Nimrod:

"Now it was Nimrod who excited them to such an affront and contempt of God. He was the grandson of Ham, the son of Noah-a bold man, and of great strength of hand. He persuaded them not to ascribe it to God, as it were through his means they were happy, but to believe it was their own courage that procured that happiness. He also gradually changed the government into tyranny-seeing no other way of turning men from the fear of God, but to bring them into a constant dependence upon his own power. He also said he would be revenged on God, if he should have a mind to drown the world again; for that he would build a tower too high for the waters to be able to reach! And that he would avenge himself on God for destroying their forefathers! *9

Although the ancient records of history apart from the Bible, do not mention anyone by the name of Nimrod, there are strong indicators pointing to a certain hero who fulfils all the criteria. In Genesis 10:8-11, we learn that Nimrod established a kingdom. Therefore, one would expect to find also, in the literature of the ancient Near East, a person who was a type, or example for other people to follow. And there was. It is a well-known tale, common in Sumerian literature, of a man who fits the description. In addition to the Sumerians, the Babylonians wrote about this person, the Assyrians likewise, and the Hittites. He was obviously the most popular hero of the Ancient Near East. We find him and his exploits described in the Gilgamesh Epic. The Gilgamesh Epic describes the first *"God is dead"* movement. In the epic, the hero is a vile, filthy, perverted person, yet he is presented as the greatest, strongest hero that ever lived.* 10 So that the one who sent the flood will not trouble them anymore, Gilgamesh sets out to kill the perpetrator. He takes with him a friend who is a monstrous half-man, half-animal-Enkidu. Together they go on a long journey to the Cedar Mountain to find and destroy the monster that sent the Flood. Gilgamesh finds him and finally succeeds in cutting off the head of this creature whose name is "Huwawa." ("Humbaba" in the Assyrian version.)[*11] Because of the parallels between Gilgamesh and Nimrod, many scholars agree that Gilgamesh is Nimrod. Continuing with the Gilgamesh fable, he did win, he did vanquish Huwawa and took his head. Therefore he could come back to Uruk and other cities in his kingdom and tell the people not to worry about YHVH anymore because he is dead. "I killed him over in the Lebanon mountains. So just live however you like. I will be your king and take care of you." It is interesting to note that YHVH has a somewhat similar sound to Huwawa. Gilgamesh did just as the "sons of god" in Genesis 6 did. The *"sons of god"* forcibly took men's wives. The epic says that is precisely what Gilgamesh did. Gilgamesh (i.e. Nimrod) may have been a Nephilim, (part human, part fallen angel, as mentioned in Genesis 6:2).

Nimrod, aka Gilgamesh, clearly is a satanic figure who epitomizes rebellion against YHVH, the Creator of the Universe. Nimrod was the founder of Babylon and as such he was the author of man-made religion. He was the "mighty hunter" who taught man through his terrifying personality the fear of man rather than the fear of YHVH. Nimrod, once boasted about having cut off the head of the One who caused the Flood.

This just goes to show that all the origins take us back to Babylon! The implication is that the EU may be a fulfillment of Daniel's prophecy, as it represents the seventh and final resurrection of this Roman Empire characterized as the feet of the image made of iron mixed with miry clay.

The Babylonian state was intensively theocratic. The kings had been preceded by high-priests, and they represented the religious as well as the civil power. At Babylon the real sovereign was Bel Merodach, the true "lord" of the city, and it was only when the king had been adopted by the god as his son that he possessed any right to rule. Before he had "taken the hands" of Bel, and thereby become the adopted son of the deity, he had no legitimate right to the throne. The Babylonian sovereign was thus quite as much a pontiff as he was a king."[*12]

From this we can see that the papacy follows this very same Babylonian pattern today, as the Pope combines the religious office of high priest or pontiff, as well as the civil office as king, his sovereign territory being located in the Vatican in the heart of Rome. More than this, the Roman Pontiff has since time immemorial considered that his right to rule stretches over all the civilized kingdoms of the world. This is why the R.C. Church refers to itself as the "Catholic and Universal Church." We find that this same concept too comes from Babylon.

"Like the Holy Roman Empire in the Middle Ages, Babylonian sovereignty brought with it a legal, though shadowy, right to rule over the civilized kingdoms of the world. It was this which made the Assyrian conquerors of the second Assyrian empire so anxious to secure possession of Babylon and there to "take the hands of Bel." Tiglath-pileser III, Shalmaneser IV, and Sargon were all like usurpers, who governed by the sword. It was only when they had made themselves masters of Babylon and been recognized by Bel and his priesthood that their title to govern became legitimate and unchallenged." *13

Babylon is to Rise From the Abyss One More Time!

The fall of Babylon occurred in 539BCE, when DARIUS took the city in one night: *"And Darius, the Mede, received the kingdom, being about 62 years old"* (Daniel 5:31).

Herodotus describes Babylon as an impregnable four corner square fortress city, with each side being 22km long. It was encircled by a wide and very deep moat, in the middle of which stood a wall that was 99 meters high and 26 meters thick, atop of which six chariots could be driven alongside of each other.

We read in Daniel 5, that in the same night Babylon fell, that Belshazzar, the pontiff-king of Babylon, was having a great feast with a thousand of his friends. He had used the golden and silver cups his father Nebuchadnezzar had stolen from the Holy Temple in Jerusalem to toast the health of the gods of Babylon. Then all of a sudden he saw opposite his throne a heavenly hand, that wrote on the wall: MENE, MENE, TEKEL, UFARSIN..........

King Belshazzar became very afraid and extremely agitated and he wanted to discover the meaning of the writing. Only Daniel was able, with HASHEM's help, to give the king the interpretation. Daniel recognized immediately that the words; "Mene, mene, tekel, upharsin," indicated measurements of weights:

MENE = 50 SHEKELS, MENE = 50 SHEKELS, TEKEL = 1 SHEKEL, UFARSIN = 25 SHEKELS—50+50+1+25 =126. The Bible also informs us in Ezekiel that a shekel is twenty GERAH'S. 20 x 126 = 2520 GERAH'S—or : <u>SEVEN TIMES.</u> Daniel then explains the interpretation to the king: PROPHETIC' e.g. SEVEN 'PROPHETIC' TIMES.

This is the writing that was inscribed: "MENE, MENE, TEKEL UPHARSIN." This is the interpretation of the matter: "Mene" (counted)— God counted [the years of] your kingship and terminated it. "TEKEL" (weighed) - you have been weighed in the scales and found wanting. "PERES" (broken up) - your kingdom has been broken and given to Media and Persia." (Daniel 5:25-26, emphasis added).

Daniel also reminded the king about the arrogance of his father Nebuchadnezzar, which had led to him having to spend seven years in madness. Just as Daniel had interpreted Nebuchadnezzar's dream, the king was declared mad for seven years. *"Seven times"* he lived as a wild beast, having to eat grass.

"Seven periods will pass over you, until you recognize that the Supreme One rules over the kingdom of man and He gives it to whomever He wishes." (Daniel 4:29b.) *"They will drive you from mankind, and your dwelling will be among the beasts of the field; they will feed you grass like oxen: and wash you with the dew of heaven, and SEVEN PERIODS will pass over you, until you recognize that the Supreme One rules in the kingdom of man, and He gives it to whomever He wishes."* (Daniel 4:22, emphasis added).

This prophetic dream of Nebuchadnezzar was twofold in its meaning in that its immediate application was to the king himself, whereas its later fulfillment would come into effect to the Babylonian Empire he ruled.

"I was watching and behold, a tree in the midst of the earth, the height of it was great. The tree grew and became strong, its height reached to the

heavens; it was visible to the end of the entire earth; In the visions of my head upon my bed, I was watching and behold! A holy angel came down from heaven. He cried out loudly, and said thus: CHOP DOWN THE TREE AND CUT OFF ITS BRANCHES; cast down its foliage and scatter its fruit; let the animals move away from under it, and the birds from its branches! HOWEVER, LEAVE ITS MAJOR ROOTS IN THE GROUND, [secured] WITH A BAND OF IRON AND COPPER."* (Daniel 4:10-12, emphasis added).

Babylon is the tree, which was cut down in 539BCE! The roots of this Babylonian tree in the meantime are protected by a band of iron and copper. You can never see the roots of a tree, as they are underground. The interpretation here is that BABYLON HAS GONE UNDERGROUND FOR SEVEN TIMES, aka, on the Biblical principle of ONE DAY FOR A YEAR. When we fast-forward 2,520 years, and add the seven years of Nebuchadnezzar's period of madness from 539BCE to our time, we arrive at respectively: <u>1982</u> and <u>1989</u>!

In the Context of Babylon, Did Anything of Significance Occur in 1982?

It was the 25th anniversary of the TREATY OF ROME! According to the Catholic Press Bureau on the 25th July 2005, Pope Benedict XVI commented on the Feast of the Apostle James, whose relics are worshipped in the famous Shrine of Santiago de Compostella, which is the destination of thousands of pilgrims from all over Europe. According to Catholic doctrine, the Apostle Saint James is the patron saint of Europe. The Pope also mentioned the Feast of Saint Brigitte of Sweden, the "female" patron of Europe, plus the Feast of Saint Benedict on the 11th of July, who was also a great patron of the old continent.*14 Thinking on those Saints, Pope Benedict said on July 25th 2005:" *It is natural to pause at a time such as this, to consider the contribution, which Christendom has made in the past, and still makes towards the building of Europe.*"

Pope Benedict XVI then urged EUROPE TO RETURN: TO HER CHRISTIAN <u>ROOTS,</u> and he commands the youth of Europe to become like yeast! He then spoke about the pilgrimage of his predecessor Pope

John Paul II, who in "<u>1982</u>" also went to Santiago de Compostella, where he performed A SOLEMN EUROPEAN ACT!

Pope John Paul II on that occasion spoke the following memorable words: *"I the Bishop of Rome and Pastor of the Universal Church address you from Santiago, "OLD EUROPE," with a cry full of love: return to yourself! Be yourself! Discover your ORIGINS! <u>RELIVE YOUR ROOTS!!!</u> Experience once again the authentic values, which have made your history glorious and your stay in other continents blessed."* During his visit of 1982, John Paul also launched a special European project, called, *"One Europe aware of his own spiritual unity, based upon the foundation of her Christian values."*

Thus we see that in 1982, exactly 2520 years after the tree of Babylon was cut down, Pope John Paul II, acting as the titular Head of Babylon, called upon the European Union, the modern day reincarnation of that evil empire to *"relive her roots!"* *15

So, What Happened in 1989?

On the World Youth Day of 1989, commemorated in Santiago de Compostella, Pope John Paul returned to the theme of EUROPE. *"A Europe which does not deny the CHRISTIAN <u>ROOTS</u> of her growth, and, who will not forsake the true humanism of the Gospel of Christ."*

A few months later, on the 9th of November "<u>1989</u>," THE BERLIN WALL (Beliner Mauer) fell down! This was also the time when the Communist system of the Soviet Union imploded. Pope John Paul II, the charismatic Polish Pope, had a lot to do with this event, by working tirelessly behind the scenes to undermine this totalitarian system. Joseph Stalin once mockingly said: *"How many divisions does the Pope have?"* Clearly, he was wrong to underestimate the power of the Papacy and the Vatican.

Note, 1989 was precisely SEVEN YEARS after the ROOTS OF BABYLON were awakened by this same Pope, the titular head of Babylon, and its mystery religion!

The year 1989 was also the 10th anniversary of the European Monetary System (EMS). The fall of the Berlin Wall that same year opened the way for German reunification on the 3rd of October, 1990. Much has happened since then, as we witness the emergence of the EU as a union of 27 mainly Catholic Nation States into one sovereign entity. It has its own Constitution in all but name, with an EU President, Foreign Minister and Diplomatic service, as well as its own Flag, (displaying the twelve stars representing the Crown of Semiramis, the Queen of heaven, and its own (Ode to Joy) EU Anthem, and Currency. We are now 23 years further on, and in just a few years more we will not be able to recognize the world, as this colossal Beast of Babylon starts to make its ghastly presence felt with especially dire consequences for all the Israelite nations of the world.

Pope Benedict XVI Visits the Temple Mount

Pope Benedict on his historic state visit to Israel in May 2009 went up to Temple Mount, and as such, he is the first pope to do so. This is the place where Antiochus Epiphanes, having desecrated the Holy Temple, raised up a statue of Zeus bearing his own likeness. Zeus was the chief god of the Greek Olympiad, who in turn was the Hellenist version of Nimrod. The pope was welcomed by the Imams and the Grand Mufti of Jerusalem, a member of the infamous Jew-hating Husseini family, who invited him to enter the mosque of the Dome of the Rock, where he kissed the Koran and joined his hosts in praying towards Mecca. As the "procurator"/ administrator of the Cult of Nimrod, he must have felt at home in this place, where one of his successors intends to place their future throne. This should be an important warning sign for the Jewish State of Israel! In the current climate of appeasement, it may not be politically correct to say so, but the plain truth is that the Roman Catholic Church never in her history has been a friend of Israel and she is not one today either. This leopard will certainly never ever change her spots! Neither will the pope's new found friend the Grand Mufti of Jerusalem for that matter, as in January 2012, Mohammed Hussein found himself encouraging the killing of Jews. Commemorating the 47th anniversary of the founding of Fatah he said: *"The hour of judgment will not come until you fight the Jews... The Jews will hide behind the stone and behind the tree. The stone and the tree will cry, 'Oh Muslim, O Servant of Allah, this is a Jew behind me, come and kill him.'" (Direct quote from the Hadith's of the prophet Mohammed.)*

It is an open secret that Rome desires sovereignty and ownership over Jerusalem and the Land of Israel. Note that Jerusalem is as important to the Vatican as it is to the Jews and Muslims. For Catholics, Jerusalem is the birthplace of Christianity and the setting of many important biblical events. The Holy City, as Catholic dogma states, is the Universal Headquarters of the Church. In his visit to Israel, Pope Benedict expressed the usual mantra calling for a Two-State [*final*] solution to the Israel-Palestinian conflict. He referred to: *"Jerusalem as a microcosm of our globalized world, this City, if it is to live up to its universal vocation, must be a place which teaches universality."* *[16] From this statement we can deduce that he, like so many other world leaders, is an advocate of the New World Order, as he uses the code words, *globalized world, universal vocation and universality.*

Just over a year later a Vatican Synod on the Middle East in its concluding remarks after two weeks of deliberations stated: *"Israel cannot use the Biblical concept of a promised land or a chosen people to justify new "settlements" in Jerusalem or territorial claims. We have meditated on the situation of the holy city of Jerusalem. We are anxious about the unilateral initiatives that threaten its composition and risk to change its demographic balance,"* the message said. Quite a statement! In a separate part of the document, a section cooperating with Jews, the synod fathers also took issue with Jews who use the bible to justify settlements in the West Bank, which Israel captured in 1967. *"Recourse to theological and biblical positions which use the Word of God to wrongly justify injustices is not acceptable,"* the document said. *"Many Jewish settlers and right wing Israelis claim a biblical birthright to the West Bank, which they call Judea and Samaria and regard as part of historical, ancient Israel given to the Jews by God."* (Quite right that they should do so!).

Asked about this last passage at a news conference, Greek-Melchite Archbishop Cyrille Salim Bustros, said: *"We Christians cannot speak about the promised land for the Jewish people. There is no longer a chosen people. All men and women of all countries have become the chosen people." "The concept of a promised land cannot be used as a base for the* *justification of the return of the Jews to Israel and the displacement of Palestinians,"* he added. *"The justification of Israel's occupation of the land of Palestine cannot be based on sacred scriptures!"* *17

If we cannot base the presence of the Jewish people in Eretz Israel on the books of the Torah and the Tanach then indeed there is little else we can stand on. This gentleman evidently wants to delegitimize the Jewish presence in the Holy land, indeed it would appear he wants to make Israel "Judenrein!"

Giulio Meotti, the Italian journalist, in an oped in Arutz Sheva in December 2011 explained how Catholic authorities in recent months have "increased their political initiatives for Catholic control over some sites in Jerusalem." In December, for example, the head of the Vatican's Council for Inter-Religious Dialog, Cardinal Jean-Louis Tauran, said that; *"peace negotiations in the Middle East must tackle the status of the holy sites of Jerusalem."* According to Tauran, *"it is time that some of Jerusalem's holy places, including the city of David, were put under Vatican charge. After all, it's practically just the Holy See who is concerned about [Jerusalem],"* Tauran stated.

Sadly, the Roman Catholic Church itself has little if any track record of being a friend to Israel, indeed it is among Israel's worst enemies!

The Ancient Assyrians are Alive Today!

There were two empires in the ancient pre-Roman world, Assyria and Babylon, who proved to be the most devastating enemies of the Hebrew nations. Think about it for a moment:

- Assyria invaded the Northern Kingdom of Israel in three devastating invasions, each of which resulted in hundreds of thousands of Israelites being slaughtered with the survivors exiled to Assyria, leaving the entire territory destitute and devoid of its Israelite population.

- The Babylonian Empire destroyed Jerusalem and the First Temple and took Judah into captivity to Babylon.

- Then Rome, the Fourth Empire to spring from Babylon, destroyed the Second Temple and murdered millions of Jews, as well as millions of Christians, prior to embracing a twisted pagan form of Christianity herself.

- Then the Roman Catholic Church, the apotheosis of Babylon, as well as the power behind the throne of the Holy Roman Empire, instigated the murderous Inquisition in which, over a period of some four hundred years, under the close supervision of its priests, an estimated 55 million Protestant Christians and Jews were tortured to death.

- Then Hitler's Nazi version of this same Empire murdered six million Jews in the Holocaust by utilizing the most obscene industrial killing process ever invented by man.

In view of this appalling track record, why would any nation be foolish enough to join this Roman Catholic European Union, which is a reincarnation of Babylon? It is high time for America and Great Britain and indeed <u>most especially for the State of Israel</u> to wake up to the threat from the European Union, where anti-Semitism has almost become a way of life. Those Hebrew nations clearly need to urgently reappraise their relationship with the EU. Great Britain needs to come out of this malign club that seeks her destruction and the tiny State of Israel would do well to put her trust in HaShem, the God of Abraham, rather than consider placing herself in the giant jaws of this man made Babylonian Euro Beast power.

The ultimate threat from the EU is far greater and even more ominous than any threat from Islamic terrorism, especially as the latter is the creation of the former. Nevertheless, with the proposed accession of some ten Muslim countries around the Mediterranean basin, this new EU Beast is destined to become at least fifty percent Islamic in any case. Therefore, the world faces the prospect of a German-led EU in a close military and economic alliance with the fanatic jihadists and the Koranic terrorists of militant Islam. Historically, the greatest threats to the survival of the Jewish people, as well as the Anglo-Saxon race, have always come from Europe! The prospect before us is that Europe's blood-spattered war-filled history is about to come to life once again. Remember, the First World War was made in Germany! The Second World War was also made in

Germany! What about the inevitability of a Third World War? Will it too be made in Germany? As a matter of historic fact, the greatest threat to the survival of the Jewish race has also come from a German-led Europe, <u>and, according to the ancient prophets of Israel, it is set to do so again!</u>

The prophet Isaiah tells us: *"Woe to Assyria, the rod of My anger; my wrath is a staff in their hand. Against a hypocritical people will I send them, and against a people that angers Me shall I charge them, to take spoils and to plunder booty, and to make them trampled like the mire of the streets"* (Isaiah 10: 5-6).

As we have already seen, HaShem has used Assyria before to correct His chosen people, and His Word indicates that this will happen again in these latter days. He warns the backsliding nations of Israel: *"Behold, I am fashioning evil against you, and I am devising a plan against you..."* Why? *"My people have forgotten Me!"* (Jeremiah 18: 11, 15).

Terrible calamities lie ahead for our grievously sinful nations! The German people are the modern day descendants of the ancient warlike "Assyrians!"[*18] The nation HaShem brings against the sinful Israelite nations is known for its haughty, master-race philosophy (Isaiah 10:8). It speaks a foreign language (Jeremiah 6:22-23 & Hosea 11:5-6). Assyria is pictured as a "Great Eagle" that carries away the house of Israel (Ezekiel 17:1-16). The eagle has for centuries been the symbol of Germany and prior to that it was the pre-eminent symbol of the Roman Empire, whilst its true origin will be found in Mesopotamia.

In the days of Abraham, Assyria was a mighty world-ruling empire. Even Abraham in his day was forced to fight against an Assyrian confederation of four kings, who had invaded the rich district of Sodom and Gomorrah, leading to the capture of Lot, the son of Abraham's brother. The names of the four kings were:

"Aramphel, king of Shinar, Arioch, king of Ellasar; Chedorlaomer, king of Elam, and Tidal, the king of Goiim!" (Genesis 14:1).

According to Flavius Josephus, those four kings were from Assyria and they had already conquered the land of Syria, as well as the land of the giants. Tidal, the king of nations, ruled in the region of Asia Minor.[*19] The name Tidal signifies TERROR, BEING AFRAID, TERRIBLE and TERRIFYING. Clearly, he was not a nice man!

However, Abraham was not afraid and trusting in HASHEM, he marched after the Assyrian armies with his small force of just 318 trained servants, and after a five day march, he divided his puny servant army and surprised that massive military force of some two hundred thousand crack Assyrian troops in the middle of the night. He not only defeated the Assyrians, but was able to capture and kill the four kings, and pursued the fleeing Assyrians to well north of Damascus. Thus in one night the invincible army of Assyria was utterly annihilated. Read all about it in Genesis 14!!! Thus was the power and might of Assyria laid into the dust. That night literally changed the history of the world! Josephus records that Abraham and his men: *"marched hastily, and the fifth night fell upon the Assyrians, near Dan...and before they could arm themselves, he slew some as they were in their beds, before they could suspect any harm; and others, who were not yet gone to sleep, but were so drunk they could not fight, ran away."*[*20] The land of Canaan was now free from Assyrian aggression, allowing Abraham and his descendants to settle peacefully in Canaan. This dramatic event also made it possible for Egypt to grow into the mightiest empire in the ancient world, without the constant danger of Assyrian aggression. It was HASHEM's wish that Egypt become the dominant power in the then-known world, in fulfillment of His plan for His nation Israel. After this battle victory the Bible has been virtually silent about Assyria for the next 1200 years. However, they did not vanish altogether. In around 700BCE Assyria appears once again as a dangerous world power, and once again they manifest their enmity towards Israel.

David reigned over the twelve tribes of the United Kingdom of Israel and he received a prophetic warning for his descendants: *"If they should profane My statutes, and not observe My commandments, then I will punish their transgression with the ROD, and their iniquity with plagues;"* (Psalms 89:31-32).

This ROD OF CORRECTION IS NONE OTHER THAN ASSYRIA, who has, as history is our witness, already transported the inhabitants of the Northern Kingdom of Israel as captive slaves in three successive invasions between 738 and 721 BCE. It is a fact of history! No other nation was involved! We have in this a clear indication. Why? Because Assyria has already done it, and going by the maxim of Solomon, they are bound to do it again! When we add to this the attack they made in the days of Abraham and Lot, plus the fact that there were three separate invasions of the Northern Kingdom of Israel, plus the further fact that they attacked the Kingdom of Judah also in the days of King Hezekiah, then we count five major aggressions against Israel. We have in this a clear historic pattern for the future; we could almost say it is a trend, as we shall see later on. Ezekiel utters a terrible warning about this:

"You, son of Man, take for yourself a sharp sword, take for yourself a barber's razor, and pass it over your head and over your beard; then take for yourself the scales of a balance and divide them. Burn one third in a fire inside the city upon completion of the days of the siege, take one third and strike [it] with a sword all around it, and scatter one third to the wind, and I will unsheathe a sword after them. Then take from there a numbered few and bind them into your hems. Then take from them once again and throw them into the middle of the fire, and burn them in the fire; from it a fire will go forth to the entire House of Israel." (Ezekiel 5:1-4).

Ezekiel is clearly addressing a yet future event, as it has not happened yet. It is hard to imagine! A third of the populations of the Israel nations destroyed by fire! This is talking here about 200 million plus casualties. Destruction on this scale can only be accomplished by nuclear weapons, and this prophecy will most certainly come to pass. It then speaks of a further third of our kinsfolk being destroyed by the sword, and this death and destruction carries on until a mere 10% of our population remains alive. The Torah confirms the fact:

"Any tithe of cattle or of the flock, any that passes under the staff [ROD], the tenth one shall be holy to HASHEM." (Leviticus 27:32, emphasis added). The Scriptures interpret themselves, and Isaiah shows us who is going to apply that terrible razor to the whole house of Israel.

"In that day the Lord will shave with a large razor those who crossed the [Euphrates] River with the king of Assyria; the head, the hair of the legs, and the beard, as well, will be destroyed." (Isaiah 7:20).

The prophet also tells us that the Assyrians are going to hit us with a stick:

Therefore, thus said My Lord HASHEM/ELOHIM, Master of Legions: " Do not be afraid of Assyria, O My people who dwell in Zion, though he will strike you with a staff and raise his ROD over you in the manner of Egypt. For in a very short while, My fury and My anger will destroy [them] for their sacrilege." (Isaiah 10:24-25, emphasis added).

Historians are almost unanimous about the warlike spirit of the Assyrians. They were a most cruel and wild race, and their soldiers were famed for their furious fighting spirit. They manifested a huge superiority over other nations in the organization of supply and in the quality of their weaponry, as well as in their strategies of attack and defense. The historian James Hastings writes in the Dictionary of the Bible: *that; "Old Assyria was the greatest war-making power in the history of the world. The entire organization of the State was based upon the continuing pursuit of war!"*

Leonard Cottrell, in his book, *"The Anvil of Civilization," writes in all the annals of mankind, it is impossible to find a people more dedicated to bloodshed and slaughter than the Assyrians. Their wildness and cruelty are without parallel except in our modern day.*[*21]

It is interesting to note that Cottrell can only find a comparative parallel with the furious cruelty of the Assyrians in our modern time. It is a fact of history that the German race in the 20th century certainly has shed much blood.

Historians have frequently referred to the Assyrians as *the Prussians of the Ancient World,* as like the Prussians they too were imbued with the spirit of militant aggression. Just as Germany saw its function during the Middle Ages to *"protect civilization against the dangers of pagan influences,"* the Assyrians in their day justified their campaign on the same grounds.[*22]

The conquered nations lived in continual fear of the Secret Police of Assyria. Her agents had a Gestapo likeness and they were incredibly devious and clever, and utterly merciless in suppressing the slightest opposition.[*23] In the Assyrian army the soldiers were purposely trained to be as ruthless and cruel as it is possible to be towards anyone who stood in the way. In their training they had to learn to ferociously attack any opposition with a disgusting barbarity and with a ruthless cruelty, and yet obtain pleasure from the act.

The historian Kalyanaram writes that the cruelty and bestiality of the Assyrians has never been equaled by any other people, because they were devoted to destruction, the spilling of blood and to bring indiscriminate slaughter to every place where they set foot

The king of Assyria was able at any given moment to call up a giant army of hundreds of thousands of well trained soldiers. It consisted of tightly organized and well disciplined troops with many specially integrated Special Forces. This gigantic army was the central method of the kings of Assyria to conquer the world. The conquest and subjugation of the world was their final goal. From the period of Shalmanezer I, the Assyrian kings gave themselves the title of *"Shar Kishati,"* which means, *"Emperor of the World!"* The word Kaiser is derived from this.

In Oded's masterpiece; *"Mass Deportations in the Neo-Assyrian Empire,* he makes the point that millions of conquered people were deported. However, they did not separate families, because they wanted to maintain community life, in order to settle them in their newly assigned areas as homogenous groups. Notice that the Assyrians thus were racially aware because they demanded that the racial identity and ethnic diversity of the people they conquered should remain intact. The victims of their aggression through those cruel deportations were taken into captivity and transported over huge and for those times historically unprecedented distances from their homelands, making it impossible for them to return.

They also operated a very large immensely efficient bureaucratic system to supervise the transport and deportations. The kings of Assyria were not a bit ashamed and did not in any way attempt to hide their barbarity. Instead they were immensely proud of their gruesome cruelty and boasted about it in all of their monuments, as any visit to the Assyrian departments of the British Museum or the Louvre in Paris will testify. After their continual and uninterrupted military successes, the Assyrians began to display a degree of superiority towards the nations they had overpowered. Gradually this attitude developed into the belief that they were THE MASTER RACE!!! Increasingly they began to exploit their prisoners as slave labor and cheap human material for their war economy in their pursuit of conquest and subjugation. After this litany of warlike signals, you may have seen the connection between the Assyrians of old and the Nazi methods of the Second World War.

After centuries of barbarity and incredible misery there came a massive revolt and with the help of large Israelite contingents from the Cimmerians and Scythians, Assyria was defeated, and her glorious capital of Nineveh was totally destroyed in 612 BCE. The prophet Nahum especially relates the terrifying militaristic nature of this empire as he speaks about this earthshaking event:

"Woe to the City of Blood; it is all deceit, full of robbery; prey departs not [from it]; the sound of the whip and the sound of rattling wheel; galloping horse and bounding chariot; the horseman raises flashing sword and glittering spear; numerous slain and heaps of corpses; there is no end to the bodies, and they stumble over their bodies. [All this] because of the many harlotries of the harlot, rich in grace, practitioner of witchcraft, who sells nations through her harlotries and families through her witchcraft. Behold, I am against you—the word of HASHEM, Master of Legions—and I will pull up your skirts over your face; and I will show the nations your nakedness and the kingdoms your shame. I will cast repulsive things upon you and make you disgusting; I will make you like dung. And it will be that all who see you will move away from you and say, "Nineveh has been ravaged; who will bemoan her?" From where can I seek comforters for you? (Nahum 3:1-7).

The historian Von Soden writes: *"At the end of the Neo-Assyrian Empire most Assyrian cities were totally destroyed and there were an unimaginable number of deaths, and it coincided with the dissolution of all former governmental order."*

The historian Oppenheim states that: *"The entire Mesopotamian civilization disappeared."*

The mighty Assyrian people and nation disappeared suddenly from the Mesopotamian area. Most historians today have simply accepted this highly illogical scenario as fact. However, such a great and mighty multi-talented people cannot just disappear without a trace! So what happened to the Assyrians after their cataclysmic defeat? Where did they go?

According to Yair Davidiy, the Israeli author, the Persian, Greek and Roman historians record that the Scythians were a large collection of tribes and nations, which were joined by the surviving Assyrians on their trek across the Caucasus Mountains into the Russian steppes. The Assyrians themselves also recorded their relationship with the Gimeri, which later became identified as the Cimmerians. In their historical cuneiform tablets they also spoke about the Scythians, and referred to them as the ISHKUZI, SAKAE, and GIMIRI, all of which were part of the ten tribes of Israel. The author recounts that when he was at school in 1950s Holland that the history book contained a whole chapter regarding the Great Peoples Land-trek Movement, which described that from around the year 600BCE, there was a continuous trek of tribes and nations which came into Europe from the East. The chapter emphasized how this massive immigration process carried on in great waves over many centuries. This great land trek coincided with the destruction of the Assyrian Empire. Ironically, those books were soon withdrawn from the curriculum, probably because the knowledge had become politically incorrect! According to Davidiy and a number of other historians and researchers, the tribes of Assyria established themselves in Austria and Germany, whilst the Israelite tribes for the most part moved on to settle in the "coastlands" of Europe and eventually from there to the "coastlands" of the world. (See: Isaiah 41:1&5; 42:10&12; 49:1; 51:5; 59:18; 60:9.) This can be verified from the above Scriptures, as well as from secular history.

The Germans themselves confirm their Assyrian heritage in the origins of one of their oldest cities. On the banks of the river Mosel, around 9 km from Luxemburg, lies the city of Trier. The Romans claim they founded the city. However, German tradition, as well as the name of the city itself tells a different story.

On the front of *"Das Rotes Haus"* is a plaque with a Latin inscription which boasts that *Trier or "Treves," is older than Rome itself! Indeed, 1300 years older! That is when–wait for it–"Trebeta," the son of Sémiramis, built and founded the city!*

"Das Rotes Haus."

This is also confirmed in the pamphlet produced by Trier's town guide. Furthermore, a German author writes in his textbook that: *"Trier was FOUNDED by TREBETA, A SON OF THE FAMOUS ASSYRIAN KING NINUS."* *24 The biblical name for Ninus is Nimrod! Here we have that ugly name again! The reason why the German city of Trier can trace its origins back to Trebeta, the son of Nimrod and Semiramis, and also to Nineveh is simply because the German people of today are the modern day descendants of the ancient Assyrians.

The Romans had a lot of trouble to contain, let alone defeat the warlike German tribes, and this is precisely the reason why they were never able to expand their empire to the east of the Rhine River. They gave those tribes a new collective name. They referred to them as: GERMANI, and thus they described the essential character of those people. GERMANI means WARMEN or WARLIKE. They had formed this opinion through their own bitter experience in fighting those ruthless warriors of the land to the east of the Rhine, as even with all the awesome might of Rome they simply were not able to defeat them.

The Romans called them Germani because of their fierce warring nature. *"Not a single neighbor of the Germans,"* wrote Emil Ludwig; *"could ever trust the Germans to remain peaceable. No matter how happy their condition, their restless passion would urge them onto ever more extreme demands."*[*25]

Emil Ludwig, in the above mentioned book, wrote, *"The history of the German kings and leaders during the Middle Ages is a story of revolt and conspiracy...In matters of torture the Germans in the Middle Ages exceeded all other nations in inventiveness."* (pp.14,33). A quick review of 20th century German history reveals that this German nature of cruelty and war did not end with the Middle Ages. A quick review of Assyrian history will also reveal this tendency towards cruelty.[*26]

Today Germany is a NATO member and close ally of America and Great Britain, and she has good relations with the State of Israel. Yet, the prophets of the Tanach indicate that Israel's allies, including Assyria, will suddenly turn into enemies (Ezekiel 23:5-24).

A good example of this is the lesson Norway had to learn to her cost when on the morning of April 9, 1940, German troops suddenly invaded their country, without provocation and without warning. Winston Churchill records that: *"Surprise, ruthlessness, and precision were characteristics of the onslaught upon innocent and naked Norway."* [*27] He further explains that: *"What stupefied the Norwegians more than the act of aggression itself was the national realization that a great power [Germany], for years professing friendship, suddenly appeared a deadly enemy... the people of Norway were dazed to find that for years their German friends had been elaborating the most detailed plans for the invasion and subsequent enslaving of their country"* [*28]

For all the talk of Berlin, after 67 years of democracy, having long forsaken military power and become a "civilian power," Germany in the past ten years has overtaken Britain and France as the world's third largest arms exporter![*29] Her state of the art weaponry is among the best in the world and her modernized army is considered the best in Europe. For many years German pilots have been trained at several bases in America. Meanwhile the armed forces of Britain, Canada and the rest of the Western democracies are being cut to the bone with all of them increasingly dependent upon the extended and overstretched forces of the U.S. The financial tsunami now in immediate prospect for the world economy will inevitably force America to greatly reduce her military forces around the world. In fact, substantial cutbacks are already taking place in the U.S Defense budget with major projects being pared down. History records that dark forces in Germany have exploited this kind of scenario before. The prophets of Israel reveal that our allies will suddenly turn on us! (See: Jeremiah 4:30; Ezekiel 23:5-10, 22-23).

A further ominous sign in the wind is the report that local authorities in Germany are to reprint "Mein Kampf" ["My Struggle"], Adolph Hitler's hate tract, for the first time since the death of the Nazi dictator in 1945. The decision by the State of Bavaria, which controls the copyright, means the book will be available again in three years, when its German copyright expires, but with content warnings throughout. It follows years of agonized debate about whether Germans remain susceptible to Nazi ideology and how to stop it reviving. The book is freely available in many other countries and is especially popular in the Muslim world. After meeting anti-Nazi activists in Nurenberg, the city that once hosted Nazi Party rallies, Bavarian Finance Minister Markus Soeder said a complete edition, with annotations throughout by historians warning against Hitler's errors, would help demystify the book. A separate edition for schools also would be issued.[*30]

Another serious cause for concern is the recent (June 2012) ruling by the District Court of Cologne that religious circumcision of a child is harmful and that a parent's jurisdiction over his child does not extend to the practice of circumcision. The Cologne ruling, which outlaws circumcision practiced for religious reasons, is a notable beachhead for the anti-circumcision camp. The court ruled that: "The body of the child is irreparably and permanently changed by a circumcision, which contravenes the interests of the child to decide later on his religious beliefs." According to the ruling, the rights of a parent to provide for children, and the rights of religious freedom, do not sufficiently justify circumcision, which the court characterized as "minor bodily harm." [*31]

The German dominated EU clearly is a global colossus in the making and already her economic and diplomatic clout is being increasingly felt around the world. The driving force behind this union from its onset was the Franco-German axis and the vision that inspired this axis of historic enemies was world domination. With the recent defeat of President Nicolas Sarkozy and the election of the anti-German Socialist President Hollande, the lynchpin partnership that held the EU together since the Treaty of Rome in 1957 is now gone. German Chancellor Merkel wasted no time in forging a new partnership with Italy's Prime Minister Mario Monti. Berlin and Rome from here on are set to dominate EU policy decisions. Once again history appears to be repeating itself, as what we see is a tentative resurrection of Hitler and Musolini's old Berlin-Rome Axis of 1939. With Italian Prime Minister Mario Monti so close to the seat of German power and Mario Draghi, another Italian, in charge of the European Central Bank, controlling the EU purse strings, we see these men, both of the same Jesuit minds, suddenly exerting huge influence over Germany. It would appear that—the Rome-Berlin Axis in formation with the unprecedented resignation of the German Pope Benedict, and his replacement by the charismatic Jesuit Pope Francis—all that now remains is for a new "Charlemagne" to appear, to lead this EU Beast power to the head of the global stage. We can only hope that the new Pope will work to forestall the day of the seventh "Roman Resurrection." Already we have seen him begin to reach out to the Jewish people in an apparent effort to build bridges of harmony and communication.

Behind all the diplomatic smiles from these EU leaders, there are among them those who harbor evil intent. Based upon the world's previous experience of European imperialism at the hands of the likes of Napoleon, Bismarck, Kaiser Wilhelm, and Adolph Hitler, this bodes extremely ill for the rest of humanity.

The EU in Prophecy

Prophecy is a sure guide to the future! The EU glorifies secular humanism and its pagan Greco-Roman heritage. A famous EU motto is: *"Of many languages, one voice."* Remember the account of the infamous tower of Babel in the book of Genesis, when all the people of the world spoke the same language? Nothing would restrain the people of Babel and they decided to make themselves as God. Their Creator, the King of the Universe, confused their language and scattered them to the four corners of the earth (Genesis 11:6). The EU concept is to deliberately reverse this process through the abolition of the nation states. She does this by subtly convincing them that their only hope of future survival lies in joining a supranational conglomerate in preparation for the establishment of a New EU-led World Order. To emphasise the Babel connection, it has chosen Pieter Breughel's famous painting of the *Tower of Babel* as one of its logos. The Tower Building [named after the Tower of Babel] houses the European Parliament. It certainly is a building of the Space Age. The seats are designed like the crew seats in the Star Trek space machines. The legislative amphitheatre is arranged in a massive hemi circle and has 679 seats, each assigned to a particular lawmaker. For example, Seat 663 is assigned to Rep Souchet, 664 to Thomas-Mauro, 665 to Zizzner and 667 to Rep Capato. While these seats are allocated to Members, one seat remains unallocated and unoccupied. The number of that Seat is 666! According to the NT Book of Revelation, this number has a particularly sinister meaning, as it describes a future world ruler who will wreak untold havoc upon the earth.

"Here is wisdom. Let him that hath understanding count the number of the beast: for it is the number of a man; and his number is six hundred threescore and six" (Revelation 13:18).

Even the design of the $12 billion European Parliament building in Strasbourg is based upon a likeness of the Tower of Babel. This begs the question—is the EU the spiritual descendent of the original Babel, and is the EU attempting to rebuild what God once destroyed? The Tower of Babel which Nimrod built in ancient Babylon was the symbol of man's first ever attempt to create a New World Order of One World Government in direct and deliberate opposition to God. When God saw mankind united against Him, He confused their speech, so that they no longer could conspire together in one language, and they were forced to stop building their diabolical political system. (Genesis 11:1-8). The EU poster that declares, *"Many tongues, one voice,"* shows the Tower of Babel with the EU "ring of stars" flag hovering above. However, the stars in this case are all portrayed as inverted pentagrams. Whereas the original five-pointed stars/pentagrams were anciently used as symbols associated with holiness and righteousness, they have over time been corrupted by occult practitioners into symbols used to represent Satan. This fact alone should make any nation wary of involvement with the EU. The European Flag portrays a circle of twelve golden stars on a blue background. In Roman Catholic symbolism twelve stars in a circle always refer to the crown of Mary, the *"Queen of Heaven."* However, in Babylonian culture, [which is what we are really dealing with in the EU], the legendary title of *"Queen of Heaven"* was given to "Semiramis," the earthly mother and wife of Nimrod, the builder of the Tower of Babel. Nimrod not only was the founder and builder of Babylon but he also built the formidable citadel of Nineveh in Assyria. (Genesis 10:8-12).

Pieter Breughel's Tower of Babel

The Covenant With Death

European Parliament Building in Strassburg

Note: the occult-tainted and inverted pentagrams

Is the EU the Mortal Enemy of America?

Note: how the design of Parliament building is deliberately modeled on the Tower of Babel

The Pergamon Altar, Pergamon Museum, Berlin

The Tower of Babel reference brings to mind the vision Daniel was called to interpret some 2500 years ago for Nebuchadnezzar king of Babylon. The king in his dream had seen a huge image of a man with a head of gold, shoulders and arms of silver, belly and thighs of brass, and legs of iron. The feet of the image were part iron mixed with part clay (Daniel 2:31-34). Daniel was given the interpretation of the great image as symbolizing four successive world-ruling empires. Most scholars, admittedly with the benefit of hindsight of actual history, recognize that the Babylonian Empire represented the head of gold, that the Medo-Persian Empire was symbolized by the shoulders and arms of silver, that the Greco-Macedonian Empire represented the belly and thighs of brass, whereas the legs of iron symbolized the Roman Empire, with one leg in the east and one leg in the west (Daniel 2:36-43).

The Rape of Europa—the Woman on the Beast

Another symbol adopted by Europe, as curious as the Tower of Babel, is the Greek myth of the "Rape of Europa." This begs the question—is Europe today being raped politically, financially and or spiritually—and by whom? In every case, a wanton woman, Europa, can be seen riding a beast. The mythical story behind the image is that Zeus, the father of the gods, spied Europa alone on the beach and lusted after her. He transformed himself into a bull of dazzling whiteness with horns like a crescent moon and lay down at her feet. She climbed on his back and he plunged her into the waves of the sea before raping her. Europa conceived a son, and after her death she received divine honors as "Queen of Heaven," whilst the bull dissolved into the constellation in the sky known as Taurus.

Both Brussels and Strasbourg EU Parliament building contain sculptures and paintings of the woman on the beast. The Charlemagne building housing the EU Headquarters in Brussels contains a massive computer called Euro Net, which is nicknamed "the Beast." Reputedly this is the first computer capable of storing the personal data of the entire world population. Throughout the EU, governments have issued stamps and coins bearing the image of the woman and the beast.

Is the EU the Mortal Enemy of America?

German telephone card—notice Islamic crescent moon symbol in the background

Notice: just 3 years after the end of WWII we see that in choosing the image of the woman riding the beast, the German leadership of the day were already planning round number three.

The Covenant With Death

Sculpture 2000 – Outside the European Council Building in Brussels!

Issued to commemorate European Parliamentary elections, this stamp shows a woman riding a beast.
Is this Revelation 17:3-5 –
MYSTERY BABYLON THE GREAT?

Is the EU the Mortal Enemy of America?

Now we can also draw upon texts written by Jews for historical insights, even though orthodox Torah Judaism does not recognize them as having a divine stamp of approval. Nevertheless, gospel texts were originally produced basically by Jewish people hoping for a messiah. Thus they contain a great deal of messianic religious Jewish culture and oral Torah. By looking to some of those texts that eventually became the Cannon of the Church, even present day orthodox Jews may observe in the writings of these messianic Jewish sects a reflection of what their culture and thinking was at the time. As such, this fourth world-ruling empire is further described in the vision of the apostle John, while on the isle of Patmos:

"So he carried me away in the spirit into the wilderness. And I saw a woman sitting on a scarlet beast, which was full of names of blasphemy, having seven heads and ten horns...And on her forehead a name was written: Mystery, Babylon the Great, the Mother of Harlots and of the Abominations of the earth." (Revelation 17:3-5 NKJV, emphasis added).

One needs to bear in mind that Babylon was at the head of all those successive empires, and thus they all represent the Babylonian mindset and system. The woman riding the scarlet beast holds sway over the seven resurrections of the fourth world-ruling Roman Empire. This final empire, according to Daniel, was to have seven revivals or resurrections, a fact amply confirmed by the history of the Roman Empire and its seven revivals in the guise of its Holy Roman Empire successors. In biblical allegory, a woman usually is a symbol of Israel, yet in this case, this, *"woman sitting on a scarlet beast,"* represents a symbol of a church that has usurped Israel's role. It is speaking of a Church that has stolen Israel's clothes through replacement theology.

In 554 CE at the behest of the Pope, the Head of the "Roman" Catholic Church:

Justinian Became the First Emperor of the Revived "Holy Roman Empire!"

Then in 800 CE the Empire was revived a second time, as the Pope placed a crown upon the head of Charlemagne, pronouncing him the 73rd Emperor of the Fourth World Empire.

CHARLEMAGNE, THE SWORD OF THE CHURCH AND ITS EMPEROR, was driven by a fanatic zeal to convert every person in his empire by force to the religion of the Roman Catholic Church. The New Encyclopedia Britannica states: *"The violence which he applied to his task of forced conversions was unprecedented even for his time in the early Middle Ages, the bloodthirsty punishments he meted out to those who would not bow to the writ of Rome, were even criticized in his own circles."* The Saxon [Israelite] tribes especially refused to submit to Rome. Even under the threat of certain death, they refused to be converted. After eighteen blood-drenched and murderous campaigns, during a period of some thirty years, including the genocide of 4,500 Saxon prisoners, Charlemagne enforced his twisted brand of Christianity with the sword. Charlemagne's problem with his Saxon [Israelite] citizens was finally solved, as the only Saxons still alive by this time had become good Catholic members of the faith.

Adolph Hitler, being somewhat of a kindred spirit, was a great admirer of Charlemagne's reign, especially his iron will and his exercise of absolute power. It was no coincidence therefore that the picture window of the main reception room at the Eagles' Nest, Hitler's hilltop fortress in Bergtesgaden, looked out upon the Untersburg, the burial place of Charlemagne.

Otto the Great, led the third revival! In 962CE, the Pope gave the Crown of the Holy Roman Empire to OTTO the GREAT, who was the first of a long list of German Emperors, and for the following 800 years his successors referred to themselves as: *"ROMAN EMPEROR OF THE GERMAN NATION!"*

Seated on Charlemagne's throne in the cathedral forecourt, the lay princes and the people pledged him loyalty and support against his enemies. *The people raised their right hands to show their assent in the election and shouted, "Victory and Salvation!"* ("SIEG und HEIL"), *a salutation of substance in that it gave the election legal force.*[*32] Much like many of his German successors, he was a ruthless soldier. During his absolute rule he enlarged the boundaries of Christendom by the force of his sword. According to the *Encyclopedia Britannica*, *"He was prone to violent explosions of uncontrolled passion, and his attitude was to* *annihilate and expunge every tendency towards independence."* *33 In every newly conquered territory he introduced new German colonies. His period can best be described as the dawn of German nationalism. This world ruling spirit of power-hungry nationalism brought many German Kings to cross the Alps to Italy seeking for everything Roman. The relationship between the German Emperors and the Catholic Popes was not without rivalry with each side seeking the supremacy. It is clear why this relationship has stood the test of time. The German Emperors have always been aware that the road to world domination goes through Rome!

Charles V, Led the Fourth Revival, as he Commenced his Reign in 1520CE.

CHARLES V presided over the greatest revival of the Holy Roman Empire during his days of power. This was also the time when the Spanish and Roman Inquisitions reached its ultimate fever-pitch in carrying out their cruel and gruesome work of persecution in all the territories under his power. Estimates vary, but it is accepted by historians that some 40 to 55 million people were murdered during the 400 years of terror, which the Inquisition had unleashed on the orders of the Roman Catholic Church.

Napoleon led the Fifth Revival From 1804CE.

After Napoleon had by military smashed the power of the remnants of the Hapsburg dynasty in the 19th century, it looked like the last vestige of the Holy Roman Empire was finally destroyed. However, historians do not recognize that the moment Napoleon so rudely grabbed the Imperial Crown out of the hands of the Pope, only to place it upon his own head in 1804, the Holy Roman Empire CHANGED HANDS. After eight centuries of German and Austrian domination, the H.R.E. experienced a short-lived revival under French domination. It was the Holy Roman Empire in disguise! Napoleon's vision was to rule over the whole world, just like the German Emperors before him, and once again it was facilitated through the Vatican in Rome.

In February 1806, Napoleon urged his uncle, Cardinal Flesh, to impress upon the Church that; "I am indeed Charlemagne, the sword of the Church and its Emperor." *34

<u>Adolph Hitler & Mussolini Axis led the sixth revival of the Holy Roman Empire.</u>

When Benito Mussolini came to power in Italy, he immediately made a Concordat with the Pope and the Vatican in 1929. It was called the Lateran Treaty. His dream was to create an Italian, say Roman Empire, and he wanted the Mediterranean Sea to become the, *"Mare Nostrum," "Our Sea."* His supporters also spoke in the same sense about the creation of a New Roman Empire! Mussolini made a pact with Hitler in 1936, which was called the Rome-Berlin Axis, and this was soon followed by "The Pact of Steel" in 1939. Despite the vaunting ambitions of Musolini, it was Hitler who played the definitive role as the Sixth Ruler of the Holy Roman Empire.

It is no accident that the six founding states of what is now the EU almost exactly comprise the territorial boundaries of Charlemagne's Holy Roman Empire. It can be no coincidence that the main religion of these same states is Roman Catholic, just as it was in the days of Charlemagne. Furthermore, it is no coincidence that the HQ of the EU Council of Ministers is located in the Charlemagne building in Brussels. In 1957, the six original members of what by then had become the European Economic Community (EEC) formally enshrined the age-old vision of a United Europe in the Treaty of Rome! The choice of venue for the signing of this historic treaty was certainly no accident. It took place in Rome, once the capital of the mighty Roman Empire, and which to this day is still the capital of Rome's spiritual descendant—the Roman Catholic Church. Paul Henri Spaak, one of the signatories to the treaty, in commenting on the signing ceremony in a BBC documentary shown sometime after the event, said: *"We felt like Romans on that day...we were "consciously" re-creating the Roman Empire once more!"*

The idea that while the Holy Roman Empire still existed—in one of its metamorphoses if not in its own person—the end of the world and the Last Judgment would be postponed, was the great theme of the medieval theologians of the Holy Roman Empire and of its poets and literary champions at critical moments in its history. This conviction concealed within itself the realization that the Holy Roman Empire was the last manifestation of an age-old sacral-political order in which "gods," men, beasts, all living things, dwelt together under the protection of one or more of the great houses. The houses were those of the world emperors, rulers whose insignia, down to the end of the Holy Roman Empire, continued to be those proper to the Emperor of the Heavens. The imperial eagle was a battle standard in the time of the earliest Mesopotamian kings, and afterwards among the Sumerians; it went into battle with the Roman legions and the troops of Frederick II of Hohenstaufen, just as in the battles of the First World War it accompanied the armies of His Apostolic Majesty the Emperor of Austria, and of the Tsar of All the Russians. The double eagle, officially incorporated into the arms of the Empire in the fifteenth century in the reign of Sigismund, is first found in Mesopotamia.*35

This just goes to show that all the origins takes us back to Babylon! The implication is that the EU may be a fulfillment of Daniel's prophecy, as it represents the seventh and final resurrection of this Roman Empire characterized as the feet of the image made of iron mixed with miry clay.

The Symbol of Satan's Throne is Located in Berlin!

The Greek word for pit is "*ABYSS,*" which means _under ground!_ This means that this powerful Beast Empire has continued underground, so that she could at regular intervals in all her gruesome power manifest herself. The Bible tells us that the last seven resurrections are inspired by a mighty Church (*the woman that rides the beast),* and that whenever this Church and the State are in agreement, we witness the ascent of the Beast of Revelation out of the abyss, which is the Holy Roman Empire. We need to understand that Satan himself is the instigator behind this Babylonian mischief, and that SATAN'S THRONE RIGHT NOW IS SITUATED IN BERLIN! In the NT book of Revelation we find the following statement:

And to the angel of the church in Pergamum write, These things says He who has the sharp two-edged sword: I know your works, and where you dwell, <u>where Satan's throne is.</u> (Revelation 2:13, NKJV).

Kaiser Willem II had the original monument shipped from Pergamum to Berlin in 1902 where it was re-erected stone by stone. It was an occasion accompanied by extravagant celebration towards the pagan gods. He called it the proudest moment of his reign.

Then in 1913 the first construction of the Ishtar Gate began in Berlin!

In Hebrew numerology Babel means SEPARATION from YHVH. In Babel was the great temple of Marduk, Baal by another name, who was also represented as the Serpent-Dragon god, an evil spirit, which was worshipped through excruciating self-torture and through human sacrifice —surely a representation of Satan himself! The entrance into the impressive ceremonial way was through the Ishtar Gate, which was decorated with 337 serpent dragon monsters, (337 is a number that signifies SHEOL or HELL). The captives of Judah would have walked through this terrifying gate to commence their 70 years of captivity in Babylon. Then just one year after its erection in Berlin:

- 1914—Germany attacks Belgium and starts the First World War, leaving 10 million dead!

- 1920—Germany becomes the center for Rationalism and the Modern Movement of Bible Criticism, coupled with the School of Liberal Theology, which denies the veracity of the Scriptures. This lying spirit of rationalism has had a huge worldwide effect in undermining faith in the Bible.

- 1930—Babylon's complete Ishtar Gate, this time inclusive of the Processional Way, is erected in Berlin.

- 1934—Hitler orders the construction of an exact copy to scale of the Pergamum Throne of Satan for his Nazi Rallies in Nuremberg.

- 1939-45—The Second World War starts with Hitler's attack and invasion of Poland. This war produced 55 million casualties, including the industrial murder of six million Jews.

- 1957—The Treaty of Rome is signed witnessing the birth of the European Union.

- 1958 –Communist East Germany requests Russia to return the Pergamum Altar, and Nikita Khrushev returns the altar to East Berlin.

- 1959—Satan's Throne is re-erected in the Pergamum Museum in East Berlin.

- 1989—The fall of the Berlin Wall.

- 1999 –The official opening of the restored Reichstag Building, and the German government moves from Bonn back to Berlin, the location of Satan's Throne.

DO YOU RECOGNIZE THE AWESOME SPIRITUAL SIGNIFICANCE OF THIS?

Iron Feet Mixed With Miry Clay

When we look at the Great Image of a Man in Daniel 2:37-43 that King Nebuchadnezzar of Babylon saw in his vision, we notice that its feet were made in part of "ceramic clay" and of "part iron." Ask any blacksmith or potter and they will tell you that iron and clay do not mix well, as the materials are not at all compatible. Consequently the Scripture states that the kingdom shall be divided, yet it will have the strength of iron in it. One possible explanation is that the iron in this kingdom represents Edom, whereas the clay represents Ishmael. The "iron" ruling influence over the ten toes of this final world-ruling empire, may reasonably be said to represent the European Union, led by Germany, which has already formed a close alliance by "mixing" with the "miry clay" of Islam and the Arab states of the Middle East. The prophet Daniel goes on to make the point that this evil combine in effect is a terrible mismatch, as iron does not mix with clay and consequently the kingdom will be partly powerful and partly fragile or broken.

It is interesting to note that in the book of Daniel, the *Aramaic* word used for "Mix" is "Arab"—meaning to co-mingle without bonding and the Aramaic word that is used for "Miry" is "Tiyn," meaning calamity, sticky dirt or a demon that must be swept away! Notice also that two distinct forms of clay are mentioned in Daniel 2:41-43. The first, which is associated with the feet, is referred to as "part potters/ceramic clay," implying a stable form of clay of the sort to mould a jar or pot, e.g., something that can hold water. Possibly this might infer a connection with the Roman Catholic Church, which historically has often had a stormy relationship with the Edomite iron rulers of Europe. The second description refers to the "Ten Toes," and it reveals a different structure, one of iron being part "MIXED with MIRY clay." This implies a rather loose pliable sticky form of clay, an unstable substance that cannot be moulded into any kind of useful vessel capable of holding water. Without too much imagination we can discern that symbolically this "miry clay" may well picture the Islamic immigration of Europe, as they "mingle" (mix—Arab) themselves into the European population, whilst refusing to cleave or culturally bond with it.*36

Once again a German Pope sat on his throne in Rome. A German-led Europe will soon mutate, like Dr. Jekyl and Mr. Hyde, into a restored Holy Roman Empire of the German Nation. Their Concordat renewed a rapidly re-Nazifying Berlin and re-paganizing Rome, which will march on Jerusalem for their Last Crusade. They will attempt to seize Jerusalem from the Jews and there crown the new king of a final world empire on Mount Zion at the Benedictine Basilica of the Dormition, constructed as an exact copy of Aachen (Aix-la-Chapelle) Cathedral build by Charlemagne 1,200 years ago.*37

Thus the SEVENTH AND FINAL RESURRECTION OF THE FOURTH WORLD RULING EMPIRE WITH ITS FEET OF IRON MIXED WITH MIRY CLAY IS EVEN NOW STANDING AT THE DOOR. However, mercifully this final revival of the Holy Roman Empire will last but a short time, as Daniel tells us how it will all end, as he concludes his interpretation of Nebuchadnezzar's dream with:

"Then in the days of these kingdoms, the God of heaven will establish a kingdom that will never be destroyed nor will its sovereignty be left to another people; it will crumble and consume all these kingdoms, and it will stand forever. Just as you saw that the stone was hewn from the mountain, not by human hands, and that it crumbled the iron, the copper, the earthenware, the silver, and the gold, so has the great God made

known to the king what will happen in the future. The dream is true and its interpretation is reliable." (Daniel 2:44-45).

The One Secret That Unlocks End-time Prophecy

To understand the prophecies of the Bible you must know the modern day identity of the characters the prophets continuously are referring to in their prophetic pronouncements. From the signs we see before us today, simply by following the daily news, we can discern a clear trend, implying the imminent collapse of the American Empire and Anglo-Saxon world rule. The prophets of the Bible forecast with absolute certainty that there will be a further battle for the birthright of the English speaking, (i.e., the Israel nations), in these end times. Once you understand that those same nations are part of the Lost House of Israel, you can begin to understand the many prophetic warnings in the Bible about this epic battle at the end of the age. Understanding the true identity of the nations the prophets variously refer to as Israel, Ephraim, or Joseph, as well as Judah, opens up the hidden mystery that unlocks those prophetic books full of utterances, which without this knowledge remain veiled in darkness and confusion. This means that those of us who have been given that understanding are under an obligation to spread the news. There is never an excuse for inaction for those who can discern the times we are in.

There needs to be an action plan to countermand the coming threat! Above all, we should not forget the power of prayer. Nevertheless, men and women of vision need to get together to avert the threat to the "Whole" House of Israel. Even as individuals, quite a lot may be achieved by taking every opportunity to lobby the Executive, as well as both the Members of the Senate and the Congress to encourage them to stand in support of the State of Israel. Those same men and women should combine to countermand and attack the multitudinous one-sided media reports about the conflict in the Middle East, which almost invariably paint Israel as the villain. Those of the Christian faith could actively declare their intent by joining some of the pro-Israel organizations, such as Women in Green, or backing the main Israeli parties against self-amputation, The National Union, Mafdal, (Bayit HaYhudi], Agudah and Shas. All of these are dedicated to freedom and democracy, but also believe in the wisdom of

Torah. They are all open-minded but not so much so that their brains fall out. To be informed one needs to look and read Women in Green, Arutz Sheva (Israel National Radio), as well as Just-peace-for-Israel. In addition, to further understand and support the reunion of Judah and Israel, everyone should back Brit-Am, PO Box 595 and KolHaTor, PO Box 1438, and SADEH, (Service Advancement Development Education of the Hebrews), which are all located in Jerusalem, Israel. One might also support the research, work and publications represented by this very book (see back page for details).

As unity is strength, the House of Israel and the House of Judah, working as one politically, spiritually and militarily, can with God's help defeat the coming inevitable onslaught of EURABIA, this looming Islamist and EU monster. If they fail to unite against their Eurabian foes, defeat will indeed be inevitable. It is only when America, Great Britain, and the Commonwealth nations that form this close Israel family alliance stand shoulder to shoulder with their Jewish brothers in the besieged State of Israel, that they stand any chance of survival. The frontline of this monumental conflict runs right through the heart of the State of Israel today. It is the duty of Joseph, alias America, Great Britain and her Commonwealth kith and kin, to help to defend the Jewish State against the whole world if need be. This also holds true for the Scandinavian and coastal nations of Western Europe where large concentrations of the other tribes of Israel are located. Whilst the rest of the world may ally themselves against them, their combined unity will be their strength. What is more, they will have the God of Israel giving them a helping hand in their battles.

CHAPTER TEN

Covenant of Death & Contract With Hell

The Oldest Title Deed in the World

What the world fails to recognize is that the Title Deed to the Holy Land is written down and recorded for all posterity in the Holy Bible. This book predates the Qur'an by a thousand years and is revered by Jews and Christians alike. It is written down in unambiguous language, giving clear boundaries and jurisdictions for the land. It is the oldest title deed in the world, which states unequivocally that the land belongs to Israel.

HASHEM said to Abram after Lot had departed from him, "Raise now your eyes and look out from where you are: northward, southward, eastward, and westward. "For all the land you see, to you will I give it, and to your descendants <u>forever.</u> "I will make your offspring as the dust of the earth; so that if one can count the dust of the earth, then your offspring too can be counted. Arise, walk about the land through its length and breadth! For to you will I give it." And Abram moved his tent, and came and dwelled in the plains of Mamre which are in Hebron; and he built there an altar to HASHEM." (Genesis 13:14-18, author's emphasis).

There is no other nation on the face of the earth that can remotely match the claim Israel has to their Land of Promise. No other nation can justify the claim to their land the way Israel can, through an Everlasting Divine Covenant. There is no clan, no tribe, or people on our planet who possess a written title deed to their land that is written by the hand of God.

On that day HASHEM made a covenant with Abram, saying: "To your descendants have I given this land, from the river of Egypt (the Nile) to the great river, the Euphrates River." (Gen. 15:18, emphasis added).

"I will ratify My covenant between Me and you and between your offspring after you, throughout their generations, as an everlasting covenant, to be a God to you and to your offspring after you; and I will give to you and to your offspring after you the land of your sojourns—the whole of the land of Canaan - as an everlasting possession; and I shall be a God to them." (Genesis 17:7-8, author's emphasis).

God Himself deeded this land to His people Israel by an eternal covenant which cannot be broken. The book also tells us who Israel is. Israel is composed of the descendants of the twelve sons of Jacob, the descendants of Abraham and Isaac, whose name was changed to Israel (Genesis 32:27-28). This makes the claim of the Palestinians totally irrelevant. It also exposes the spurious claims of Islam as false. The truth is that nothing can change the irrevocable Word of HASHEM, the Holy One of Israel, the Almighty Creator of the Universe and Ruler over All things.

The prophets of the Bible forecast the ultimate future scenario for these two intrepid sons of Joseph and their fellow Israelite tribesmen, as according to the prophets of Israel their destiny is to be reunited with their Jewish kinsmen of the tribe of Judah into one nation.

The prophet Ezekiel gave the most emphatic prophecy on the future reunion of Judah and Israel:

The word of the HASHEM came again to me saying, "Now you, Son of Man, take for yourself one piece of wood and write upon it, 'For Judah and for the children of Israel, his comrades'; and take one piece of wood and write on it, 'For Joseph, the wood of Ephraim and all the House of Israel, his comrades.' "Then bring them close to yourself. One to the other, like one piece of wood, and they will become <u>united</u> in your hand."

"Thus said the LORD HASHEM/ELOHIM: "Behold, I am taking the wood of Joseph, which is in the hand of Ephraim, and the tribes of Israel, his comrades, and I am placing them and him together with the wood of Judah, and I will make them into one piece of wood, and they will become one in My hand..... will make them into ONE NATION in the land, upon

the mountains of Israel, and one king will be a king for them all; they will no longer be TWO NATIONS, and they will no longer be divided into TWO KINGDOMS, ever again" (Ezekiel 37:15-17 & 19,22, emphasis added).

This is the messianic age the Bible speaks of—an age of true peace when finally, *"swords shall be turned into ploughshares and spears into pruning hooks."*

What the world fails to recognize is that the establishment of the State of Israel is in accordance with God's plan and purpose. When this remarkable nation, having just suffered the loss of one third of its population in the immediate aftermath of the Holocaust, after an absence of some two thousand years re-established her sovereignty on the soil of her ancient homeland in 1948, it was a twentieth century miracle! This clearly was a supernatural event unequalled in the entire history of the world! Yet, ever since that day, and true to past form, the nations of the world have sought to destroy the tiny Jewish State. What they fail to recognize is that this State came into being as part of a Divine Process, which was forecast in the Bible. What sticks in the craw of mankind is that the Jewish State proves the existence of the Creator of the Universe. Ultimately His Divine plan is to restore the Davidic Kingdom and reunite the Two Houses of Israel. The re-establishment of the State of Israel in 1948 is one of the greatest political miracles in the history of the world, and this fact alone signifies that we live at the dawn of the glorious Messianic Age to come.

Any nation or individual which dares to come against this Divine plan will be laid waste in the dust of the ground, just as anyone who in any way curses the State of Israel, in turn is cursed by YHVH, the Eternal and Almighty God of Israel. This is true for both Jew and Gentile alike.

The Spirit of Jihad is in Our Blood!

"Because you have had an ANCIENT HATRED, and have shed the blood of the children of Israel by the power of the sword at the time of their calamity, when their iniquity came to an end, therefore as I live, says the LORD God, "I will prepare you for blood, and blood shall pursue you;

since you have not hated blood, therefore blood shall pursue you." (Ezekiel 35:5-6, emphasis added).

The reference above to the *"ancient hatred"* refers to the family feud brought about through the envy of Ishmael, the son of Hagar, born out of resentment of Isaac, the son of Abraham, being chosen as the true heir of Abraham. As the resentment welled up in Ishmael's breast some four thousand years ago it morphed into a root of bitterness, which today has resurfaced in the hearts of the Palestinian Arabs, as well as in the hearts of nearly the entire Islamic world.

Under the evil rule of Arafat and his successor Abu Mazen, e.g. Mahmoud Abbas, the indoctrination of the Palestinians has become total. The PLO leadership has raised a generation so thoroughly schooled in Jew hatred, that the process has now become absolutely irreversible. The present generation of Palestinians has become infested with a jihad spirit which is now openly calling for the genocide of the Jews. Their leaders have literally brainwashed their people through a constant media diet of hateful Nazi inspired diatribes against Israel and the Jews. Most Palestinians are simply pawns in a greater game, one in which their rulers are continuously stoking up the embers of Jew hatred. There was a notorious incident some years ago in Cairo in September 1997, which perfectly illustrates the spirit behind the irrational hatred of the Muslims towards the Jews. Saber Farahat Abu el-Ela and his brother Mahmoud emptied their automatic weapons on a busload of German tourists in the middle of Cairo in broad daylight, killing nine Germans and injuring a score more. At his arrest, Saber said: "I thought they were Israelis! I would have liked to kill two hundred of them as Jihad is in my blood!" We see this same jihad spirit at work today in the blood of three and four year old Palestinian children who are taught to hate and kill the Jews even in the Palestinian play schools.

The Sardine and the Shark

One is reminded of a Jewish ballad that tells the story of a sardine swimming off the shores of Eilat. On his way, he meets a shark and humbly says the normal greeting, SHALOM (peace). To avoid any clash, the sardine then gives up its tail, some fins, some scales but it seems to avail him nothing. Now for a real and lasting peace, he surrenders everything. The shark nods in agreement and utters the word SHALOM (peace), opens his mouth and swallows the sardine whole. All the other fish in the whole wide sea are in agreement that a lasting peace has finally been achieved. This is the lasting peace the Islamic world is looking for and this is precisely what their mantra "Land for Peace" is all about. To their mind, it is simply a means to an end for them. So much for the iniquitous *"LAND FOR PEACE"* policy, which is enshrined in the Oslo Peace Accord, signed between the Israeli government and the Liberation of Palestine Authority, otherwise known as the PLO. The whole concept of trading land in exchange for peace is a total travesty in itself. The Palestinian enemy is in effect dictating: *"If you give me another chunk of land, I will tell my terrorists to stop killing your women and children."* What absolute madness! It is unbelievable! Please tell me, how can any sane person fall for that one? Apart from all of this, the main issue is that the land is not Israel's to give away in the first place! The land belongs to God! Now, this may not be a very popular concept in our world today; it is nonetheless an absolute fact. This is what the Torah tells us: *"But the land must not be sold beyond reclaim, FOR THE LAND IS MINE; you are but strangers resident with Me."* (Leviticus 25:23). In view of their actions one is inclined to wonder if the leaders of the Israeli government have ever read the book. One may be pretty sure that whatever land the Israeli government has already given away in exchange for a peace that never materializes, HaShem, the Holy One of Israel, is bound sooner or later to take all of His land back!

I Give You my Land if You Stop Beating My Wife and Children

So, what is the world's latest plan for rescuing the Middle East Peace Process? The answer is always the same.... Apply more pressure on Israel! The US administration, the E.U. and the other Quartet members, ably assisted by the world's media continuously picture the Israelis as the intransigent ones. The policy is to constantly apply pressure to try to twist the arm of the Israeli government into giving away more land in exchange for peace! The whole so-called "Land for Peace" concept is utterly ludicrous. The world is effectively assisting Israel in its own suicide. The United States is leading the nations of the world compelling Israel to commit voluntary euthanasia! This is really what the *"Land for Peace"* plan is all about.

The policy is akin to your rather nasty neighbor coming up to you and saying *"I want you to sign over the title deeds to your back garden and if you let me have it, I will stop beating your wife and children."* This is effectively what *"Land for Peace"* means in practice. The Palestinians are trading *"land" for "peace."* They are saying to their Israeli neighbors, you give us the "land" we want and we will leave you alone and give you "peace." So the naïve Israelis believed them and gave them Gaza, and do you know what? NO PEACE. If anything, terrorist attacks grew worse. So the Israelis, being heavily leaned on by their American and European allies, give the Palestinians Jericho and certain cities, as well as autonomy over substantial territory in the so-called West Bank, and do you know what? Surprise, surprise, there was still no peace, as terrorist attacks grow even worse than before. So, the Israeli government, now under the most severe and intensive pressure from their allies in the West, give the Palestinians the city of Hebron, which houses the tombs of the great patriarchs, Abraham, Isaac and Jacob. This is really an emotive and very big concession for the Israeli government, but for the sake of peace, and because of the heavy international pressure they are under, they are reluctantly prepared to make it. And do you know what? This is getting monotonous and boring! There is still no peace. In fact, the enemy unleashes the worst suicide bombing campaign of all time, hitting Tel Aviv and also the very heart of Jerusalem. Once again the Israeli government comes under the most unrelenting pressure from Uncle Sam, the European Union, Russia and who knows who else and she decides to make a really big concession. This time she agrees to use her own army to forcibly evict her own citizens from Gush Katif in the hope that her sacrifice will be appreciated by the enemy, and that she will now finally be left in peace. And do you know what? You've guessed it! There was no peace! Instead the enemy rained some twelve thousand rockets on her cities.

Are we getting the picture? If the man who is beating your wife and your children gets your back garden by doing so, why should he stop? It makes no sense for him to stop, because if he carries on beating your wife and children, only harder, he can get your garage as well. When he has got your garage, he will be encouraged to go for your front garden next. Once he has forced you to give him your front garden, he will start beating your wife even harder and he may even decide to kill one of your children, because he is really after your house in the first place. Your neighbor is clever enough to know that if he demanded you give him your house right at the beginning, you would have never given it to him. This guy has been to school, he has picked up a bit of elementary psychology, so consequently he asks for something quite small at first, something that perhaps you can do without and that you do not want to make a big issue over and certainly something that you do not want to go to war over. The problem comes, once you have given in to his first demand, he will never stop until he has got the shirt off your back! This is the essence of the Oslo Accord.

A Covenant of Death and A Contract With Hell

Israel has an unfortunate history of making covenants with other nations. Every time these covenants have ended in tears. The Northern Kingdom of ancient Israel made a covenant with Egypt, as a counterbalance to the ominous threat emanating from the Assyrian Empire. The prophet Isaiah had warned them repeatedly against their folly but the princes and the rulers, instead of heeding the prophets warning, scorned and mocked him, by saying: *"We have made a covenant with death and with Sheol we are in agreement. When the overflowing scourge passes through, it will not come to us, for we have made lies our refuge, and under falsehood have we hidden ourselves."* (Isaiah 28:15). *[Rashi]*, explains the latter phrase as: *"We have hoped in idols to conceal us."*

The prophet Isaiah then gave God's verdict on this covenant, as he stated the following:

"Your covenant with death will be annulled, and your agreement with Sheol will not stand; when the overflowing scourge passes through, then you will be trampled down by it. As often it goes out it will take you; for morning by morning it will pass over, and by day and by night; it will be a terror just to understand the report." (Isaiah 28:18-19).

The words; *"as often it goes out it will take you,"* imply that the overflowing Assyrian scourge will pass through them more than once.

History confirms that the Assyrians invaded the Northern Kingdom three times. Each time it was accompanied by a genocidal slaughter, after which the survivors were removed and taken into captivity.

Later on the southern kingdom of Judah made the same terrible mistake first under King Jehoiakim, and then by King Zedekiah, the 21st king of Judah, leading to the second Babylonian invasion, the destruction of Jerusalem and the glorious Temple of Solomon in 586BCE, as well as the seventy years of the Babylonian exile.

Even those heroic leaders of the Maccabaeus revolt against Antiochus and his Hellenistic Empire made the mistake of seeking a covenant when Judas, know as Maccabaeus, made a treaty of friendship and alliance with Rome. Jonathan later on confirmed and renewed the treaty and he in turn was followed by Simon, son of Mattathias, who sent Numenius to Rome with a large gold shield, worth a thousand minas, to confirm the alliance with the Romans. This too proved to be a Covenant with Death and a Contract with Hell, and we all know how it ended, as the rest is history.

The Zohar [Exodus 7b] predicts that in the end of days certain Jews in Israel will make an alliance with the enemies of the Jewish people. The modern State of Israel has made the same mistake again in signing the Olso Accords with the PLO, as it too is a Covenant with Death and a Contract with Hell. The PLO already has its own covenant which predates the Oslo Accords by nine years. Their own national covenant consisting of some 33 articles, calls for the eradication and extinction of the Jewish State of Israel. The extraordinary thing is that they are quite open about their intent!

- Article 15: *The liberation of Palestine is a national duty to repulse the Zionist, imperialistic invasion from the great Arab homeland and to purge the Zionist presence from Palestine.*

- Article 19: *The partitioning of Palestine in 1947 and the establishment of Israel is fundamentally null and void.*

- Article 20: *The Balfour Declaration, the mandate for Palestine, and everything that has been based upon them, are deemed null and void. Claims of historical or religious ties of Jews with Palestine are incompatible with the facts of history....*

- Article 21: *The Palestinian Arab people, in expressing itself through armed Palestinian revolution, rejects every solution that is a substitute for a complete liberation of Palestine.*

The Israeli Left, which like the ancient Israelites; *"Has made lies their refuge, and has hidden them selves under falsehood,"* is in a total denial of reality. The Left claims that, in Hebrew, the initials PLO represent the "Palestine Liberation Organization." In Arabic it says: *"Muznasmat Tahrir Falastin,"* the true meaning is: *"Organization for the Liberation of Palestine!"* This means they intend to take all of the land! Therefore, at the signing ceremony of the Oslo Accords, the Israeli government signed an official agreement with a terrorist organization whose national Covenant was committed to the destruction of the Jewish State! Despite solemn assurances made at the time to the contrary, that covenant has never been changed. If future historians ever want to look for the most perfect example of a nation signing a Covenant with Death, surely the Oslo Accords will prove to be the ultimate definition thereof.

The Threshold Covenant

Man's first dwelling place was the cave, or the tent or hut in which he made his home. The threshold and the hearth of that dwelling place was the boundary of his earthly possessions. It was the limit or sacred border of the portion of the earth over which he claimed control, and where his family were under the special protection of the deity with whom he was in covenant. Therefore, the threshold was hallowed as a place of covenant worship. As families were formed into tribes and communities, they came to have a common ruler or priest, and his dwelling place was counted by all as the center of covenant with their deity, and when they worshipped that deity there, they worshipped at the threshold altar of his sanctuary. Thus the threshold was the place of the altar, in both house and temple.

When a man acquired property rights beyond his dwelling place, and people gained control over portions of land more extensive, the boundary limits of their possessions were extended. The protecting deity of the region thus bounded was recognized as having sway in that domain, and those who were dwellers there were in covenant relations with him.

Therefore, the boundary line of that territory was considered its threshold, and as such was held sacred as a place of worship and of sacrifice.

A private landmark was a sacred boundary, and was a threshold altar for its possessor. To remove or disregard such a local threshold was an offense not only against its owner, but against the deity in whose name it had been set up. It is interesting to observe that in Jewish homes all over the world this custom is still upheld through the placing of the Mezuzah on the doorpost just above the threshold. This same Mezuzah contains a written reference to the protecting deity, e.g. the Holy One of Israel. However, at the same time it must be pointed out that the sole motivation for the Jewish practice of placing a Mezuzah on the doorposts of their homes and gates is because of their dedicated obedience to the commands of the Torah. The Hebrews were commanded to dedicate their doorways to the One Living God, as a reminder of their covenant with HASHEM, the Holy One of Israel. Deuteronomy 6:4-9 & 11:13-21, *"You shall write them on the doorposts of your house and on your gates."* To this day those covenant words are encased in the Mezuzah and affixed to the side posts of every door in the house. On the outside of the written scroll in the Mezuzah, the Divine name, SHADAI, - "the Almighty," is visible. This name stands for the "Guardian of the dwellings of Israel," whose name is thus invoked above the altar of the threshold of the entrance way. Every observant Jew, as often as he passes a Mezuzah will touch the Divine Name with the finger of his right hand, puts it to his mouth and kisses it, saying, *"The LORD shall preserve my going out and my coming in from this time forth, and forever more!"*

At a time of grave crisis in the early history of the children of Israel, after their sin with the golden calf, Moses stood "in the gate of the camp," when he would execute judgment in the name of HASHEM; *Then Moses stood AT THE GATEWAY of the camp, and said, "Whoever is for HASHEM, join me!"—come to me!" And all the Levites gathered around him.* (Exodus 32:26, emphasis added). The *"gate"* or *"entrance"* to the camp signified its threshold. Moses then instructed them in verse 27: *"Let every man put his sword on his thigh and pass back and forth from "gate" to "gate" in the camp……* The Levites were thus instructed to go from threshold to threshold to execute HaShem's judgment upon the guilty.

The Pesach offering too was a threshold covenant, as is intimated by the text in Exodus 12, where Moses instructs all the elders of Israel to: *"Slaughter the pesach-offering. You shall take a bundle of hyssop and dip it into the blood that is in the basin, and touch the lintel and the two doorposts with some of the blood that is in the basin, and as for you, no man shall leave the entrance [THRESHOLD] of his house until morning. HASHEM will pass through to smite Egypt and He will see the blood that is on the lintel and the two doorposts; and HASHEM will pass over the entrance [THRESHOLD] and He will not permit the destroyer to enter [CROSS YOUR THRESHOLD] your homes to smite.* (Exodus 12:22-23, emphasis added).

Notice, it says that no one is to leave/cross over the entrance/threshold of his house and that HASHEM Himself, having observed the blood on the doorposts and lintel will pass over/cross over the entrance/threshold into the house.

The common understanding of the term Passover in connection with the exodus from Egypt is that it was, on HASHEM'S part, a passing by those homes where the doorways were blood-stained, rather than entering them. Yet this meaning does not seem justified. HASHEM did not merely spare His people when He visited judgment on the Egyptians. <u>He covenanted anew with them by passing over or crossing over, the blood-stained threshold right into their homes,</u> while His messenger of death went into the houses of the Egyptians! It seems this interpretation is confirmed by the modern observance of the Pesach Seder, where at a certain stage of the feast the outer door is opened and an extra place is set at the table, in the hope that God's messenger [Elijah] will cross the threshold, and enter the home as a welcome guest.

According to Jewish tradition it was on a Passover night that HASHEM entered into a cross-over covenant with Abraham on the boundary of his new possessions in Canaan. It was on a Passover night that Lot welcomed the angelic visitors into his home in Sodom. It was also during a Passover season that the Israelites crossed the threshold of their new home in Canaan, when the walls of Jericho fell down. The blood colored thread on the outer window of the house of Rahab was a symbol of the covenant of the Hebrew spies with her and her household. The protection of the Israelites against the Midianites, and the Assyrians, the Medes and the Persians, and again the final overthrow of Babylon, all these events were said to have been at the Passover season. All these examples indicate that the Passover covenant was considered a cross-over covenant, and a covenant of welcome at the family and or the national threshold.

The Pesach sacrifice took place on the threshold of the homes of the Israelites on the threshold of a new year, when Israel began anew in all things! Above all it was recognized as the rite of marriage between HASHEM and Israel. That first Pesach night was the night when HASHEM took to Himself in covenant union the "Virgin of Israel" (Jer. 31:4), and became a Husband to her. From that time onwards any recognition of or affiliation with another god, is called "whoredom," "adultery," or "fornication." It seems to be in recognition of this truth that this first Pesach in Egypt represented the rite of marriage between HASHEM and Israel, that Solomon's Book, "Song of Songs" is read in the Synagogue at the Passover service. It was the "virgin of Israel" who certified the marriage covenant union by the bloody stamp on the doorway. Hence it was a feminine symbol in the form of a bunch of hyssop that was dipped in the blood and used for striking onto the doorposts and lintel of the home.

We find a further example of this same principle in the book of Judges when all Israel was aroused to do judgment against the sin of the tribe of Benjamin against the concubine of the Levite: *Her master got up in the morning, opened the doors of the house, and left to go on his way, and behold - his concubine wife was fallen at the entrance of the house, with her hands on the threshold!* (Judges 19:27, emphasis added).

People have often been puzzled as to why Samson picked up the city gates of Gaza, where his enemies were laying in wait to kill him. It had to do with the threshold covenant! He took hold of the gates of the city and pulled it up by its doorposts and carried it upon his shoulders for quite a distance right up to the top of a hill facing Hebron. He was carrying the gates and was thus extending the threshold of the city. As long as he had the gates his would-be murderers could not touch him, because whilst you are within the gates of the city you are entitled to hospitality. (See: Judges 16:1-3).

Boaz, *"had gone up to the gate,"* to meet the elders there, when he would covenant to do justice by Ruth and the kinsman of Naomi. (Ruth 4:1-10, emphasis added).

A most significant example of the threshold covenant concerns the release of a Hebrew bondsman. After six years of continuous service, he must be released in the seventh year. Yet, if his servant wishes to remain, his master shall take him to the place of judgment at the gate of the city, after which he shall bring him to the threshold of his property and pierce the servant's ear with an awl at the doorpost, and he shall serve him forever. Some of the blood will fall onto the threshold and thus the master and servant appeal together at the threshold altar of the master's property in witness of their sacred covenant. (See: Exodus 21: 2-6).

Daniel's post of honor in Babylon was *"in the gate of the King,"* as a judge in the king's name. (Dan. 2:29). A just and righteous man is, *"him who reproves in the gate..."* (Isaiah 29:21, emphasis added). There are literally hundreds of examples in the Tanach which highlight the importance of gates, doorposts and thresholds, all of which signify the boundaries of the house, the city and the land.

All over the Middle East today, people still understand the significance of a threshold covenant, as well as the importance of landmarks and boundary stones.

The most important covenantal boundary or threshold in all of Judaism is the Kotel, as to all intents and purposes it is the threshold of the Holy Temple! In some respects it is fair to say that all of East Jerusalem too comprises the threshold of the Holy Temple. This explains the reason why the Palestinians, with the enthusiastic encouragement of the whole wide world, want this bit of real estate more than any other! The U.N. wants it and has declared Jerusalem an international city! The Roman Catholic Church wants it to set up a Vatican Mark II from which to dominate and control the world! The Palestinians want it so that they can claim the prize of this holy site for Allah, which will finally complete their conquest and desecration of all the holy sites in Israel. Any Israeli government that dare surrender this holiest of all covenantal places will be twice cursed by YHVH, the Elohim of Abraham, Isaac and Jacob! Why? Because those men and women will in effect be committing high treason not only against the State of Israel but also against the Throne of Heaven itself.

The Torah places similar emphasis on the sacredness of local landmarks, and a curse was pronounced against him who would dare to remove such a threshold altar. *"You shall not move a boundary of your fellow, which the early ones marked out, in your inheritance that you shall inherit, in the land that HASHEM, your God gives you to possess it."* (Deut. 19:14). It was a reproach to the children of Israel that there were those among them who would disregard sacred property rights. In fact one of the curses written on the summit of Mount Ebal, [the Mountain of Blessing], after Israel had taken possession of Canaan, was: *"Cursed is the one who moves his neighbors' landmark."*

As Abram approached the southern boundary of Canaan he remembered the promise of HASHEM, that he and his seed would possess that land, but as yet he was childless. He naturally desired some tangible assurance, in accordance with the traditional customs of the threshold covenant, that God's promises to him would be made good. Then YHVH responded with these directions, apparently in accordance with a well-known method of covenanting among men: *"Take to Me three heifers, three goats, three rams, a turtledove, and a young dove."* [Abraham seems to have understood exactly what was to be done with these animals for sacrifice.] *"He took all these to Him: he cut them in the center, and placed each piece opposite its counterpart. The birds however he did not cut up. So it happened: The sun set, and it was very dark. Behold - there was a smoky furnace and a torch of fire* [a blazing light as a symbol of the Shekinah presence], *which passed between these pieces.* [It crossed the blood on the threshold]. And the record adds: *On that day HASHEM made a covenant with Abram, saying:"To your descendants I have given this land, from the river of Egypt to the great river, the Euphrates River: the Kenite, the Kenezzite, and the Kadmonite, the Hittite, the Perizzite, and the Rephaim, the Amorite, the Canaanite, the Girgashite, and the Jebusite."* (Genesis 15:9-10; 17-21, commentary & emphasis added).

Thus Abram was assured that HASHEM had covenanted the land to him and that the Eternal Creator of the Universe would protect his boundaries. When we consider the great solemnity of this Divine Covenant, is it not a great sin for successive Israeli governments, whilst in rank appeasement mode, to have given portions of this same land to their enemies? Regardless of the pressure they might have been under at the time, if we go by the Words of the Torah they are without excuse! The prophet Hosea has something very pertinent to say about this very situation, as he addressed the leaders of Judah directly, he says: *"The officers of Judah were like those who shift the boundaries: upon them I will pour my wrath like water."* (Hosea 5:10). Remember that ancient curse of Mount Ebal? *"Cursed is the one who moves his neighbors' landmark."* It would be bad enough if those appeasing politicians had moved the boundaries of their own nation. However, as the Land of Israel belongs to HASHEM, the leaders of those same Israeli governments, encouraged by their left-wing media, have placed themselves under a double curse! The nation and its collective leadership need to repent over these terrible sins. As a first step, a good move would be to utterly repudiate the Oslo *"Land for Peace"* charade and call it by its true name: *a Covenant with Death and a Contract with Hell!*

A most alarming trend in Israeli political and media circles is the desire to commit the nation to join the European Union. Israel already is an associate member of the European Union. A recent [2011] Israeli opinion poll recorded an 83% vote in favor of EU membership. Telltale signs of government policy have long been evident by the adoption of the blue strip on the rear of all Israeli car number plates, which is an EU requirement for all the current 27 members of the union. Another subtle sign is that Israel's zip codes too are in conformity to those prevailing in the EU. There is also the extraordinary fact that the Israeli government has joint cabinet meetings each year with Germany, the veritable engine of the European Union, and indeed she has even signed a so-called anti-terrorism treaty with that nation, which requires the parties to come to each others' assistance in case of need. She has also received a number of German Dolphin class submarines which have been heavily subsidized by the German government. Just recently, in November 2011, Angela Merkel and Benyamin Netanyahu met in Europe where the agreement was signed for the delivery to Israel of the sixth submarine. This is one way in which Germany has been buying Israel's friendship. We may well forgive the Germans for what they have done to our people in WWII, but we cannot forget! In view of the past history, is it really wise to get into bed with, and engage in such a close partnership with the German nation? If this process is not reversed by a future government, it will lead the nation to once again sign *a Covenant with Death and a Contract with Hell!* Sadly, if the leaders of the nation are foolish enough to enter into a covenant with the European Union, the prophets of Israel assure us that this covenant will be a million times worse than the deadly Oslo Accords; it truly will be the Ultimate Covenant with Death!

On the Mountains of Israel

It was on the mountains of Israel that God entered into a covenant with Abraham, Isaac and Jacob. The mountains of Israel are located around what is called the Highway of the Patriarchs, a route that goes all the way from Elon More in the north to Beer-sheva in the south. This is the very heartland of the Bible where most of the ancient history of Israel has taken place, from the time of the patriarchs on down to King David to the heroic exploits of the Maccabees. These are the mountains of Judea and Samaria which the prophet Ezekiel lovingly describes as; *"the ancient heights of Israel."* However, the world's media has come to refer to this area as the "West Bank," a term entirely devoid of any spiritual significance. This is the territory the world's leaders have designated for the establishment of a Palestinian State. It is because this piece of land is sacred to the God of Israel and His chosen people that they wish to place these ancient biblical heights in the blood soaked hands of the greatest Jew-haters in the world today. The Palestinians in turn, including Mahmoud Abbas, have already declared their intent to ethnic "cleanse" the mountains of Israel of all Jews. The so-called "two-state solution" is spawned by jihadist demons who are seeking the destruction of the Jewish nation. Sadly, the post Zionist secular Jews in combination with the powerful organs of the Israeli left wing, have been blinded by their desire to be like the other nations, and are actively supporting this tragic process in the idle and vain hope that peace will ensue.

What most Israelis, as well as the peoples in the west, do not realize is that this whole issue revolving around the possession of the "Mountains of Judea and Samaria," represents the most intense spiritual battle raging in the world today. In effect, it is a battle between good and evil! If, through lack of will on the part of Israel's leaders, evil is permitted to win, it will signal the end of the State of Israel. The two-state solution will not only place all of Israel's strategic high ground into the hands of the nation's murderous arch-enemies, it will also reduce the remaining territory at the center to an utterly indefensible width of just 9 km. If this is not an act of national suicide, what else would you call it? The surrender of Austria, the Sudetenland, followed by the sacrifice of the democratic Republic of Czechoslovakia only served to whet Hitler's appetite for more and greater conquests. *"Those who cannot learn from history are doomed to repeat it."* *2 Today's jihadist radicals have sadly embraced Neo-Nazi views and seek, much like Hitler before them, to make the world Judenrein (free of Jews).

If the hopelessly nihilistic Israeli left wing and the world's nations are to succeed in foisting this two-state solution onto Israel, it will be their last anti-Semitic act to rob these God-given mountains from the Jewish people. This act will bring terrible judgment on all nations and persons involved.

"For behold, in those days and at that time, when I will bring back the captivity of Judah and Jerusalem, I will gather all of the nations and bring them down to the Valley of Jehoshaphat and I will contend with them there concerning My people and My possession Israel, that they dispersed among the nations, and they divided up My land." (Joel 4:1-2).

Have You Ever Heard of a Jewish Government Expelling Jews?

There is one further important side to the planned "give-away" of the biblical heartland mountains of Israel, including the surrender of East Jerusalem, in that it involves the wholesale uprooting and enforced removal of hundreds of thousands of Jews from their rightful homes. For any Israeli government to even contemplate such utter madness is beyond reason or comprehension. The cruel deportations from Gush Katif in Gaza in 2006, should serve as a valuable lesson to the nation. In this wholesale retreat, nearly 10,000 Jews were forcibly removed from their homes, resulting in the loss of their jobs and the destruction of their businesses and communities. Many of those evicted to this day are still unemployed. All of this was done for no logical reason. For no Arab leader has stated that they view the unilateral surrender as a step towards peace. Instead, the leadership of the Palestinian Authority said it would move the front line for their fighters closer. The surrender left a dismal legacy. Most of the affected people, some seven years after the event, are still living in caravans or other such temporary housing. Many of the children still suffer from the psychological trauma of being evicted from the security of their homes by their own government. The event also created psychological problems for the IDF soldiers involved in this cruel and most pointless exercise.

The expulsions from Gush Katif were done in the cause of appeasement and were meant to bring investment capital from Europe and the U.S. as a pay-off for surrender, while in turn obligating the Arabs to continue to pass their petro dollars on to U.S. and European companies. The surrender was a huge coup for the enemy that greatly emboldened Hamas, which immediately embarked on an unprecedented missile barrage into southern Israel. Thus, Israel was left with lots of pain for no gain, whilst the architects of the exercise suffered all kinds of terrible tragedies. Hopefully their successors will not make the same mistake and learn the lesson from their colleague's fate!

We know from history that throughout the ages the Jews have been expelled from many nations. We know King Edward of England did it. We know Philip II of Spain did it on a massive scale. We know the King of Portugal soon followed suit. We also know, in more recent times, that Stalin's murderous regime did it in a truly epic way. What we up to now have never known is that a Jewish government would ever do such a thing to Jews! Who would have believed such a thing could ever happen?

Those Settler Heroes of Israel

Nevertheless, the biblical mountains of Israel today are held fast by a most tenacious people. They are a generation that is prepared to fight for the Land of Israel imbued with the faith that it is our God-given inheritance. Their men and women have captured the vision of Joshua, who in his time cried out to his people: *"How long will you wait, to come and take possession of the land that the Lord, God of your fathers has given you?"* (Joshua 18:3). The world knows them as settlers, a term which is deliberately intended to be derogative, as it is meant to convey a most primitive obstructive group of bearded religious fanatics living in caravans, huts or caves. The term settlement itself implies a rather primitive community with the barest minimum of facilities, yet the truth is something else altogether. Most of their settlements are veritable garden cities, towns and villages, which are beautifully kept with excellent roads, pavements and housing that would be the envy of many nations. Many a village community in the country side of England or small town in New Hampshire in the United States would be proud to have similar facilities. The beautiful settlement communities of Eli, Shiloh, Kedumim, Karnei Shomrom, Beit El, as well as most of the others boast three trash collections per week and are immaculately kept with beautiful parks and gardens. All of them are accessed by a superb bus service. They have splendid community halls, synagogues, and schools, and many wonderful play grounds for their children. Thus, the picture conveyed to the outside world is simply a case of left-wing propaganda and totally off-key. It also needs to be understood that even Tel Aviv once began life as a settlement, and so did most cities and towns in Israel as well as in the United States of America.

These heroic Jewish settler pioneers, are utterly despised by the secular left-wing Israeli press, and the whole global community of nations considers them to be an obstacle to peace. Baruch Hashem! What a blessing that there are people of principle who are standing in the way of a wholesale surrender of the land to the avowed enemies of Israel. They have cultivated the land and planted orchards and vineyards and brought industry and employment to the barren mountains of Samaria. These people ought to be celebrated as national heroes; instead, they are hated and vilified by the whole world, including by many in the State of Israel. The world hates those settlers because they simply will not play ball with the global agenda and leave the Biblical Heartland of their patriarchal fathers Abraham, Isaac and Jacob. These visionary people are filled with a holy fire. They are men of God and women of valor, who are ready to die at any moment for their belief. Surrounded as they are by Muslim enemies, who given the opportunity will steal their cattle, burn their crops and kill their families, yet they have such peace and are imbued with the faith to move mountains. On top of this, even their own government will carry out regular night time pogroms against them by forcefully evicting them from their beds prior to bulldozing their properties. All of this they take in their stride without any rancor or bitterness. If ever there was a no-win situation, with their own government and all of the world's nations and media ranged against them in one united chorus of hatred, they surely must constitute the most classic case ever! Nevertheless, HASHEM loves no-win situations! In fact you only have to read the Tanach to see that He specializes in them! Just read the account of Moses and the children of Israel trapped in a high mountain pass with the deep waters of the Red Sea in front and the murderously mighty Egyptian army closing in behind, to realize how HASHEM likes to bare His Mighty Arm in order to deliver His people Israel.

It seems the settlers are denied the most basic human rights when the IDF soldiers and the Israeli Border Police raid their homes without any warning in the dead of night. Most of the time the sheer size of those police forces is out of all proportion to the job they have come to execute, as sometimes they number as many as four hundred men. All of them are dressed to intimidate in black clothing, wearing visors, bullet proof vests and carrying tasers, teargas, and heavy clubs, as well as their sidearms. They come with powerful searchlights and bulldozers. Men and women with their babies and young children are forced to leave within minutes out of their beds, as their homes are brutally razed to the ground in front of them. A recent practice has been to bring neighboring Palestinian Arabs in to carry out the demolitions, who naturally rejoice in the misery being inflicted upon those settlers by their own government. They laugh and smirk at the misfortune they are helping to bring. This kind of behavior by the Israeli government needs to be condemned by all of civilized society, as it smacks of the way that fascist governments treat their citizens. Recently, Arutz Sheva [Israel national News] quoted the comment of a top officer in the Israeli Police who slammed the Defense Ministry's decision to allow Arab workers to participate in the demolitions of buildings in new neighborhoods conducted by the IDF, police, and Border Guards. Last September [2011] Arutz Sheva reported that Palestinian Arab workers participated in the demolition of Migron. According to witnesses, the Arabs laughed and joked while pulling apart structures, making fun of the Jews who were being "exiled" from the site. The officer criticized the inclusion of Arabs in the demolition and evacuation of Migron, terming it "heartless."

The officer also criticized the recent late-night eviction of families from Mitzpeh Avichai by Yassam Police, which is Israel's elite force of police Commandos usually employed on anti-terrorist operations. It is a travesty that these kinds of forces are employed against babies, women and young children. The eviction took place in the pre-dawn hours of a very cold night, with residents, including numerous children roused from their sleep and thrown out into the cold. *"I am very sorry that the operation was conducted as it was,"* the officer told Arutz Sheva. *"You cannot throw families out in the freezing cold in the middle of the night. It's just not right."* What do you think?

CHAPTER ELEVEN

Appeasement Leading to Divine judgment

Whereas Britain started out in active support of the establishment of a Jewish homeland in the last days of the 19th and early days of the 20th century, she later changed her mind and reneged on a number of promises to the Jewish leaders. It must be said that she also reneged on a number of promises made to Arab leaders, as she tried to please both sides; she ended up pleasing no-one. Her major problem was that she found herself facing a disastrous war with Hitler's Germany and her position was virtually impossible. In the end she compromised her position out of political expediency. In mitigation one can say that Britain's primary concern was to somehow keep the lid on the seething unrest brewing in the Islamic quarters of her empire, as finding herself in a life and death struggle with Nazi Germany, she simply could not afford the manpower to deal with any insurgency, let alone with multiple insurgencies.

In the aftermath of World War Two, the newly elected Labor government brought a sea-change in British politics, as the new government was unsympathetic to the maintenance of her far-flung colonial empire. Furthermore, the effects of pressure from Arab leaders together with prospects for lucrative opportunities for the expansion and development of the Middle Eastern oilfields also played their part. The truth is that Great Britain played a perfidious game in the years leading up to the independence of the State of Israel. She had reneged on numerous promises. Furthermore, the Foreign and Colonial Office favored the Arabs, a sentiment shared by many of her senior officers on the ground in Palestine. Her approach to the conflict raging between the Jews and the Arabs was patently uneven, where she prevented the arming of the Jews on the one hand, whilst at the same time allowing the Arabs to access whatever arms they wanted. Finally, one of the blackest days for British honor came when she shamefully prevented thousands of Jewish Holocaust survivors from reaching safe haven in their Promised Land, by using military force. With Britain having thus totally dishonored her calling under God, it is perhaps not surprising that the British Empire started to unravel in 1948, the very year in which the Jewish State of Israel was born. That same year Britain lost the *"Jewel in the Crown"* of her Empire, as the Indian subcontinent, comprising some 400 million of her subjects, became independent. Almost every other colony and overseas possession was subsequently given its independence, leading to the closure of the Foreign and Colonial Office, and the end of the Empire in 1966. Once again this goes to show the truth of HASHEM's promise to Abraham: *"I will bless those who bless you, and him who curses you I will curse!"*

The United States, having started out equally well as Israel's stalwart supporter, has since, much like Great Britain before her, under Arab pressure and through political expediency, compromised her calling. She has compromised her Divine calling to be Israel's champion and protector by foisting the "Land for Peace" Oslo Peace accord onto the Jewish nation with a view to imposing the so-called two-state solution. Thus, she is forcing Israel into submission to a globalist agenda whose hidden purpose is the eradication of the Jewish state. The political impetus behind this political act of betrayal was simply to appease the world of Islam, propelled by America's need for oil. This disastrous policy can only lead to the detriment of the State of Israel. Thus America is cursing her brother Judah. By her actions she is cursing her only true and most loyal friend in the whole of the Middle East, as well as the only seasoned democracy in the Middle East, simply because she fears the combined opposition of the rabidly anti-Semitic axis of Islam, the European Union and Russia. America is thus cursing what God has blessed! As such she invites the sure judgment of YHVH, the Almighty GOD of Israel.

American Presidents Do Not Grovel to Anyone

It has been a longstanding tradition that America Presidents do not bow before any Sovereign or foreign Potentate. This is especially so, as it befits the dignity of the Commander in Chief of the most powerful, freedom loving and most magnanimous nation on earth. Ever since her victory in the Revolutionary War of Independence, America has never been subservient to any nation.

For this reason, it was all the more shocking to see President Barack Hussein Obama virtually prostrate himself before King Abdullah bin Abdul Aziz, the absolute ruler of the Kingdom of Saudi Arabia, at the London G20 Summit in April 2009. The House of Saud unquestionably is one of the world's most repressive, racist and anti-Semitic regimes. The Saudi Arabian police state also is the fountainhead of Wahabism, the most extreme sect of Islam, which the Kingdom has ceaselessly promoted with hundreds of billions of U.S. dollars these past fifty years. The sinister purpose behind this effort is to promote their Islamist faith in order to undermine and destroy the foundational pillars of our Western democratic societies.

The question therefore is: Of all the world's undemocratic potentates, why did America's new President bow before him in this groveling way? One of the keys lies in the fact that King Abdullah is the Keeper of Islam's Two Holy Mosques and Saudi Arabia is the cradle of Islam! Clearly, the worlds' 1.4 billion Muslims were the target audience for Barack Hussein's submissiveness. Furthermore, ever since the president's humbling himself before Abdullah, Barack Obama has steered the United States on a cowardly course of submission and appeasement.

America Has Made Common Cause With Islam!

The United States of America today is treading on thin ice! When the President of the United States is prepared to grant East Jerusalem to the emerging Jew-hating terrorist neo-Nazi Palestinian State, whose only raison d'être is the total annihilation of what they scornfully refer to as the "Zionist entity," he is in effect spitting in the eyes of God! For those same Palestinians teach their nursery school children that, *"to kill a Jew is to go to heaven!"* Hamas, the evil Muslim Brotherhood offshoot, whose thoroughly corrupt leadership is currently in control of Gaza, considers the State of Israel, *"an alien cancer,"* to be mercilessly excised from the *Muslim* Middle East. Americans should beware of what Muslims in the Middle East chant in their demonstrations, as the common cry goes: *"First we kill the Saturday people; then we kill the Sunday people."* The graffiti on the walls of Gaza repeat the above warnings to its Christians.* And PLO flags displayed in the traditionally Christian Arab town of Bethlehem and Beit Sahour in December 1993 carried the same printed message: *"On Saturday we will kill the Jews; on Sunday we will kill the Christians!"**** [1]

What was so significant about President Barack Obama's benchmark speech at Cairo University in June 2009, is that he invoked his rarely used Muslim middle name, Hussein, as well as the Qur'an, to lend extra emphasis to his statement, that, *"America has a common cause with Islam,"* and never will be at war with the faith.** [2] The President's speech changed the natural order as it had existed up to that point in time. It changed everything! Before the Cairo speech, *"America had common cause with Israel,"* After the speech, hey presto: *"America has a common cause with Islam!"*

To say you have common cause with another party in effect means that you are on the same page with those people. It means that you are in agreement with Islam! For Muslims the "cause" of Islam is all too clear, as the Qur'an states that the cause is to bring the world into subjection to Allah. The reality is that every Muslim is given a divine mandate (from Allah): to conquer the world for Allah. (Sura 8:39). In other words the "true" Muslim has no choice but to engage in jihad, *(Holy War)*, against all non-Muslims until the entire world is Islamic. Therefore, when the leader of the world's only superpower clearly and purposely aligns himself and his nation with a religious system that has been terrorizing the world for the past forty years, one ought to sit up and take notice. Islamic terrorists, out of religious duty, have to date, (30/11/11), in the name of this so-called religion of peace, carried out more than 17,995 deadly terror attacks since 9/11 *[3]

Most ironically, just prior to President Barack Hussein Obama's speech in Cairo, on June 1st 2009, the President proclaimed June the

"Lesbian, Gay, Bi-sexual and Transgender Pride month." This is in commemoration of the 40th anniversary of the Stonewall Inn riots, which marked the beginning of the LGBT rights movement in America. The President on this occasion declared himself a, *"Partner," of the Lesbian, Gay, Bi-Sexual and Transgender movement.* How low can a man sink in his quest for votes and power? One doubts if his new found Islamic friends will approve of Barack Hussein's *"partnership"* with these strange bedfellows? Muslim society is not exactly noted for its tolerance in this area! In fact the Muslim fundamentalist view is one of militant bigotry and extreme homophobia. Then just a few days later the President made *common cause with Islam.* In his every act ever since he has shown his constant contempt of Israel's interest.

President Barack Hussein Obama—The Servant of Allah!

President Obama's *"COMMON CAUSE WITH ISLAM"* declaration implies a seismic change of U.S. policy, which sets both him and the United States of America on a collision course with the ALMIGHTY GOD OF ISRAEL. The President clearly does not understand that the State of Israel is in a covenant relationship with God. Destroy the nation of Israel, and you destroy the concept of a covenant-keeping God. Destroy Israel and the demonic religion of Islam will claim the victory. Thus in coming against Israel, President Obama has become the servant of Allah and the lackey of Islam! Who would have thought that any President of the United States would ever stoop so low to take such an abominable step?

Fox News, on its website, also reported that during his speech to the Muslim world, the US President bluntly recognized Hamas, (*which has called for the destruction of Israel*), as a partner in creating a Palestinian State.

For good measure President Obama added the words, *"and will never be at war with the faith."* Presumably this was to help his Islamic audience to understand that if and when the Islamic nations decide to launch their inevitable genocidal attack upon the Jewish State of Israel, America will not lift a finger to intervene!

President Mahmud Ahmadinejad, just before he took office in July 2005, gave an interview extolling suicide bombers. He also declared that Islam would take over the world. He went on to say: *"Is there an art that is more beautiful, more divine, and more eternal than the art of martyrdom. The message of the Islamic Revolution is global, and is not restricted to a particular place and time...Have no doubt, Allah willing, Islam will conquer what? It will conquer all the mountaintops of the world."* Iran not only finances terrorism overseas, it extols it! A leading member of its powerful revolutionary guard has declared that anti-western terrorism is a God-dictated instruction. *"I made a pact with God, with the blood of martyrs and with this nation that I will prepare, with God's help—and harsh strategies and doctrines—<u>to uproot the Anglo-Saxon race!</u>"* *4

Can we not see how the Jews and the Anglo-Saxon race are placed side by side by the enemies of Israel? The same Ahmadinejad, the Holocaust-denying President of Iran, refers to Israel as a, *"stinking corpse,"* that needs to be removed from the earth! Can you see how the Jewish and the Anglo-Saxon races of the West are hated by these people? They make no secret of the fact that they have marked both groups for extermination! It appears that the powers that motivate our enemies are aware of America's Israelite ancestry - why else put the U.S. in the same class as the Jews?

The U.S. is Cursed With a President Who is All Mouth and No Trousers

Most people in the West are well aware that Iran is furiously developing nuclear weapons with the very same purpose in mind. They hardly make any secret about their agenda, which is Hell's own agenda, to eradicate the Jewish people, as defined by their faith in the One True God, and to wipe the State of Israel from the face of the earth. President Ahmadinejad recently stated that; *"The Israeli Zionist regime is a rotten tree that will be removed in one storm. He is talking about a nuclear storm,"* and President Obama was and indeed still is willing to do business with this psychopath! He has no idea how utterly pathetic he looks in the eyes of his Islamic enemies! They interpret his outstretched hand of friendship to Iran as weakness, and his Islamist enemies hold him in utter derision for what they perceive as his unmanly cowardice. They despise him all the more for the fact that he, being the leader of the most powerful nation on earth, will not stand up to them like a real man. A British slang expression describes this kind of unmanly behavior very well as it says: *"He is all mouth and no trousers!"* In the meantime the American government has time and time again threatened Iran weakly about applying sanctions against her, and the Iranians and their growing band of allies just laugh at this because they know is it all just *"mouth and no trousers,"* as nothing ever happens.

President Obama is the Enemy of Israel!

At a time when Fatah, the "allegedly" moderate Palestinian Authority, has forged a unity government with Hamas, the Muslim Brotherhood terrorist group that runs Gaza, President Obama, once again embraced the ultra-terrorist agenda in his, *"Moment of Opportunity,"* speech addressed to the Muslim world on May 19th, 2011. Obama stated that:

"The United States believes that negotiations should result in two states, with permanent Palestinian borders with Israel, Jordan, and Egypt, and permanent Israeli borders with Palestine. We believe the borders of Israel and Palestine should be based on the 1967 lines with mutually agreed swaps, so that secure and recognized borders are established for both states. The Palestinian people must have the right to govern themselves, and reach their full potential, in a sovereign and contiguous state."

Thus the President of the United States tells the world that he is prepared to carve out a terrorist state, by sacrificing 40% of the land-mass of Israel, America's only reliable ally and friend in the Middle East. Does the State of Israel really need friends like these? The fact is that those pre 1967 borders Obama mentioned would cut Israel to just nine miles wide at the center. These same borders were once referred to as Israel's, *"Auschwitz borders,"* by Abba Eban, the redoubtable former foreign secretary. It clearly would make the country completely indefensible! The President is pressuring the Jewish State to commit national suicide and has once again embraced the murderous cause of Muslim terrorists. As the President is a highly intelligent man, one can only conclude that he is consciously setting the stage for a second Holocaust. He also requires that the Palestinian state must be a contiguous state meaning that Israel itself will have to be cut in half, so that the ultra Jew-hating koranic terrorists of Gaza maybe connected to the equally ultra Jew-hating terrorists of the West Bank. In case there is any doubt about which side President Obama was batting for, seated in the front row next to the Secretary of State was Imam Mohamed Magid, the president of the largest Muslim Brotherhood organization in the U.S. This person was there at the White House's insistence despite the well known fact that Muslim Brotherhood's creed is: *"Allah is our objective. The Prophet is our leader. Qur'an is our law. Jihad is our way. Dying in the way of Allah is our highest hope!"* These are the same "good" people who on the day prior to their victory in Egypt's parliamentary election staged a special *"kill the Jews"* rally in Tahrir Square in downtown Cairo.

In his speech Obama revealed himself as an enemy of the Jewish people. The pre 1967 borders also require a re-division of Jerusalem, Israel's religious and historic capital, which predates Islamic claims by 2000 years. The moment the Muslims are in charge of East Jerusalem, Islam, this *"death-cult"* religion of war and intolerance, will dictate that all Christians and Jews will immediately be denied access to its holy sites. All American Jews must now decide where they stand with this openly anti-Israel President. Are they for him or against him? (A Jew who contributed to or voted for Obama in 2012 has voted for the destruction of Israel! Such a person is a JINO—a Jew-In-Name-Only!

Obama Embraces the Muslim Brotherhood

The Obama administration once again showed its true colors on the eve of the 4th of July, the proud day marking the birth of the nation no less, to both announce and admit that they are embracing the Muslim Brotherhood. This is the extremist international Islamist organization that has the destruction of the United States, Israel and all the other parts of the Free World as its explicit objective. This is an extremely ominous development both for America and for Israel, as the Muslim Brotherhood objective, in their words, is as follows:

"A kind of grand jihad in eliminating and destroying the Western civilization from within, sabotaging its miserable house with their, [i.e. Americans'], hands and the hands of the believers so that it is eliminated and God's religion,[Islam],is made victorious over all other religions." *5

According to the former Deputy Assistant Secretary of Defense for Nuclear Forces and Arms control Policy in the Reagan Administration, who heads the Center for Security Policy, and respected author Frank J Gaffney, Jr., the Muslim Brotherhood has a "phased plan" of five distinct phases to accomplish its mission in America:

PHASE ONE: Discreet and secret establishment of leadership.

PHASE TWO: Phase of gradual appearance on the public scene and exercising and utilizing various public activities.

PHASE THREE: Escalation phase, prior to conflict and confrontation with the rulers, through utilizing mass media. Currently in progress!

PHASE FOUR: Open public confrontation with the government through exercising the political pressure approach. This phase includes training on the use of weapons domestically and overseas in anticipation of zero-hour.

PHASE FIVE: Seizing power to establish their Islamic Nation under which all parties and Islamic groups are united.*6

Once again, as the President undoubtedly is well informed and is without question a highly intelligent man, one can only conclude that he is aware of the declared aims of the Muslim Brotherhood, and in view of his wholesale promotion of Brotherhood officials to key positions in his government, that he fully supports them. Remember the saying; *"You can tell a man from the company he keeps!"* The question really ought to be asked because, if he really does support the Muslim Brotherhood's aims, is America currently cursed with both a President and a State Department who are prepared to commit treason against their own nation? With all the evidence stacking up against the President, the other question that needs to be posed is: *"Why have impeachment proceedings against this president not yet been instituted?*

Why is Obama in Bed With the Muslim Brotherhood?

Dr. Essam Abdallah, an Egyptian liberal intellectual, in an article published October 2011 in the leading pan-Arab journal Elaph, expressed his bewilderment at certain reports coming out of Washington:

These reports reveal the depth of the below-the-surface coordination between the Council on American Islamic relations (CAIR), Hamas Hezbollah, the Iranian regime and the Muslim Brotherhood in Egypt, Syria, Tunisia, Libya and Jordan. This bloc of regimes is now becoming the greatest Islamist radical lobby ever to penetrate and infiltrate the White House, Congress, the State Department and the main decision making centers of the U.S. government. All of this is happening at a time when the US government is going through its most strategically dangerous period in modern times because of its need to confront the Iranian Mullah's regime, which is expanding in the Middle East, as well as penetrating the United States via powerful and influential allies.

In a follow up article Abdallah asked the question:

Why aren't the West in general and the United States Administration in particular clearly and forcefully supporting our civil societies, and particularly the secular democrats of the region? Why were the bureaucracies in Washington and in Brussels partnering with Islamists in the region and not with their natural allies, the democracy promoting political forces?

Steve Emerson of the Investigative Project on Terrorism said of the article: "This is one of the most important articles I have read in years." He then made <u>allegations</u> of his own:

It was just revealed that FBI Director Mueller secretly met on February 8, 2012 at FBI Headquarters with a coalition of groups including various Islamist and militant Arabic groups who in the past have defended Hamas, Hezbollah, and have also issued blatantly anti-Semitic statements. At this meeting, the FBI revealed that it had removed more than a thousand presentations and curricula on Islam from FBI offices around the country that were deemed "offensive." The FBI did not reveal what criteria was used to determine why material was considered "offensive" but knowledgeable law enforcement sources have told the IPT that it was these radical groups who made that determination. Moreover, numerous FBI agents have confirmed that from now on, FBI headquarters has banned all FBI offices from inviting any counter-terrorist specialists who are considered "anti-Islam" by Muslim Brotherhood front groups.

Emmerson stated that this comes as no surprise to him, as in August of 2011, after making the case, I wrote, "To my mind, the alliance between the Obama administration and the Muslim Brotherhood is the cornerstone of Obama's New Middle East policy."

So while Obama is supporting the Nazi inspired Muslim Brotherhood, he is keeping Israel under his thumb. Isi Leibler takes exception to all this and reminds everyone that:

This organization [The Muslim Brotherhood] represents one of the most fanatical and dangerous of the radical Islamist groups in the region, with a dark record of violence and terrorism embedded in its DNA. It is rabidly anti-Western, anti-Christian, anti-Semitic, committed to imposing sharia law and a global Caliphate—and willing to employ any means to further its objectives.

Many would argue that Obama is also "anti-Western, anti-Christian, [and] anti-Semitic." Judging by his policies, they would be right!*7

Al Qaeda's founders, Abdullah Azzam, Osama bin Laden, and its top leader Ayman al-Zawahiri were all members of the Muslim Brotherhood, or were trained by it.*8

"Throughout history, Allah has imposed upon the [Jews] people who would punish them for their corruption. The last punishment was carried out by [Adolph] Hitler... Allah willing, the next time will be at the hands of the believers." *9

Islamic Prophecy Re Obama, "He-is-with-us!"

Maybe the definitive answer as to why President Obama has gone to bed with the Muslim Brotherhood is answered by an Islamic Prophecy about Barack Hussein Obama!

The question has made the rounds in Iran since 2008, the year of Obama's bid for the Presidency of the United States. At this time, a pro-government website published a Hadith [tradition] from a Shiite text of the 17th century. The tradition comes from Bahar al-Anvar (meaning Oceans of Light) by Mullah Majlisi, a magnum opus in 132 volumes, and the basis of modern Shiite Islam. According to the tradition, Imam Ali Ibn Abi-Tlib (the prophet's cousin and son-in-law), prophesied that at the End of Times and just before the return of the Mahdi, the Ultimate Savior, *a "tall black man will assume the reigns of government in the West." Commanding "the strongest army on earth," the new ruler in the West will carry "a clear sign" from the third Imam, whose name was Hussein Ibn Ali. "Shiites should have no doubt THAT HE IS WITH US!"*

In a curious coincidence Obama's first and second names—Barack Hussein—mean, "the blessing of Hussein," in Arabic and Persian. His family name, Obama, written in the Persian alphabet, reads O Ba Ma, which means "HE IS WITH US"—the magic formula in Majlisi's tradition. Thus, in this prophecy we have a double witness that Obama is a Muslim, or at the very least one who supports the Muslim cause, and as such utterly unfit to hold his high office. This more than anything else explains why he is in bed with the Muslim Brotherhood—the simple answer is that he is one of them! All of his actions since his election confirm the fact.

Identifying the Evil at the End of Days

There was a brief period of time of unity among the people of Israel at Mount Sinai, when the twelve tribes of Israel received the Torah. This unity lasted until the death of Moses, and before his death he was able to tell the assembled nation what would befall them at the end of days. He said they would stray from the Covenant of Torah, and that if they angered the Holy One of Israel through the work of their hands, then evil would befall them at the end of days. The only other time this phrase is used in the five Books of Moses, when Hagar is told that she would have a son, and she should name him Ishmael. This word is normally connected to proclaiming and voicing something. It is used here to tell us that when evil befalls the children of Israel, it was proclaimed in heaven and does not happen by chance. So, just what is the connection between Ishmael and the end of days? The connection is that the descendants of Ishmael are the evil that will befall the people of Israel at that time.

The "work of our hands" has a gematria of 501, and "the evil that will befall us" also has a gematria of 501. So, what could we possibly have dome that would anger God? With our very own hands, we finance and work to put the wrong people in power over us. This action results in our downfall. By putting in power leaders in Israel who don't believe in God, we help bring about a spiritual collapse. And by electing dangerous leaders in America and other countries, we assist in bringing our physical and moral downfall. We vote for these people, we put them in power, and we raise money for them. This inappropriate work of our hands will bring evil upon us in the form of Ishmael.

The shocking fact is that 501 is also the gematria of Barack Hussein Obama, and thus with our own hands we have taken a descendant of Ishmael and placed him in the White House, just seven years after 9/11. He indeed is the evil that will befall us at the end of days, the evil that Moses spoke of to our ancestors. How do we know that he is dangerous? Not only is his name the same gematria as Ishmael, evidencing that he is a Muslim (although he denies it), he also has a further connection to a wave of impending evil against the Jews and the rest of the world. At a Jewish Passover Seder we spill a drop of wine when we mention each of the ten plagues, and also when we mention the abbreviation of those plagues. Well this abbreviation of the ten plagues also has a gematria of 501, the same as Barack Hussein Obama. Obama and radical Muslims will bring much havoc, destruction and confusion to the world as all the ten plagues did to Egypt. This message has been encoded in the Haggadah (the account of the Exodus) for nearly 2000 years for today.

—*Excerpts from an article by Joel Gallis and Dr. Robert Wolf*

Ayatollah Khamenei and Hamas Both Praise Obama

Further confirmation was given by an Associated Press report dated March 8th 2012, which quoted Ayatollah Ali Khamenei, warmly praising U.S. President Barack Obama for saying that diplomacy, and not war, can resolve the dispute over Tehran's nuclear ambitions. Iran's top leader said, *"These words are good words and an exit from delusion."* The Associated Press noted that the accolade from the ayatollah was "one of the rare cases in which Iran's top leader praised an American leader." The truth is that Obama's words are nothing of the sort and the ayatollah knows full well that the Presidents words are not an exit but rather an entry into delusion! Khamenei and most other top leaders of the Islamic Republic regularly refer to America as the "Great Satan," whom they vow to destroy. Ayatollah's praise for *[he-is-with-us]* Obama comes as a direct result of the president giving Iran the ingredient it needs most to finish its first nuclear weapons: TIME! The reality is that Khamenei's rare outburst of praise for President Obama includes recognition that his anti-war stance has given Iran a "window of opportunity."

The Jerusalem Post Magazine of May 18, 2012 in an op-ed by Josh Hasten referred to an election controversy in 2008 caused by Aaron Klein's WABC radio show. Klein conducted a radio interview with Hamas leader Ahmed Yousef in which Yousef reveals that Hamas was openly endorsing Obama's candidacy! As a result of Klein's shocking interview the then Republican candidate John McCain cited the Hamas endorsement numerous times. When we see the avowed arch enemies of the United States heap praise and support on President Obama, should this not fill all the citizens of America with alarm? It's a bit like the Boston strangler heaping public praise on the head of the police department for allowing him to carry on his murderous campaign unhindered by the police under his jurisdiction. In such a case should the citizenry of Boston not be justified in calling for the dismissal of their Chief of Police?

A "Stranger" in the White House!

This brings to mind a prophecy Moses spoke out just prior to his death, when he warned his people of the curses for rebellion and disobedience that would come upon them. Moses directed his solemn warning at the children of Israel: *"The stranger who is among you will ascend above you higher and higher, while you descend lower and lower."* (Deut. 28:43).

This prophecy is as valid today as it was in the day Moses spoke it out. Can we not see how it perfectly fits in with the situation prevailing in America today? America is steeped in sin; in fact, she openly revels in it, and has rebelled against all that the Almighty Creator God of Israel stands for, as she has trampled on all of His commandments. She is now cursed with, *"A STRANGER" in the White House, and that is why with Obama's active support, the Muslim Brotherhood will rise higher and higher. Because America's leaders and this present generation have despised the Law of God, YHVH will allow Obama's re-election to enable his Islamist friends and Muslim associates to bring in and subject America to their sharia law, and consequently the nation will descend lower and lower!*

Just listen to what Obama's Koranic friends are saying about you! Grand Ayatollah Ali al Sistani, Islam's most influential Shiite cleric, makes even more explicit the dehumanizing leitmotif of Muslim scripture. Relying on centuries of Shia scholarship, he teaches that non-Muslims should not be touched, much less associated with. They are considered in the same category as "urine, feces, semen, dead bodies, blood, dogs, pigs, alcoholic liquors, and 'the sweat of an animal who persistently eats filth.'"*[10]

Is it not highly ironic that the United States government considers this same Sistani to be her key "moderate" ally in the new Iraq?

Unless the nation repents in dust and ashes there is no hope for America—without wholesale top-down repentance - the nation is utterly doomed! Does anybody really think that the American government will publicly confess and admit its mistakes? Does anybody think the President will ask God for forgiveness and follow in Abraham Lincoln's footsteps by calling for a national day of fasting and prayer? Does anybody seriously think that both houses of Congress will beg God's forgiveness by rescinding all the laws which are in flagrant breach of the Torah? If you do not think this is a likely scenario, then I challenge the reader to read the rest of Deuteronomy Chapter 28, from verse 44 to 68, which in the most vivid detail describes the future that now awaits the American nation.

Two Minutes to Midnight on the Iranian Threat

All of this is happening at a time when the State of Israel faces the worst existential threat since its foundation in May 1948, and this at the hands of a maniacal religious psychopath in charge of Iran. Were Iran to equip high speed ballistic missiles with nuclear warheads, Mahmoud Ahmadinejad would suddenly be in a position to accomplish in about six minutes what it took Adolph Hitler nearly six years to do—kill more than six million Jews! This appears to be just what Ahmadinejad has in mind when he says that Israel is; *"heading toward annihilation"* and *"one day will vanish."* *11

Iran's Blueprint for the Destruction of Israel!

Recently, [February 2012], the Iranian government through a website proxy, has laid out the legal and religious justification for the destruction of Israel and the slaughter of its people. The doctrine includes wiping out Israeli assets and Jewish people worldwide. Calling Israel a danger to Islam, the conservative website Alef, with ties to Iran's supreme leader, Ayatollah Ali Khamenei, said the opportunity must not be lost to remove this *"corrupting material."* It is a *"jurisprudential justification"* to kill all Jews and annihilate Israel, and in that, the Islamic government of Iran must take the helm. The article written by Alireza Forghani, an analyst and strategic specialist in Khamenei's camp, now is being run in most state-run sites, showing that the regime endorses this doctrine. One Friday, in a major speech at prayers, Khamenei announced that Iran will support any nation or group that attacks the *"cancerous tumor"* of Israel. Iran's Defense Ministry announced the following weekend that that it test-fired an advanced two-stage, solid-fuel ballistic missile and boasted about successfully putting a new satellite into orbit, reminding the west that its engineers have mastered the technology for intercontinental missiles even as the Islamic state pushes its nuclear weapons program.

The commander of the Revolutionary Guards, Brig. Gen. Seyyed Mehdi Faradi, stated in August that the Safir missile, which is capable of transporting a satellite into space, can easily be launched parallel to the earth's orbit, which will transform it into an intercontinental ballistic missile. Western analysts did not believe this would happen until 2015. Historically, orbiting a satellite is the criterion for crediting a nation with

ICBM capacity. This means that Iran now has the ICBM means to deliver destruction on Israel and soon will have nuclear warheads for those missiles.

In order to attack Iran, the article says, Israel needs the approval and assistance of America, and under the current passive climate in the United States, the opportunity must not be lost to wipe out Israel before she attacks Iran.

Under this pre-emptive defensive doctrine, several Ground Zero points of Israel must be destroyed and its people annihilated. Forghani cites the last census by the Israel Central Bureau of Statistics that shows Israel has a population of 7.5 million citizens of which a majority of 5.7 million are Jewish. Then it breaks down the districts with the highest concentration of Jewish people, indicating that three cities, Tel Aviv, Jerusalem and Haifa, contain over 60 percent of the Jewish population that Iran could target with Shahab 3 ballistic missiles, killing all its inhabitants.

Forghani suggests that Iran's Sejil missile, which is a two-stage rocket with a trajectory and speed that make it impossible to intercept, should target such Israeli facilities as the Rafael nuclear plant, which is the main nuclear engineering center of Israel; the Eilun nuclear plant; another Israeli reactor in Nebrin; and the Dimona reactor in the nuclear research center in Neqeb, the most critical nuclear reactor in Israel because it produces 90 percent enriched uranium for Israel's nuclear weapons.

Other targets, according to the article, include airports and air force bases such as the Sedot Mikha Air Base, which contains Jericho ballistic missiles and is located southwest of the Tel Nof Air base, where aircraft equipped with nuclear weapons are based. Secondary targets include power plants, sewage treatment facilities, energy resources, and transportation and communication infrastructures.

Finally, Forghani says, Shahab 3 and Ghadr missiles can target urban settlements until the Israelis are wiped out. He claims that Israel could be destroyed in less than nine minutes and that Khamenei, as utmost authority, the Velayete Faghih [Islamic Jurist], also believes that Israel and America not only must be defeated but annihilated."[12]

Notice the disgustingly cold and matter of fact way their detailed plans are outlined in the above article. Who can possibly doubt the absolute commitment Iran has to the total annihilation of Israel?

Islamists the world over reckon they have a warrant for the genocide of the Jews, which is signed by Allah, the god of the Islamic death-cult. These Islamic jihadists are planning another Holocaust, and President Barack Hussein Obama, in his infamous Cairo speech, formally gave them the *"go ahead,"* signal, and left them to understand that America would not stand in their way! Furthermore, by his every cowardly action of appeasement since that fateful day, he has signaled to the enemy that he will not move a finger to stop them.

Message From the White House: "DON'T ROCK THE BOAT!!!"

Even as the clock is already set at two minutes to midnight before the State of Israel becomes history, the President is doing everything to try and prevent Israel from staging a defensive pre-emptive first-strike at Iran's nuclear plants. The message from the White House, the Pentagon and the State Department is screaming at Israel, *DON'T ROCK THE BOAT!* Washington is literally invading Israel, sending over every top dog they can think of from the Chairman of the Joint Chiefs of Staff, General Martin Dempsey, to Tom Donilon, the U.S. National Security Adviser, to the Director of Intelligence Tom Clapper, all this to apply maximum pressure and to cajole, blackmail, threaten and intimidate the Israeli government, all of it designed to coerce them not to act in their own defense. They are calling on Israel to be patient, sit back and let those toothless sanctions of ours work. In between the lines the message is: don't you Jews dare to defend yourself! The consequences could be catastrophic! Really? To whom, Mr. President? The fact is that the Obama administration is in a huge panic, not about Iran but about Israel, and is doing everything in its power to prevent its supposed ally from implementing a pre-emptive strike in its own defense. The White House battle against Israel is in full swing. The New York Times, the leftwing mouthpiece of the Obama Administration, has already began a "blame Israel in advance gloom and doom" scenario by publishing a classified war simulation exercise by the United States which estimated that a strike on Iran would lead to a regional war which would draw in the United States and leave hundreds of Americans dead. At the same time, rising gas prices are already being blamed on Israel! This whilst nothing has happened yet! Can you imagine what a furor they would direct at Israel if something really does happen?

Israeli MK Aryeh Eldad, in a speech given in the U.S. in the fall of 2011, when Israel was intending to act against Iran militarily, said word came down from the White House that, "If you act alone, you will remain alone!" Because Israel is so dependent on the U.S. for resupply of weapons and munitions in a prolonged war, this threat changed the calculus immediately. It is true when Mahmoud Abbas was threatening to go to the U.N. for recognition, the Obama administration lobbied around the world for negative votes. But at the same time, Obama threatened Netanyahu that Obama would withhold his veto if Israel took punitive action against the PA by annexing some of the territories or by withholding funds. Finally, he used the same threat to get Israel to instruct AIPAC to lobby Congress not to punish the PA by withholding U.S. funds, which they were planning to do.

Almost every day the scenario worsens for Israel, as a report from Associated Press dated February, 25, 2012, cited Mohammad Hejazi, the deputy head of Iran's Armed Forces, that the Islamic republic might launch pre-emptive missile strikes against Israel. Yet, the Obama administration continues to act as though Israel is the real problem, not Iran! Who cares about those six million Jews in Israel? Just don't rock the boat! Clearly, the truth is that Israel now stands all alone!

The Head of the IDF (Israeli Defense Forces), Aviv Kochavi, informed the audience at the January 2012 Herzliya Conference on Israeli policy, that Israel's enemies have 200,000 missiles aimed at Israel, which can reach all parts of Israel—even the ostensibly safe "center" of Tel Aviv and its suburbs. The rockets and missiles are largely located in Lebanon and Syria, with a smaller amount in Gaza—and in Iran, as well, which has thousands of missiles that could reach Israel. "Every tenth house in Lebanon is now a weapons depot," Kochavi said.*[13] Avi Kochavi's assessment did not include the scores of thousands of missiles in Egypt's

Armed Forces, which will soon be controlled by the new Muslim Brotherhood government. Egypt's substantial missile inventory is administered by eighteen Tactical Missile Brigades, and, most of her short to medium range missiles are carried on mobile launchers. Egypt also has a meaningful quantity of Intercontinental Ballistic Missiles (ICBMs). A Muslim Brotherhood-led Egypt, with her formidable, super-modern American-armed Forces, are bound to participate in the next, now imminent, FOURTH ARAB-ISRAEL WAR!

The New York Times, the leftwing poodle of the U.S. government, in mid February 2012, joined the chorus of naysayers from the White House and the State Department, advising Israel against an attack on Iran. The Times expressed serious doubts about Israel's military capability to cripple Iran's nuclear weapons program. Their bleak analysis was headed as "Iran Raid Seen as a Huge Task for Israeli Jets," and said that Israel would have to deploy at least 100 fighter jets to destroy Iran's nuclear complexes. The article also expressed doubt about whether those planes could manage the distance to Iran and back, and it cited the viewpoint of several leading U.S. military analysts. The consensus was that it would be a monstrous challenge for Israel to breach Iran's airspace and attack its nuclear facilities.

Lone Support From Germany

In stark contrast to this negative viewpoint from the New York Times, the German "Die Welt" newspaper expressed confidence that the Israeli air force could decimate Iran's principal nuclear installations. Hans Ruhle, former director of the German defense Ministry planning department, said that Israel is militarily capable of setting Iran's nuclear weapons program back by a decade or more. In the analysis titled "How Israel can destroy Iran's nuclear program," Ruhle cited German defense experts to defend his optimistic view. "Israel's Air Force is first class," wrote Ruhle. "Their pilots are conditioned from the history of Israel and the constant dangers faced by the Jewish state."

The following Tuesday, the Jerusalem Post published an article juxtaposing the U.S.'s bleak outlook on the matter with Germany's optimistic perspective. As the U.S. declines, it is bound to leave Israel increasingly isolated in the fast Islamizing Middle East. It is not unrealistic to expect the Jewish nation to turn to Germany for defense help. Sadly, it is a move that, if she does decide to go that way, she will in time come to greatly regret. There is a particular warning given by the Prophet Hosea: *"Ephraim saw his ailment and Judah his wound; and Ephraim went to Assyria and [Judah] sent [tribute] to the king of Jareb—but he will not be able to cure you nor to heal your wound."* (Hosea 5:13) Judah's wound is the "Oslo Accord," the so called "peace accord" between Israel and the terrorist entity commonly referred to as the Palestinian Authority. King Jareb means king of contention and is another name of Assyria, whereas, as we have already seen, the German nation is descended from ancient Assyria. In a previous chapter we have already established the fact that she has also had some extremely adverse influence upon the Muslim world, having deliberately and consciously inculcated her diabolic Nazi Jew hatred into the Islamic world. Both of these factors, when coupled with the Holocaust, provide the most powerful reason for Israel to shun any German advances. For the State of Israel to get into bed with the European Union would indeed be "the ULTIMATE COVENANT WITH DEATH AND CONTRACT WITH HELL." This essentially is the urgent warning of this book. Israel would do better to put her trust in God than put her trust in man! King David had learned this lesson, as he stated: *"Do not rely on nobles, nor on a human being, for he holds no salvation"* (Psalm 146:3).

Obama Has Got Israel's back—Watch the Knife!!!

At the 2012 AIPAC convention in Washington DC, President Obama famously quoted that he had got Israel's back! Meaning that Israel was not to worry about the Iran situation, as he, Obama, was at Israel's back! The question is: should Israel feel safe with a treacherous guy like Obama at their back? Surely, by now, after all the adverse treatment they have received from this president, Israel's leaders should be concerned about the knife in Obama's hand! True to form, within weeks of his speech his administration had started openly leaking classified Israeli information through official channels, forewarning Israel's enemies and making an Israeli pre-emptive attack on Iran that much more difficult. Mark Perry, the former "unofficial advisor" to Yasser Arafat, the arch-terrorist and former

Chairman of the Palestine Liberation Organization, writing in Foreign Policy Magazine wrote an "informative article" in which he quoted high-level officials from the Obama administration. *He stated that those officials now believe that the "submerged" aspects of the Israeli-Azerbaijani alliance—the security cooperation between the two countries —is heightening the risk of an Israeli strike on Iran.* He went on to say: *"In particular, four senior diplomats and military intelligence officers say that the United States has concluded that Israel has recently been granted access to airbases on Iran's northern border. To do what, exactly is not clear. "The Israelis have bought an airfield,"* a senior administration official told me in early February, *'and the airfield is called Azerbaijan.'"*

By revealing such sensitive highly-classified information, the element of surprise has been removed from a possible attack coming from Iran's northern border. According to John Bolton, the former U.S. Ambassador to the United Nations, we can assume with some confidence that Iran was not focused on the risk of Israeli bases in Azerbaijan, so hearing about it from US administration sources is a gift beyond measure. And one can confidently assume that if that leak is not enough to make Israel bend its knee, more public revelations directed by the White House are only a matter of time. Even now, Obama advisers could be revealing additional information to other governments behind closed doors. Not only is this not the way to treat a close ally facing an existential challenge, it is directly contrary to America's national interests. Israel is not the threat, Mr. President; Iran is!*14

Israel Has Been Betrayed in the House of Her Friends

Appeasement is a supreme act of cowardice! You can be sure that America's enemies recognize weakness when they see it! Islamic terrorists the world over are rejoicing as they sense that the planet's only superpower is now in wholesale retreat before them. In the meantime, Israel knows she has been betrayed in the house of her friends. Despite the regular hypocritical political lip service paid by the U.S. government to the close bonds between the two countries, the sad reality is that America never ceases from pressurizing the Jewish State into making suicidal concessions to her sworn enemies. With the onset of Obama's presidency the familial bond of brotherhood between America and the Jewish State of Israel is now broken. It is a terrible and most shocking realization, but deep down Israel now knows and is fully aware that she has been abandoned by the government of the United States of America.

Yet, people fail to realize the ancient prophecy of Zechariah, who prophesied the end of the brotherhood between Judah and America: *"Then I broke My second staff, Hobelin, to annul the brotherhood between Judah and Israel."* (Zechariah 11:14).

Previous American administrations have always appreciated that Israel is the front line holding back the Islamic juggernaut. The truth is, if Israel falls, the U.S. and her dwindling band of allies, may very well feel the brunt of the assault to come, which might pale into insignificance when compared to what she faced during both World Wars. The prophet Zechariah makes the consequences for anyone who would mess with the status of Israel or Jerusalem very clear:

"And it shall happen in that day that I will make Jerusalem a very heavy stone for all peoples; all who would heave it away will surely be cut in pieces, though all the nations of the earth are gathered against it. (Zechariah 12:3).

America, consider yourself warned! If you pursue your present course of appeasing the enemies of the State of Israel you will most certainly be cut to pieces! You will be stripped of your power and global supremacy and you will be overrun by your enemies!

"Together They Shall be Against Judah"

As we have seen in chapter seven, the Prophet Isaiah prophesied that Manasseh would devour Ephraim and that Ephraim would devour Manasseh, not only in the Revolutionary War of Independence, but also during the subsequent Civil War. In this way these two brothers and sons of Joseph truly were, *"devouring the flesh of their own arm."* The truth is that the Prophet Isaiah goes on to add an ominous afterthought to his prophecy, much like a sting in the tail. The additional text is as follows: *"Every man shall eat the flesh of his own arm. Manasseh shall devour*

Ephraim, and Ephraim Manasseh; <u>together they shall be against Judah!</u>" (Isaiah 9:21, editor's emphasis).

Thus both Isaiah and Zechariah foresaw what would happen in our day. It should be noted that both prophets pronounced their prophecies after the secession between the two houses of Israel had already taken place. In fact the kingdom of Israel was no more, as it had been overrun by the Assyrian invaders, who had deported the entire population to the territory of the Assyrian Empire. Only the house of Judah remained.

Isaiah's statement, *"<u>together they shall be against Judah!</u>"* could not possibly have applied to the time of either the American War of Independence, or to the subsequent Civil War, as Judah only became a national entity with the creation of the State of Israel in 1948. In any case, in those heady days of the Revolutionary War and the Civil War both Great Britain and the United States of America were pro-Judah, as the early stirrings of Christian Zionism were having a positive effect in both nations. We have also seen in chapter eight how both Great Britain, (i.e. gentile Ephraim), and America, (i.e. gentile Manasseh), have served as Providence's instruments in bringing about the rebirth of the Jewish State in the Promised Land. Isaiah's prophecy therefore by definition is speaking of a much later time period. Sadly, is this not what we are seeing today, as America in cowardly appeasement mode stands ready to jettison and desert Judah in favor of the evil Islamic juggernaut? Those Islamic nations are even now hungrily baying for the blood of every Jewish citizen of the State of Israel.

Great Britain in turn has made a Covenant with Death and signed a contract with hell by voluntarily giving up her sovereign independence as a nation, and submerging herself into the European Union, which ever since the OPEC Oil Embargo of 1973, has become the lackey and bedfellow of the Arab League. Thus we also see the final part of Isaiah's prophecy fulfilled in our day, as even Manasseh (U.S.A.) and Ephraim (Great Britain) are both taking sides against Judah by consorting with and giving comfort to her most ferocious enemies. Zechariah gave his prophecy some 2,500 years ago, after the Jews had recently been released from their Babylonian captivity in the days of King Cyrus of the Persian Empire, at the time the Northern Kingdom of Israel was nowhere to be

Appeasement Leading to Divine Judgment

seen, as the ten tribes of Israel were still scattered into the four corners of the earth. Nevertheless, his prophecy that; *"the brotherhood between Judah and Israel would be broken,"* therefore is also clearly meant for our day!

Thus these prophecies are being fulfilled in real time before our own eyes, as both nations, much like Pontius Pilate, have publicly washed their hands of the Jewish nation so that the inevitable crucifixion of the Jews may begin. You may be sure that America and Great Britain will be held accountable and will pay a most terrible price for this betrayal of their brother Judah.

Why Do So Many Bad Things Keep Happening To The United States?

Consider for a moment: things have not gone terribly well for America in the past ten years or thereabouts! Who can deny it? The nation has suffered the 9/11 catastrophe when, for the first time in U.S. history, fortress America was breached, and breached not by a mighty nation of superior arms, but breached by a bunch of terrorists. Can you believe it? How humbling is that? It is no coincidence that this worst terrorist attack in American history happened after U.S. President Bill Clinton attempted in the dying days of his administration to divide Jerusalem in his ill-fated Camp David initiative. The terrorists struck soon after his successor took office.

Since then, the nation suffered the calamity of the Katrina disaster in New Orleans. Scores of ever more disastrous hurricanes and tornadoes have hit her shores. Ongoing extreme droughts are taking a terrible toll, causing out-of-control wild fires, and just recently the country was being blitzed by a financial tsunami the like of which the world has never seen. Great financial institutions have fallen into the dust like ninepins and the country found itself staring into the abyss of major recession, which is absolutely certain to lead to the mother of all depressions. The once invincible car industry has become a total train wreck, only to be "temporarily" resuscitated through a massive cash transfusion funded by the hapless taxpayers of America. Property values have tanked throughout the nation and unemployment and house repossessions continue their downward spiral. This is not to speak even of the soldiers who are dying in far away foreign fields, fighting wars in Iraq and Afghanistan. This, whilst the consensus of informed opinion says that the war in Afghanistan is a particularly hopeless quest! A war which, based upon both past and present experience, simply cannot be won, whereas anybody with only an ounce of common sense can see that the only ultimate beneficiary of the wars in Iraq and Afghanistan is Iran, America's greatest enemy.

Another most *"inconvenient truth"* is that the American economy is staggering under the weight of the size of the National Debt, which at the time of writing exceeds $100 trillion. The nation has no chance of ever repaying this debt and the world is fast losing confidence in the once "Almighty U.S. Dollar." America has become the greatest debtor nation in the history of the world, and she has to rely on foreigners to buy her bonds to sustain her utterly unsustainable debt trajectory. The writing is on the wall for those who can see it, as one day those same foreigners will lose confidence and stop buying her bonds. Even now, her enemies are actively planning the moment when they, in a coordinated move, will pull the rug from underneath the U.S. Dollar, as the world's only reserve currency. When this happens, it will create total panic leading to Armageddon for the American economy.

Has anyone ever heard of the Ogallala Aquifer? The Ogallala Aquifer is absolutely critical to food production in the United States of America. It is an enormously large underground lake that stretches from South Dakota all the way through northern Texas covering around 174 thousand square miles. The bad news is that this gigantic aquifer is drying up with potentially disastrous consequences for the country's future food supplies. The Aquifer is being drained at the rate of 800 gallons per minute. That amounts to a staggering 1.15 million gallons per day.

If the current drought conditions continue and the depletion is not reversed, the era of pivot irrigation in the region could be over. This means that the Great Plains, which has served as one of the largest food baskets of the nation, would quickly turn into the Great American Desert. Thus, America could well see a return to the Dust Bowl days of the 1930s. As of July 2012, the U.S. Department of Agriculture has declared the current Midwest Drought to be the Biggest Natural Disaster. A Natural Disaster has been declared in 26 States as drought sears 1016 U.S. counties affected by the drought, wildfires and other disasters.

Have you heard what's been happening to the bees? Nature is playing some very strange tricks all of which have an impact upon our survival. For the fourth year in a row the American honeybee has been in trouble, as more than a third of all bee colonies have failed to survive the winter. An annual survey by the Apiary Inspectors of America and the U.S. government's Agricultural Research Service, the number of managed honeybee colonies in the United States fell by 33.8% last winter. When you consider that a full one-third of what we eat depends upon honeybee pollination, this ominous trend has the potential of quickly turning into a disaster affecting our very survival.

What of the floods in May 2011, when half of the North American continent has been subject to flooding in the Mississippi drainage pattern? Up and down the Mississippi, the floods were near biblical, as the mighty River swelled to more than three miles in width. Large agricultural areas (more than 6.8 million acres) were under water for weeks on end. Vast swaths of infrastructure—homes, factories, roads, railways—were submerged. The weather forecasters said it will take weeks for the water to drain away. Then it will take months, or even years to clean up. As a direct consequence, a lot of people and many businesses were ruined. A major disaster unprecedented in its scale, and an untold number of people and businesses will have to start life all over again.

Epic flooding along the Missouri River has forced mass evacuations and threatened to inundate two nuclear power plants in Nebraska. Meanwhile, other parts of the United States are dealing with some of the most extreme droughts since the dustbowl of the 1930s, and the tinder-dry conditions have led to massive and uncontrollable wildfires. Already this year, millions of acres have been burned in many separate fire incidents so far this year (June, 2013). The most recent one destroyed over 500 homes near Colorado Springs and took the lives of two people. According to the National Interagency Fire Center, the numbers of calls and fires has doubled the annual average over the past decade.

Violent storms have unleashed scenes of apocalyptic destruction. The deadliest tornado season in 60 years ravaged the United States in just the first six months of 2011, leaving 542 victims dead. In 2012, there were 939 with 70 deaths and so far in 2013 there have been 43 deaths in 573 outbreaks. In the meantime, scientists, such as Jon Gottschalck, head of the forecast operations at NOAA's Climate Prediction Center, is warning that more extreme weather is expected in the coming months. The human and economic toll has been staggering and unprecedented.

Considering what you have read in this chapter about America's cowardly policies of appeasement and her treatment of Israel, her most trusted and loyal friend, do you think it is fair to pose the question "Why Do So Many Bad Things Keep Happening to The United States of America?"

Reason Why Things Are Not Going Well For America!

People come up with all sorts of reasons for this sad state of affairs, but none of them really hits the button. Consider what could be the reason for these disasters. The nation is not just suffering from one isolated disaster, but myriad calamities, all coinciding at the same time. What on earth can be the reason for America's sudden change of fortune?

The prophet Isaiah speaking in the end-time context of Israel pronounces God's judgment as follows: *"For the nation and kingdom which will not serve you shall perish, and those nations shall be utterly ruined."* (Isaiah 60:12).

These are strong words: any nation that comes against Israel, or any part of it, will perish and will be utterly ruined! Just as the once mighty British Commonwealth lost her empire by hurting the emerging Jewish nation, so it was with the Spanish empire and more recently with the Soviet Union and so it might be with America too! The surest way for America to lose her wealth, power, global status and yes, even her freedom, is for her to appease the enemies of the Jewish State of Israel. Sir Winston Churchill once famously said: *"An appeaser is one who feeds the crocodile hoping it will eat him last!"*

Appeasement was the policy that emboldened Hitler and two fine democratic and free nations were sacrificed to him! President Obama's policy is one of appeasing America's most deadly enemies, whilst at the same time alienating her closest allies. President Harry S. Truman was the first foreign head of state to recognize the State of Israel. He had the courage to lead the world in acknowledging the revival of the tiny nation "reborn" out of the ashes of the Holocaust. He said: *"I had faith in Israel even before it was established. I knew it was based upon the love of freedom, which has been the guiding star of the Jewish people since the days of Moses."* For 64 years Israel has been America's one true friend and strategic ally in the Middle East. Since Harry Truman, all US Presidents have considered the support of Israel as not only a moral imperative, but also believed that a secure and strong Israel is in America's self-interest.

Now, in his attempt at appeasement of the Islamic world, and through his projection to them of himself as a kosher Muslim, Obama has joined the "kick-a-Jew" club. The President has ceased America's position of being the honest broker in the Middle East conflict between Israel and the world of Islam, by taking the Palestinian position and effectively becoming their spokesman. This reminds one of an ancient Arab proverb which says: *"The enemy of my enemy is my friend."* In the case of Israel's formerly close relationship with the United States government, the reverse of this proverb applies, in that *"The friend of my enemy is my enemy!"* When we reflect on America's ancestry and its close association with Manasseh, the "birthright" son of Joseph, it makes her betrayal all the more heinous. It is a case of Joseph betraying his brother Judah! You can be sure that this fratricidal sin will not go unpunished! Terrible Divine Judgment is coming upon America that will be manifested by Awesome Acts of God, there is a high probability that the American people will turn against their current President, and rue the day they ever elected him to his high office.

America, what are you waiting for? You have so much to lose! As a nation, you have lost belief in the Creator of the World and you have trampled on His instructions. Because of this, your belief and trust in your institutions have been taken away from you. This is the reason why the heaven-sent Angel of Death continues to visit God's judgment on your financial institutions and industries, and why you will witness the systemic collapse of the entire banking and monetary system, the erosion of which is even now in progress. On the U.S. dollar, the nation used to proudly proclaim the motto "IN GOD WE TRUST." The question is, which God? For sure going by the conduct of Wall Street, the Federal Reserve, your Bankers and your Government, it cannot possibly refer to the One and Only Creator of the Universe, the God of Israel. Clearly your God is a pagan god called Mammon, the god of hedonistic materialism! It would be more honest if you printed on your dollar bills a motto that reflects the truth. A more accurate motto would be "IN GREED WE TRUST!" Once the U.S. dollar has collapsed, the god of Mammon you have idolized and worshipped for so long will, with great suddenness, be thrown into the dust, leaving the nation destitute. This is the stark and inevitable future that is staring America in the face right now! All of the above is said in tough love born out of heartfelt concern for the future of your nation. These admittedly hard comments are made in the sincere hope of helping all Americans wake up to the dire state of the nation, as well as to the importance of returning to the divine Creator and Author of all of our lives.

When the economy implodes, do you want to see violent civil commotion erupting throughout the major cities of your land? You probably will not have to wait long because it will soon be all too real. Do you want to witness the unimaginable death and devastation of an earthquake on the San Andreas Fault line? Do you want to witness a mega quake in the New Madrid Fault line affecting the Mid West, devastating the states of Missouri, Iowa, Wisconsin, Indiana and Illinois, as well as Mississippi and the East Coast? Do you think the unthinkable is not possible in modern-day America? You had better think again! Consider the mega droughts going on in the South. Think on the mysterious departure of a full one third of all the pollinating bees. On top of this we have the alarming prospect of the vital Ogallala Aquifer drying up. These are all signs and they are telling us that if these trends continue that famine is already an all-too-real possibility for America in the near future. The common consensus amongst the world food scientific community is that the world is only one crop failure away from famine! The Swine-flu pandemic reared its ugly head some years ago, and we know it was greatly overhyped at the time, which has led to massive complacency, thus setting the stage for ugly surprises in the near future. Health officials around the world are only too aware that a much worse scenario of an Avian-flu pandemic, plus who knows what else, may even now be waiting in the wings eager to take its toll. The tottering economy plus the weird weather patterns we are now experiencing almost every week, with freak storms, hurricanes, tornadoes and floods hitting the nation from all sides, all speak of the fact that God has taken His blessing off the nation. The question is: What is it going to take before any one of us gets the picture?

Consider for a moment the worst case scenario: Do you want to wait for the day when your enemies perpetrate the ultimate unthinkable—a first-strike nuclear attack on America's major population centers? Be sure that your enemies have been planning this very scenario for many years! They are planning a nuclear holocaust preceded by a gigantic cyber attack, in order to paralyze all your defenses. All of these calamities and more will be in store unless the nation repents, which implies that all of these disasters may be avoided if the American people will but turn about and change direction. The choice therefore is in your own hands! The Prophet Ezekiel conveys the very heart of the Holy One of Israel as He laments the destruction of His people:

'As I live - the word of the Lord HASHEM/ELOHIM—[I swear] that I do not desire the death of the wicked one, but rather the wicked one's return from his way, that he may live. Repent, repent from your evil ways! Why should you die, O House of Israel?' (Ezekiel 33:11, emphasis added).

America Like the Titanic Maybe Heading For the Rocks

American society, much like the Titanic, is fatally holed below the waterline and facing impending destruction. While many, with the recent implosion of the economy, are undoubtedly concerned about the state of the nation, yet the temporary upturn has encouraged most still to believe in the indestructibility of the ship of state. America's decadent, "anything goes" culture has infected the whole world and her sins have reached the heavens. The truth is that America has lost her moral compass. The Judeo-Christian value system, that has so successfully guided the nation since its foundation, has been eroded almost to oblivion. It has been replaced by a Godless creed of secularism where there are few moral absolutes, leaving only a system of ethical relativism to guide the affairs of the nation. The country appears to be unwilling to recognize the ultimate reality of our Creator GOD and His Kingdom. Those who discern the danger seem helpless in the wake of the secular tsunami of hedonistic humanism and materialism sweeping the nation. The country needs to recognize that its national survival at the very least depends upon a return to the faith of its founding fathers.

The fathers of the nation understood that the strength and survival of the country depended on the continued presence of the providential hand of God. Those who take the words of the Bible seriously are looked upon scornfully as extremists today by the elites of the establishment. They fail to recognize that on that basis George Washington, Thomas Jefferson and most of the founding fathers of the nation were extremists to a man. Yet, over the past forty years, U.S. legislators, courts and judges, influenced by the liberal doctrines of secularism, have been hell-bent on sandblasting all references to God from the public domain. They have created an extraordinary situation where, to publicly acknowledge God is now deemed unconstitutional! The legislators and the courts have thus in their wilful arrogance created this affront to God, regardless of the fact that the men who wrote the constitution were men who had a profound respect for the God of the Bible. They saw an absolute link between faith in God and the success of the Republic. George Washington himself stated: *"It is impossible to rightly govern the world without God and the Bible!"*

Thomas Jefferson famously related the following:

"God who gave us life gave us liberty. And can the liberties of a nation be thought secure when we have removed their own firm basis, a conviction in the mind of the people that these liberties are a gift from God? That they are not to be violated but with His wrath? Indeed I tremble for my country when I reflect that God is just, and that His justice cannot sleep forever." * 15

If Thomas Jefferson could see our day, he would indeed tremble at the moral bankruptcy of the nation. Just like the Hebrews of ancient times, America has been given great blessings, and just as those ancient Hebrew ancestors broke their covenant with the Eternal God of Israel, America too has let God down in a big way. Make no mistake, God is not mocked. Just as ancient Israel was made to pay the price, so America will today, as God is not a respecter of persons and by His own admission He does not change (See: Malachi 3:6). Dr. Ezra Stiles, the seventh president of Yale College, often spoke of America as a "modern-day Israel." In referring to George Washington, Dr. Stiles made this significant statement:

"Whereupon Congress put at the head of the spirited army, the only man on whom the eyes of all Israel were placed. Posterity, incredulous as they may be, will yet acknowledge that this American Joshua was raised up by God for the great work of leading the armies of this American Joseph—now separated from his brethren—and conducting these people to liberty and independence." * 16

Ground Zero: "The Spiritual Birthplace of America!"

It was in St Paul's Chapel in Manhattan that America was dedicated to God by George Washington, the first President of the United States of America. This first ever inauguration of a U.S. President did not take place in Washington DC nor in Philadelphia. Instead, Lower Manhattan in New York City was awarded the honor of being the first capital of America! America was born not on July 4th but instead in a manner of speaking was conceived on July 4th. America was born as a fully formed nation on April 30th 1789. On that day for the first time, America had a Constitution, a House of Representatives and a President with executive powers over a duly constituted government. It was the birth of the United States as a fully fledged nation. On that day, the Government, the House, the Senate and the President all gathered in the Capital at the Federal Hall (Latin for "Covenant" Hall). It was the inauguration of George Washington. It was the nation's Dedication Day.

Now often in the Bible, the threshold of a new beginning brings promises and warnings and prophetic truths: Moses at the Jordan River, Solomon at the dedication of the Temple. So after being sworn in on the steps of the Federal Hall, Washington issued the first Presidential address. His words were short and in midstream they contained a solemn warning:

"We ought to be no less persuaded that the propitious smiles of heaven can never be expected of a nation that disregards the eternal rules of order and the right which heaven itself has ordained."

The warning was that America's future blessing would, as with ancient Israel, hang on its relationship to God. If America should begin to depart from God's eternal rules, its blessings, its prosperity, and its protection should be removed.

After finishing his address and giving his warning, President Washington led the American government in its first act of kneeling before that same God. He led all his officials, his Vice President, the Senators, as well as the House of Representatives on foot for a "Thanksgiving Service" at St. Paul's Chapel just a stone's throw away. Thus, the entire government of America was kneeling before God. As they prayed, they committed the nation into God's hands. Hence, on that auspicious day of April 30th, 1789, that little Chapel became the ground upon which America was consecrated to God. The Chapel even to this day is known as St. Paul's Chapel, where George Washington's pew is preserved. The words on the plaque above the President's pew read as follows:

"Almighty God, we make our earnest prayer that you will keep the United States in Holy protection!"

What most Americans do not know is that the place where George Washington knelt in prayer on the day of the nation's birth was on a plot of land that today is better known as, *"Ground Zero!"* It was in the place where the whole government of the United States 212 years previously had prayed for God's protection, that His Divine protection was lifted on September the 11th, 2001, on a day of judgment now better known as 9/11. It all took place on the same ground where America was consecrated to God.

It was right there at the corner of *"Ground Zero"* they all prayed. The Islamic terrorists had no idea they were touching the very place where America was dedicated to the God of Israel and where God's favor and protection were prayed for; the very place that was so closely linked to Washington's prophetic warning that His Divine favor and protection would cease the moment the nation turned its back on God and His righteous laws. As history is our witness, in that same place on September 11th 2001, God lifted His Divine Hand of protection over the nation in the most dramatic and public way possible, allowing the enemy planes to crash into the twin towers. Thus unspeakable terror struck the first capital of the United States, as well as the financial capital of the world. The whole world stood in shock and amazement as they witnessed the unthinkable happen in real time in front of their eyes on their TV screens. Soon the clouds of death and destruction covered Manhattan including the little Chapel of St. Paul's...yet this one building was spared. Not even a single window was broken in the spot where America was dedicated to God.

The Sycamore Tree: A Symbol of Judgment

It is referred to as the *"miracle of ground zero!"* In the graveyard behind St. Paul's Chapel stood a large sycamore tree which was felled by a large steel beam that came flying through the sky from one of the twin towers. The sycamore tree took the full force of the blow thus protecting the chapel that stood on the ground of America's consecration, whilst all around was debris and devastation. What few realize is that the sycamore tree in the Bible is referred to as a symbol of judgment. King David speaks about this in Psalm78:43-47, referring to the judgment exacted upon Egypt. The sycamore trees are mentioned again by the prophet Isaiah in the context of judgment coming upon Samaria, the capital city of the Northern Kingdom of Israel.

"The Lord sent a word against Jacob, and it has fallen on Israel. All the people will know—Ephraim and the inhabitants of Samaria—who say in pride and arrogance of heart:

The bricks have fallen down,

But we will rebuild with hewn stones;

The sycamores are cut down,

But we will replace them with cedars

Isaiah 9:8-10

Isaiah says: *"all the people will know!"* Never before was a truer word spoken! All of the people did know! Never before was such a catastrophic act of judgment executed in such a public way in that it could be viewed live on the TV screens of the whole wide world. The entire world community was witness to America's terrible humiliation! The prophet goes on to say that Ephraim, (generic name for the ten tribes of Israel), and the inhabitants of Samaria, (the capital city of the former kingdom of Israel), continue in pride and arrogance of heart. The truth is that in the aftermath of 9/11, he might as well have said the same about America and the city of New York! The world did witness amazing acts of courage and sacrifice in the rescue efforts following the disaster, and the heroic efforts of the New York Fire Service inspired many people. It is also undeniably true that people were shocked and greatly sobered by the event, yet there was not a sign of the nation turning back to God in heartfelt repentance. To the contrary, what the world witnessed instead was pure defiance. It is highly ironic that those prophetic words of Isaiah, which so epitomized the pride and the arrogance of heart of America's ancient Israelite ancestors, were used verbatim a number of times in the immediate aftermath of the event.

No Sign of Humility, Only Excess Pride!

Just one day after 9/11, on Wednesday September 12[th,] 2001, a transfixed nation and world waited and watched events with great suspense. Senator Tom Daschle gave the Joint Response of the Nation on the Senate floor in Washington DC, which was broadcast to the people of America and the world, as recorded in the Federal Register. Having expressed his pain, sorrow and anger he went on to quote: *"But there is a passage in the Bible, from Isaiah, that I think speaks to all of us at times such as this: "The bricks have fallen down, but we will rebuild with dressed stone, the fig trees have been felled, but we will replace them with cedars!"*

If ever there was a misapplication of Scripture, this surely must be one of the best examples ever, as the focus of Isaiah's message was to administer a stern rebuke to Israel for their lack of humility and contrition. In the aftermath of 9/11 what was on show in the reaction of America's leaders was sorrow, anger and defiance. Isaiah had rebuked ancient Israel for their pride and arrogance of heart and his words cut to the heart of what is wrong with America today.

In the same Senate meeting Senator John Kerry remarked: *"And I believe one of the first things we should commit to—with Federal help that underscores our nation's purpose—is to rebuild the towers of the World Trade Center and show the world that we are not afraid—we are defiant!"*

At the Citywide Prayer Service at Yankee Stadium on September 23rd, 2001, Mayor Rudy Giuliani stated: *"The proud Twin Towers that once crowned our famous skyline no longer stand. But our skyline will rise again. In the words of President George W. Bush, "we will rebuild New York City." To those who say our city will never be the same, I say you are right. It will be better!"*

The first stone to be used in the construction of the 1,176 ft. Freedom Tower was hewn from New York granite and lowered by crane in a ceremony on July 4th, 2004. The then-Governor of New York, George Pataki stated: *"Today, we the heirs of that revolutionary spirit of defiance lay this cornerstone."*

In this same spirit, the rebuilding of New York City's "Freedom Tower" to replace the "twin towers" began with a *"dressed stone"* ceremony. Furthermore, in yet another ceremony just over a year previously on November 22nd, 2003, a crane lifted a large *"cedar tree"* into the hole left by the slain sycamore three. Thus by this extraordinary series of parallel coincidences, the leaders of New York portrayed the same pride and arrogance of heart, as did their ancestors in ancient Israel. Their response to God's judgment-call on both occasions was to repeat the defiant actions portrayed in Isaiah's words:

"The bricks have fallen down,

But we will rebuild with hewn stones;

The sycamores are cut down,

But we will replace them with cedars."

Isaiah 9:8-10

In the wake of terrible destruction, the words of America's rulers were to make the above vow. Isaiah had prophesied that Israel's reaction both ancient and modern would take the form of a vow of arrogance! *[17]

Can we not see the connection? The prophet Isaiah specifically addressed his words to the Northern Kingdom of ancient Israel. To remove all possible doubt he mentions: *"All the people will know—Ephraim and the inhabitants of Samaria."* (Isaiah 9:9). Samaria was the capital city of ancient Israel. The question is: Why would the application of this prophecy so perfectly fit the modern day 9/11 tragedy, if there was no correlation between ancient Israel and the citizens of the modern day United States of America? Furthermore, in Chapter 6 we covered the remarkable warning from this very same chapter of Isaiah 9, about Ephraim and Manasseh *"devouring the flesh of each others arms!"* We have seen how this prophecy has been fulfilled, not only in the history of America's Revolutionary War of Independence, but also in the Civil War. Thus, this further prophetic utterance regarding *"the bricks have fallen down,"* as written down and recorded once again in Chapter 9 of the Book of Isaiah, provides us with additional evidence that America and Great Britain and her Commonwealth daughters are Israelite nations. Isaiah's dual prophecies thus add to the reams of evidence that America and Great Britain are descended from Manasseh and Ephraim, the "birthright" sons of Joseph.

Let there be no mistake; 9/11 should not be in vain. We must draw lessons and learn from it. Most people did not even for one moment seem to comprehend that the shocking events of 9/11 denoted that America has entered a period of Divine judgment.

CHAPTER TWELVE

The Divine Hand of Protection Has Been Withdrawn

A Call to Repentance

The terrible events of 9/11, that great day of infamy, should serve as a warning to America. Is it any wonder God is angry, since your leaders are busily dividing the land which He covenanted to the children of Israel, the descendants of Abraham? Oil and investment capital from oil are ruling the day. Can man annul that which God has decreed by an eternal covenant? The tragic events of 9/11 clearly indicated that God's Divine Hand of Protection had been removed. In other words, God is temporarily withdrawing His sponsorship of the United States in order to ultimately bring the nation back to Him. What this means is that He is giving the enemies of America free reign to attack, to hurt, and to destroy, in the hope that the nation, through all its consequent suffering, will come to its senses and repent. Once again, the words of President Abraham Lincoln convey the voice of prophecy, as they apply so perfectly to our time today. It is because today the moral slide in America is so much worse than it ever was in Lincoln's day, that his words surely bear repetition:

"We have been the recipients of the choicest blessings of heaven. We have been preserved, these many years, in peace and prosperity. We have grown in number, wealth and power as no other nation ever has grown; but we have forgotten God! We have forgotten the gracious hand which preserved us in peace, and multiplied and enriched and strengthened us; and we have vainly imagined, in the deceitfulness of our hearts, that these

blessings were produced by some superior wisdom and virtue of our own. Intoxicated with unbroken success, we have become too self-sufficient to feel the necessity of redeeming and preserving grace, too proud to pray to the God that made us."

Abraham Lincoln led the nation in the crucible of the Civil War and called for a nation-wide day of fasting and prayer. The American people responded and God heard from heaven and the tide of war was turned from that moment. Thus Abraham Lincoln gave not only an enduring example but also a formula to the nation today, as to how further calamities may be averted, and, as to how America's fortunes may be restored. The dire scenario confronting America in the near future clearly demands a call to genuine repentance for the whole nation. The prophet Joel speaks with moving eloquence on this same theme, as He expresses the very heart of God:

"Now, therefore," says the LORD, "Turn to Me with all your heart, with fasting, with weeping, and with mourning. So rend your heart, and not your garments; Return to the LORD your God, for He is gracious and merciful, slow to anger, and of great kindness; and He relents from doing harm. Who knows if He will turn and relent, and leave a blessing behind Him." (Joel 2:12-14).

The fact that GOD, the Almighty Creator, has removed His Hand of protection over America is highly significant. It is significant because the spirit world understands your true origins, and their demonic aim has always been to destroy the covenant people of Israel. These dark forces understand only too well the link between the Jews and the Anglo-Saxon, Celtic, and related peoples. It is only the tribes of the lost house of Israel who are largely blind to the fact. Without wholesale national top-down repentance, those dark forces will continue to heap calamity upon calamity and disaster upon disaster upon America and the other nations where the ten tribes are concentrated, until those nations are utterly ruined and laid low. Nevertheless, further catastrophic disasters can still be averted, as even at this late hour it may still be possible to turn back, for God says: *"If My people who are called by My name will humble themselves, and pray and seek My face, and will turn from their wicked ways, then I will hear from heaven, and forgive their sin and heal their land"* (2 Chronicles 7:14).

The Lifting of the Veil

The veil that has been placed over the face of the Lost House of Israel is being removed! As this veil vanishes, the world will discover the true face of Israel. America and Great Britain, Canada, Australia and New Zealand, plus the coastal nations of northern Europe amongst others, form an intrinsic part of that face. Their Israelite heritage in time will become recognized throughout the world. The reality of gentile America's Israelite ancestry will become self-evident to the point where no one will question it any longer.

Wake up, America, Wake up Europe & Wake up Israel!

Wake up, gentile America! You need to go back to your Hebrew roots! Your Puritan forefathers believed in America's "Manifest Destiny," the belief that God had ordained a special role and purpose for the American people. The "Pledge of Allegiance" *"One nation under God,"* expresses this same sentiment of America's "Manifest Destiny." As we have already indicated, by embracing this extraordinary concept, Americans have indeed subliminally adopted an exclusively Israelite or even a Jewish concept of being, *"the Chosen People."* Please recognize that your destiny is different from that of other nations. May your blindness soon be healed! Open your eyes! Look into the mirror of your history and understand that you are part of Israel! Get a grip, America! Remove the veil and recognize your ancestry! Blow the dust off your Bibles and be cured of your collective amnesia! Come on America, check it out and realize your true origins! Remember the ancient paths of your Hebrew ancestors and return to your fathers Abraham, Isaac and Jacob. Why does all this matter? It matters because God has not forgotten His Covenant promises to Abraham. Remember, those promises were meant for "all" the descendants of Abraham. That includes YOU and all of those who dwell with you!

The nations of Europe also need to wake up! This is especially true for Great Britain, whose leaders have followed the despicable example of

Esau, by selling the "birthright" of their sovereign independence for nothing to the European Union. In the case of Esau, he at least got a bowl of soup out of his abominable act, whereas the U.K. received zero! This once-great nation, descended from Ephraim, the "birthright" son of Joseph, possessor of the greatest empire that ever ruled the world, is now reduced to subservience, with eighty percent of her laws being dictated to her by the unelected and unaccountable Commission in Brussels, the seat of the European Union. The other mainly Israelite nations, such as Norway, Sweden, Finland and Denmark, as well as the Netherlands and Belgium, and northern France, have also despised their God-given heritage in that they too have been willing to surrender their sovereign independence to the totalitarian supra-national EU consortium. The best advice for those nations is to "GET OUT OF BABYLON!" Get out whilst there is still time, and return to the God of your fathers Abraham, Isaac and Jacob. Make that decision! Be strong and of good courage and return to the "ancient paths," and the faith of your fathers!

Listen, Judah! Let the Prophets of Israel speak!

Last but not least, we come to the Jewish State of Israel, whose courageous people have fought war after war ever since its miraculous foundation in 1948. Today, your people have become so fatigued they seem willing to take what appears to be the more attractive option, as at least in joining the EU, so the thinking goes, she will find some security being part of a much greater combine. Having lived in the eye of the storm for nearly six and a half decades, many in the nation are suffering from battle fatigue and its secular Torah-less leadership has lost its vision. The Prophets of Israel administer a stern warning to Judah about this very situation, therefore: *"Listen for once, Judah! Let the Prophets of Israel speak!*

The first word comes from the prophet Hosea, and it is specifically addressed to the leaders of the State of Israel: *"The officers of Judah were like those who shift the boundaries: upon them I will pour my wrath like water."* (Hosea 5:10).

The prophet Hosea then goes on to indicate how His wrath will be manifested in the days to come:

"I will be like a moth to Ephraim, like rot to the House of Judah. Ephraim saw his ailment and Judah his wound; and Ephraim went to <u>Assyria</u> and [Judah] sent [tribute] to the king of Jareb [EU?] - but he will not be able to cure you nor heal you of your [Oslo-Accord?] wound. For I am like a lion to Ephraim and like a lion's whelp to the house of Judah. As for Me, Me, I will mangle and I will go; I will carry off and no one will rescue. I will go, I will return to My place <u>until they will acknowledge their guilt</u> and seek My face; in their distress they will seek Me." (Hosea 5:12-15, emphasis added).

The prophet Isaiah too has an admonition for the house of Judah: *"The LORD will bring the king of <u>Assyria</u> upon you and your people and your father's house - days that have not come since the day that Ephraim departed from Judah."* (Isaiah 7:17, emphasis added). This prophecy still awaits fulfillment, as to date it still has not come to pass.

For a final warning Isaiah goes on to say:

"Therefore, behold, the LORD is bringing upon them the mighty and abundant waters of the [Euphrates] River, the king of <u>Assyria</u> and all his glory, and it will rise above all its channels and overflow its banks. It will pass through Judah, flooding as it passes, and reaching to the neck; and its wingspread will be the full breath your land, O Emmanuel. (Isaiah 8:7-8, emphasis added).

Hopefully, you will heed the word of the prophets and learn not to put your trust in man, especially if he is of Roman or Assyrian origin, as is the case with the European Union. Hopefully too, you will have learned from your forefathers and not make the same mistake in seeking protection in alliances with other nations. Remember, all those alliances brought your ancestors nothing but a vale of tears. If, regardless of the lessons of your own history, as well as the warnings of the Prophets, you do decide to join the European Union for commercial gain and for greater security, remember, you will be signing a Covenant with death and a Contract with hell!

This book is written out of love and a heartfelt concern for both houses of Israel. The author's desire is, first of all, to make both houses aware of each other's existence and especially aware of the fact that through the

Patriarchs of Israel they share a common ancestry. At the same time he wishes to warn all the modern day sons of Jacob of the severe trials that lie ahead, in the sincere hope that at least some will take note and consider the path of repentance. Only wholesale repentance and penitence from the leadership of our nations down to Mr. average citizen can avert the disasters already decreed in Heaven. My earnest hope is that our nations will heed the call.

The Union of Jacob

The "Union of Jacob" is about the restoration of the whole house of Israel. It speaks about the restoration of the Tabernacle of David! (Amos 9:11). It will be a time when, after three thousand years of separation, the house of Judah and the house of Israel come together into one United Kingdom of Israel. It is the ultimate union of all the tribal sons of Jacob into one nation under God. It also represents the final fulfillment of the covenant of the Creator of Heaven and Earth, made with Abraham, Isaac and Jacob, the Hebrew patriarchs of Israel. This is about the ultimate family reunion when all the tribal sons of Jacob become reconciled to each other and reunite into one Kingdom. This is the grand Messianic vision proclaimed by all of the great prophets of Israel--a union that is to last forever! It is through this United Kingdom of Israel that all the nations of the earth will be blessed. This glorious Kingdom will be in place for as long as, *"the stars remain, and the heavens send down dew upon the earth."*

Prayer of Repentance

Our Father, our King, we have sinned before thee.

Our Father, our King, we have no king except thee.

Our Father, our King, deal with us (kindly) for the sake of thy name.

Our Father, our King, annul every severe decree against us.

Our Father, our King, annul the designs of those who hate us.

Our Father, our King, frustrate the counsel of our enemies.

Our Father, our King, cause every oppressor and adversary to vanish from us.

Our Father, our King, close the mouths of our adversaries and of those who accuse us.

Our Father, our King, remove pestilence, sword, famine, captivity and destruction from the children of thy covenant.

Our Father, our King, withhold the plague from thy heritage.

Our Father, our King, forgive and pardon all our iniquities.

Our Father, our King, blot out and remove our transgressions from thy sight.

Our Father, our King, erase in thy abundant mercies all records of our guilt.

Our Father, our King, bring us back in perfect repentance to thee.

Our Father, our King, rend the evil sentence decreed against us.

Our Father, our King, remember us with a good remembrance before thee.

Our Father, our King, inscribe us in the book of redemption and salvation.

Our Father, our King, inscribe us in the book of forgiveness and pardon.

Our Father. our King, cause our salvation soon to flourish.

Our Father, our King, hear our voice, spare us, and have compassion on us.

Our Father, our King, receive our prayer with mercy and favor.

Our Father, our King, open the gates of heaven to our prayer.

Our Father, our King, we pray thee, turn us not away empty from thy presence.

Our Father, our King, remember that we are but dust.

Our Father, our King, may this hour be an hour of mercy and a time of favor before thee.

Our Father, our King, have compassion on us, on our children and our infants.

Our Father, our King, do it for the sake of those who were slain for (proclaiming) thy holy name.

Our Father, our King, do it for the sake of those who were slaughtered for (proclaiming) thy unity.

Our Father, our King, do it for the sake of those who went through fire and water for the sanctification of thy name.

Our Father, our King, avenge before our eyes the blood of thy servants that has been shed.

Our Father, our King, do it for thy sake, if not for ours.

Our Father, our King, do it for thy sake and save us.

Our Father, our King, do it for the sake of thy abundant mercies.

Our Father, our King, do it for the sake of thy great, mighty and revered name by which we are called.

Our Father, our King, be gracious to us and answer us, for we have no (good) deeds of our own; deal charitably with us and save us *[1]

Bibliography

A HISTORY OF THE AMERICAN PEOPLE, by Paul Johnson, published by Phoenix Press, London, 2000

AMERICA'S LAST CALL: On The brink Of A Financial Holocaust, by David Wilkerson, published by Wilkerson Trust Publications, Lindale, Texas, U.S.A. 1998

ANCIENT MESOPOTAMIA, by L. Oppenheim, published by University of Chicago Press, Chicago & London, 1964

ASSOCIATES FOR BIBLICAL RESEARCH, By Dr, David Livingston, published by ABR's Bible and Spade, U.S.A. 2001

ANTIQUITIES OF THE JEWS, by Flavius Josephus, translated by William Whiston A.M., London

A PORTRAIT OF THE STARS AND STRIPES, by Bud Hannings, published by Seniram Publishing Inc. Glenside, PA., U.S.A. 1988

BABYLONIANS AND ASSYRIANS—*LIFE AND CUSTOMS*, by Professor A.H. Sayce, published by John C. Nimmo, London, 1891

BABYLON IN EUROPE: What Bible Prophecy Reveals About The European Union, by David Hathaway, published by New Wine Press, Chichester, United Kingdom

BARACK OBAMA'S TOP TEN INSULTS AGAINST BRITAIN; Extracts from article by Nigel Gardiner, The Telegraph (U.K.) World, Last updated March 1st, 2010

BETRAYED: The Conspiracy to Divide Jerusalem, by Mike Evans, published by Bedford Books, Bedford Texas, copyright 2008 Bedford Books.

BEYOND BABYLON: Europe's Rise and Fall, by David Ben Ariel, published by Publish America, LLLP, Baltimore, U.S.A. 2004

BLOWING THE WHISTLE—One man's fight against fraud in the EUROPEAN COMMISSION, by Paul van Buitenen, published by Politico's Publishing, London 2000

CIVIL WAR ALBUM: Complete Photographic History of The Civil War, by William C Davis and Bell L Wiley under the direction of The National Historic Society, Tess Press, New York.

COMMENTARY ON THE OLD TESTAMENT, vol. 1, by C.F. Keil, and P. Delitzch, published by Eerdmans, Grand Rapids, U.S.A., 1975

CROMWELL: Our Chief of Men, by Antonia Frazer, published by George Weidenfeld & Nicolson Limited, London, Great Britain 1973

EIGHT HARBINGERS OF JUDGMENT, article by Rabbi Jonathan Cahn, Beth Israel Worship Center, Box1111, Lodi, NJ 07644, 2009

EMPIRE OF DEBT—The Rise of an Epic Financial Crisis, by Bill Bonner and Addison Wiggin, published by John Wiley & sons, Inc., U.S.A. 2006

EPICenter—Why the Current Rumblings in the Middle East will Change your Future, by Joel C. Rosenberg, published by Tyndale House Publishers Inc., Illinois, U.S.A., 2005

ERRAND INTO THE WILDERNESS, by Perry Miller, published by Harvard University Press, Cambridge Massachusetts and Cambridge England, Thirteenth Printing, 2000

EUROPE'S FULL CIRCLE—Corporate Elitism and the New Fascism, by Rodney Atkinson, published by Compuprint Publishing, 1 Sands Road, Newcastle upon Tyne, Great Britain

EURABIA—The Euro-Arab Axis—by Bat Ye'or, published by Maddison —Teaneck, Fairleigh Dickinson University Press, U.S.A. 2005

Bibliography

GEORGE III: AMERICA'S LAST KING, by Jeremy Black, published by Yale University Press, Newhaven CT U.S.A.

GESENIUS HEBREW GRAMAR, Editor E. Kautsch, published by Oxford: Clarendon, 1910

GRAND DESIGN: A European Solution to German Reunification, by Franz Jozeph Strauss, published by Weidenfeld and Nicholson, London, 1965

GREAT BRITAIN—Her Calling and Hidden Ancestry, by Stephen J Spykerman, published by Mount Ephraim Publishing, Eastbourne, England 2004

HISTORY BEGINS AT SUMER, edited by S.N. Kramer, published by Doubleday, Garden City NY, 1910

HOW OBAMA EMBRACES ISLAM'S SHARIA AGENDA, by Andrew C McCarthy, Encounter Books, New York, New York, 10003, 2010

IN SEARCH OF: THE ORIGIN OF NATIONS, by Craig M White, published by History Research Projects, Australia, 2002

I.O.U.S.A.—One Nation. - Under Stress. - In Debt. By Addison Wiggin and Kate Incontrera, published by John Wiley & Sons, Inc., Hoboken, New Jersey, USA

IS ISLAM A GLOBAL THREAT?—By Victor Mordecai, published by Victor Mordecai, Taylors, South Carolina, U.S.A. 1997

ISRAEL: The BLESSING or the CURSE, by John McTernan & Bill Koenig, published by Hearthstone Publishing, Oklahoma City, OK 73101 U.S.A. 2002

ISRAEL'S TRIBES TODAY, by Steven M Collins, published by Bible Blessings, Royal Oak, MI, U.S.A. 2005

JEWISH ANTIQUITIES, BOOK III, by Flavius Josephus, published by Cambridge MA: Harvard University Press, Loeb Classics, 1998

ORIGIN—You too are from Israel—You too are the People, by Yair Davidiy, published by Russell-Davis Publishers, Jerusalem, Israel, 2002

PHILISTINE: - The Great Deception, by Ramon Bennett, published by Shekinah Books Ltd. P.O.Box 846 Keno, Oregon 97627.

POLITICIDE—The Attempted Murder of the Jewish State, Volume three, by Victor Sharpe, published by LULU, U.S.A. 2011

REFLECTIONS ON THE REVOLUTION IN EUROPE—Immigration, Islam and the West, by Christopher Caldwell, Doubleday Books, Random House Inc., London, 2009

SHORT HISTORY of the ENGLISH PEOPLE, by John Richard Green, published by Macmillan & Co, London and New York, 1895

SYMBOLS OF OUR CELTO-SAXON HERITAGE, by W H Bennett, published by Herald Press Limited, Windsor, Ontario, 1985

THE AMERICAN DREAM: Stories from the Heart of Our Nation, by Dan Rather, published by Harper Collins, New York, NY U.S.A. 2001

THE AMERICAN JEREMIAD, by Sacvan Bercovitch, published by University of Wisconsin Press, Madison, Wisconsin, U.S.A.

THE AMERICAN PROPHECIES—Ancient Scriptures Reveal Our Nation's Future, by Michael D Evans, published by Warner Faith, New York, U.S.A. 2004

THE AMERICAN REVOLUTION: A People's History, by Ray Raphael, published by Harper Collins, New York, NY, U.S.A. 2002

THE ANCIENT ORIENT, by W. Von Soden, published by Willim B Eerdmans, Michigan, (1994).

THE ANVIL OF CIVILISATION, by Leonard Cottrell, published by New York: New American Library 1957

THE AUTOBIOGRAPHY OF BENJAMIN FRANKLIN, by Benjamin Franklin, published by Barnes & Noble Publishing Inc. New York, U.S.A. 1994

THE AUTOBIOGRAPHY OF MARTIN LUTHER KING, edited by Clayborne Carson, published by Abacus, Time Warner Books UK, London, 2000

THE AUTHORIZED SELICHOT—For the Whole Year, Translated and annotated by Rabbi Abraham Rosenfeld, published by The Judaica Press, INC., New York, 1978

THE CHUMASH—THE ARTSCROLL SERIES/STONE EDITION, published by Mesorah Publications, Ltd., Brooklyn, NY, U.S.A. 1993

THE DEATH PACT—How National Socialism and Islamism formed an alliance in Germany and together plotted the Holocaust, by Rosamund Streseman, published by Christen an der Seite Israels, Gemany Nov. 2011

THE DISINTEGRATING WEST, by Mary Kaldor, published by Penguin Books, New York, New York 10022 U.S.A.

THE DOWNING STREET YEARS, by Margaret Thatcher, published by Harper Collins, London, 1993

THE EAGLE AND THE SHIELD: A History of the Great Seal of the United States, - 1976, by Patterson, Richard S & Richardson, Dougall, Published by the Office of the Historian, Bureau of Public Affairs, Department of State

THE EXHAUSTIVE CONCORDANCE OF THE BIBLE, by James Strong, published by Mac Donald Publishing Company, McLean, Virginia, U.S.A.

THE GATHERING STORM, by Sir Winston Churchill, published by Cassel, London, 1948

THE GILGAMESH EPIC and OLD TESTAMENT PARALLELS, by A. Heidel, published by Chicago: University Press, 1963

THE GRAND CHESSBOARD—American Primacy and it's Geo-Strategic Imperatives, by Zbigniew Brezinski, Published by Basic Books, New York, 1998

THE GRAND JIHAD—How Islam and the Left sabotage America, by Andrew C McCarthy, Encounter Books, New York, New York, 10003, 2010

THE GREAT GERMAN NATION—Origins and Destiny, by Craig M. White, published by Author House, IN, U.S.A., 2007

THE GREAT SEAL of the UNITED STATES—Its History, Symbolism and Message for the New Age, by Paul Foster Case. Published by Builders of the Adytum, Ltd. Los Angeles, 1976

THE GERMANS: DOUBLE HISTORY OF A NATION, by Emil Ludwig, published by Little, Brown and Company, Boston, U.S.A., 1941

THE HIDDEN ANCESTRY OF AMERICA AND GREAT BRITAIN, by Stephen Spykerman., published by Mount Ephraim Publishing, England, 2004

THE HISTORY OF THE SEAL OF THE UNITED STATES, by Gaillard Hunt, republished by Kessinger Publishing LLC, 2010

THE HISTORY TODAY COMPANION TO BRITISH HISTORY, Edited by Juliet Gardener & Neil Wenborn, published by Collins & Brown Limited, London, 1995

THE HOLY BIBLE—KING JAMES VERSION, published by Oxford University Press, London W1

THE HOLY ROMAN EMPIRE—by Friedrich Heer, translated into English from the original German by Janet Sondheimer, published by George Weidenfeld & Nicolson Ltd circa 1968, London, England

THE ISLAMIC INVASION—Confronting the World's Fastest Growing Religion, by Robert A Morley, Las Vegas, NV, 1992

THE ISLAMIC TSUNAMI—Israel and America in the Age of Obama, by David Rubin, published by Shiloh Israel Press, Israel, 2010

THE KING WHO LOST AMERICA: A Portrait of the Life and Times of George III, by Alan Lloyd, published by Doubleday Books, Random House Inc. 2009

THE LAST OF THE GIANTS: Lifting the Veil on Islam and the End Times, by George Otis, JR., published by Chosen Books, a Division of Baker Book House Co., Grand Rapids. U.S.A.

THE LIFE AND TIMES OF WASHINGTON: Portraits of Greatness - by Mario Rivoire, published by The Hamlyn Publishing Group Ltd, England, 1967

THE NEW KING JAMES VERSION - Copyright 1982, Thomas Nelson Inc.

THE PRINCIPALITY AND POWER OF EUROPE: Britain and the emerging Holy European Empire, by Adrian Hilton, published by Dorchester House Publications, Rickmansworth, U.K.

THE PURITAN ORIGINS OF THE AMERICAN SELF, by Sacvan Bercovitch, published by Yale University Press, Newhaven, 1975, U.S.A.

THE REAL MESSIAH, by Rav. Dr. A Kaplan, published by NCSY, Orthodox union, NY, U.S.A.

THE ROTTEN HEART OF EUROPE: The Dirty War for Europe's Money, by Bernard Connolly, published by Faber and Faber, London, Boston, 1995

THE SECOND WORLD WAR—Volume 1, *"THE GATHERING STORM,"* by Winston Churchill, published by Houghton Mifflin Co, Boston, U.S.A.

THE SECRET DESTINY of AMERICA, by Manly P. Hall, published by Philosophical Research Society Inc., Los Angeles, 1944, 1972

THE SWORD OF THE REPUBLIC: The United States Army on the Frontier—1783-1846, by Francis, Paul Prucha, Macmillan, New York, 1969

THE TRIBES—The Israelite Origins of Western Peoples, by Yair Davidiy, Third Edition, - Russell-Davis Publishers, Jerusalem, Israel 2004

THE TWO BABYLONS—or the Papal Worship proved to be the Worship of Nimrod and his Wife, by Alexander Hislop, published by S.W. Partridge & Co (A. & C. Black, Publishers, Ltd., London, 1916

THE WINNING OF THE WEST,—Volumes I, II, III, & IV, by Theodore Roosevelt, published by Bison Book Edition, University of Nebraska Press, U.S.A. 1995

TO AMERICA: Personal Reflections of a Historian, by Stephen E Ambrose, published by Simon & Schuster, New York, NY, U.S.A. 2002

WARFARE—RENAISSANCE TO REVOLUTION 1492-1792, by Jeremy Black, published by Cambridge Illustrated Atlas, Cambridge University Press, Cambridge, U.K. 1996

WARFOOTING: 10 STEPS America Must Take to Prevail in the War for the Free World, by Frank J. Gaffney, Jr., published by Naval Institute Press, Annapolis, Maryland, U.S.A., 2006

WHAT'S THE MESSIAH WAITING FOR? By John Hulley, unpublished manuscript, Israel 2005

"WHO ARE YOU, AMERICA?—TIME TO LIFT YOUR PROPHETIC VEIL" By Stephen Spykerman, published by Mount Ephraim Publishing, 2nd edition, England, 2010

WHO'S JERUSALEM?—by Eliyahu Tal, published by The International Forum For A United Jerusalem, Jerusalem, Israel, Copyright 1994 by Eliyahu Tal

YOU DON'T HAVE TO BE JEWISH TO BE A ZIONIST—A Review of 400 years of Christian Zionism, by Eliyahu Tal, published by; A Millennium Publication of the International Forum for a United Jerusalem, Israel

ZONDERVAN NASB Wide Margin—New American Standard Bible, published by Zondervan, Grand Rapids, Michigan U.S.A. 2002

Unless states otherwise, all Scriptural references are from The Stone Edition TANACH, the ArtScroll Series, published by Mesorah Publications, Ltd., New York, 1998. Emphases are the author's.

ABOUT THE AUTHOR

STEPHEN J SPYKERMAN was born in September 1940 during the Nazi occupation of Holland. His parents were Catholics of Jewish origin and he was the fourth son of seven children with a Dutch father and an English mother. The family escaped the Holocaust due to his parent's Catholic religion plus the fact that his mother was English and thus she was seen as the English rather than the Jewish woman. Stephen's early years were full of excitement and danger, as their house for some time became the emergency headquarters for the Dutch resistance in his region. His father was arrested by the Nazi authorities and held for some time in a special prison for people who were considered influential in their local communities. His parents also sheltered Henny Cohen, a Jewish woman, who was hiding whilst on the run from the Nazis. At the same time their formidable children's nanny worked as courier for the Dutch resistance.

Having received a solid general education, he spurned the higher education his parents had hoped for and entered the world of retail fashion at age nineteen. After working in his hometown for a few years he left to try his luck in London, where he trained as a tailor in various high-class fashion houses. Whilst he was aware that his maternal grandfather had been a renowned tailor in London, he did not realize at the time that he was following a family tradition going back for at least five generations. Then in 1965 he married Virginia Edwards, and after the second of his four children was born, he left the fashion industry to take up a more lucrative career in financial services. During a successful career he pioneered a number of new schemes and concepts in charitable giving and seminar selling, and became an international speaker in his field. His interest in public speaking led him to direct his own public speaking club. In the years prior to his retirement in 1997, he became involved in a Speakers Bureau, after which he and a colleague set up their own International Speakers Bureau in London.

Once retired from day to day business he started writing books and founded Mount Ephraim Publishing as a vehicle for his work. To this day he continues to give lectures. Stephen Spykerman is a consummate communicator and has addressed audiences and conferences in Great Britain, Canada, the United States, Ireland, France, Belgium, the Netherlands, Israel, Malta and Cyprus. Stephen and Rabbi Avraham Feld share the same vision for the restoration of the two divided houses of Israel and the establishment of the United Kingdom of Israel. They first met at a conference at the Hilton Hotel in Jerusalem, where Stephen had been invited to speak in the year 2000, and have been firm friends ever since. This book is their first major collaborative effort.

"The Covenant with Death!"- is Stephen's eighth book to date, which includes much of the fascinating American heraldic material of an earlier work by the title, "Who Are You, America?"

THE COVENANT WITH DEATH

"The Covenant with Death," concerns America's connection with Israel both ancient and modern. This work contains an urgent heart stopping message affecting the immediate future of every citizen of the State of Israel as well as the United States of America. It contains an astounding message for our time, as it brings the revelation of an ancient secret about America's true ancestry and heritage.

This work implies that President Obama's Cairo, *"Common cause with Islam,"* declaration signifies a seismic change of U.S. policy, which sets both him and the United States of America on a collision course with the ALMIGHTY GOD OF ISRAEL. The President clearly does not understand that the State of Israel is in a covenant relationship with God. Destroy Israel and the demonic religion of Islam will claim the victory. Thus in coming against Israel, the current President has become the servant of Allah and the lackey of Islam!

The author makes the point that appeasement is a supreme act of cowardice! Islamic terrorists the world over are rejoicing, as they sense that the office of the American Presidents has become "all mouth and no trousers." That the planet's only superpower is now in wholesale retreat before them. In the meantime, Israel knows she has been betrayed in the house of her friends. With the onset of the current administration, the familial bond of brotherhood between America and the Jewish State of Israel is now broken.

This book reveals the hidden meaning behind America's colorful heraldry and the dramatic illustrations are a visual feast in this astounding work. After you have seen them and understood the sensational secrets hidden within the U.S.A.'s heraldic symbols, you will never again be able to look at either *the Great Seal of America* or *the Presidential Seal* in the same light again.

The Covenant with Death contains an astonishing truth, as it provides conclusive evidence that the ancient Assyrians are still around today! Remember your biblical history, how those warlike Assyrians invaded and defeated the northern kingdom of Israel and took the ten tribes of Israel into captivity? Would you be surprised to know that their modern day descendants reside in Germany? Prepare yourself for the Germans will soon be on the warpath again! They started WW I and II and are about to start World War III through a new European Union in close alliance with Islam.

The author also proves a clear link between Germany and radical Islam, a secret association that actually began long before Hitler under the German Kaiser Wilhelm II and the then German Foreign Office, which has continued to have an influence, often hidden, to this day. The author also reveals the sinister agenda behind the secret EURABIA Covenant made between the EU and Islam in the aftermath of the Opec Oil Embargo of 1973. Learn about the ultimate *Axis of Evil*!

This work contains a most urgent warning about the dangers of the European Union, which is set to launch the final resurrection of the Holy Roman Empire. The book provides many fascinating insights into the bloody history of the Holy Roman Empire, including the malignant role played by the Papacy and the Roman Catholic Church throughout its history right up to our present day. It also furnishes absolute proof that the formation of the EU represents the fulfillment of a Nazi dream for global conquest.

The Covenant with Death warns of perilous times ahead for the State of Israel as well as for America! This book is a must read for every Israeli and American citizen. It is a work of the greatest importance, as it carries a most urgent warning message for our nations. In the final analysis the Jewish as well as the American peoples should both look to Moses and the prophets of Israel, who in the perilous times of their days gave both Judah and America the formula, as to how disaster might be avoided and how the nation's fortunes might be restored. As such, this work, despite its serious content, conveys a most incredible message of hope.

> *"If My people who are called by My name*
> *will humble themselves, and pray*
> *and seek My face, and will turn from*
> *their wicked ways, then I will hear*
> *from heaven, and forgive their sin*
> *and heal their land"*
> (2 Chronicles 7:14)

ENDNOTES

Chapter 1

* 1 See; Rav. Dr. A. Kaplan, "The Real Messiah," [NCSY, Orthodox Union, NY, NY] for further details and enlightment).

* 2 Orthodox Jewish Art scroll Stone edition of the Chumash/Tanach

Chapter 2

* 1 Josephus Antiquities of the Jews (Book X ch.9).

* 2 Israel's Lost Empires, by Steven M Collins.

Chapter 3

* 1 Chumash p.281

* 2 Extracts from Barack Obama's top 10 insults against Britain, by Nile Gardiner, The Telegraph (U.K.) World, last updated March 1st

   2010

Chapter 4

* 1 ISRAEL'S TRIBES TODAY by Steven M Collins pp. 182-183.

* 2 ORIGIN, by Yair Davidiy - Russell-Davis, Jerusalem p96.

Chapter 5

* 1 Feliks p.9

* 2 Source: Center for Arms Control and Non Proliferation, February 20, 2008.

* 3 Source: usgovernmentspending.com/defense budget.

* 4 Numbers Rabah 2;5.

* 5 THE TRIBES, (2004) p.127, Russell-Davis Publishers, Jerusalem.

* 6 (Numbers 2;7),

* 7 THE TRIBES, (2004) p.409 & 434, Russell-Davis Publishers, Jerusalem.

Chapter 6

* 1 Wikipedia.org/American Civil War

Chapter 7

* 1 From the Manuscript: "What is the Messiah waiting for?" by John Hulley.

* 2 From the Manuscript: "What is the Messiah waiting for?" by John Hulley.

* 3 From the Manuscript: "What is the Messiah waiting for?" by John Hulley.

* 4 From the Manuscript: "What is the Messiah waiting for?" by John Hulley.

* 5 Israel Ministry of Foreign Affairs

Chapter 8

* 1 Dr Tony Corn, "The Real Politic behind the European Financial Crisis." Small Wars Journal, November 29, 2011.

* 2 The Gathering Storm, *Ibid., p.93.*

* 3 The Grand Design, p.9.

* 4 (Ibid., pp. 40, 92).

* 5 (Ibid., pp 77).

* 6 The Grand Design, p.104.

Endnotes

* 7 The Grand Chessboard, p.63

* 8 (Ibid., pp 73-74)

* 9 CDU/CSU paper, Reflections on Europe, Sept. 1, 1994.

* 10 Matthias Küntzel. Djihad und Judenhass. Freiburg 2003 Page 17 ff

* 11 Küntzel, ibid. P. 23

Chapter 8—end notes continued

* 12 Küntzel, ibid. P.33

* 13 cf. http://www.zeit.de/1990/37/der-traum-vom-grossen-arabien.

* 14 Article by Azmul Fahimi Kamaruzaman. The Emergence of the Egyptian Muslim Brotherhood in Palestine:

* 15 Matthias Küntzel ibid. P. 36

* 16 http://wahrheitgraben.wordpress.com/2009/02/27/die-juden-im-koran/

* 17 http://de.wikipedia.org/wiki/%E1%B8%A4arb%C4%AB

* 18 Quoted from a speech by the Grand Mufti by Matthias Künzel in Djihad und Judenhass, ibid P.39

* 19 Article in the "Zeit" newspaper 7. Sept. 1999. Klaus von Münschhausen. Der Traum von grossen Arabien, P.2.

* 20 http://www.zeit.de/1990/37/der-traum-vom-grossen-arabien

* 21 cf. Wolfgang G. Schwanitz. Die Berliner Djhadisierung des Islams—Wie Max von Oppenheim die islamische Revolution schürte. P.19 ff. In: Konrad-Adenauer-Stiftung e.V.(Hg). Auslandsinformationen, Sankt Augustin, 10. Nov. 2004. Also at: http://www.kas.de/db_files/dokumente/auslandsinformationen/7_dokument_dok_pdf_5678_1.pdf

* 22 cf. http://de.wikipedia.org/wiki/Halbmondlager

* 23 cf. http://www.dradio.de/dkultur/sendungen/laenderreport/567079/

* 24 cf. Wolfgang G. Schwanitz. Die Berliner Djhadisierung des Islams. ibid. P. 27

* 25 cf. http://www.jafi.org.il/JewishAgency/English/Jewish+Education/German/Israel+und+Zionismus/ Konzepte/Britisches + Mandat.htm

* 26 cf. Gerhard Höpp: Der Koran als "Geheime Reichssache." Bruchstücke deutscher Islam-Politik zwischen 1938und 1945. www.zmo.de/biblio/nachlass/hoepp/01_22_057.pdf

* 27 From a very special story of a notorious bomb maker who was trained by the SS, reported by Ulrich Sahm. http://bit.ly/pVawLG

* 28 U. Sahm: Fawzi al Kutub-The darkest character in German-Jewish-Israeli-Palestinian history.ibid.

* 29 cf. Wikipedia Article http://de.wikipedia.org/wiki/Mohammed_Amin_al-Husseini

* 30 cf. Statements from the Eichmann trial: http://www.nizkor.org/hweb/people/e/eichmannadolf/ transcripts/Sessions/Session-016-03.html 22Complete text at: http://atlasshrugs2000.typepad.com/atlas_shrugs/2010/02/mufti_jewish_genocide.html

* 31 Complete text at:http:/atlasshrugs2000.typepad.com/atlas shrugs/2010/02/mufti jewish genocide.html

* 32 The complete document at: http://www.ns-archiv.de/verfolgung/antisemitismus/mufti/in_berlin.php (underlining by the author)

* 33 The conclusion of Klaus von Münchhausen. ibid. P.4. http://www.zeit.de/1990/37/der-traum-vom-grossen-arabien

* 34 cf. Klaus von Münchhausen. ibid

* 35 cf. Article by Matthias Küntzel, Über die europäischen Wurzeln des Antisemitismus im gegenwärtigen IslamischenDenken. http://www.matthiaskuentzel.de/contents/ueber-die-europaeischen-wurzeln-desantisemitismus-im-gegenwaertigen- islamischen-denken

* 36 cf. Article by Matthias Küntzel: Von Goebbels zu Ahmadinejad. Tribüne, Heft 186, Dezember 2010.

* 37 cf. Article by Matthias Küntzel: Von Goebbels zu Ahmadinejad. Ibidem

* 38 Matthias Künzel, Von Zeesen bis Beirut. www.matthiaskuentzel.de/contents/von-zeesen-bis-beiruthttp://www.matthiaskuentzel.de/contents/von-goebbels-zu-ahmadinejad

* 39 See also: http://www.dradio.de/dkultur/sendungen/ausderjuedischenwelt/1291589/

* 40 cf. http://atlasshrugs2000.typepad.com/atlas_shrugs/2010/02/mufti_jewish_genocide.html

* 41 cf. Article in the "Zeit" newspaper 7.Sept.1999 by Klaus von Münchhausen: Der Traum vom großen Arabien. http://www.zeit.de/1990/37/der-traum-vom-grossen-arabien

* 42 cf. Article by Titus Lenk: Die SS-Mullah-Schule und die Arbeitsgemeinschaft Turkestan in Dresden. http://web.europenews.dk/de/node/40168

* 43 cf. Article in the "Zeit" newspaper 7.Sept.1999 by Klaus von Münchhausen: Der Traum vom großen Arabien P. 5. http://www.zeit.de/1990/37/der-traum-vom-grossen-arabien

* 44 cf. Article in the Canadian Jewish Chronicle January 31,1947 at http://atlasshrugs2000.typepad.com/atlas_shrugs/2010/02/mufti_jewish_genocide.html

* 45 Ian Johnson. Die vierte Moschee—Nazis, CIA und der islamische Fundamentalismus. Klett-Cotta, 2011

* 46 cf. Hans-Jürgen Döscher: Die verdrängten Seilschaften des Auswärtigen Amts. Propyläen Verlag, 2005.

* 47 cf. Johannes Gerloff: Die Palästinenser. SCM Hänssler: 2011, P.54f.

* 48 cf. http://www.efg-hohenstaufenstr.de/downloads/texte/plo_charta.html

* 49 Matthias Küntzel. Djihad und Judenhass; Freiburg 2003. Page 114 ff

* 50 cf. "Spiegel" 36/2002, P. 117.

* 51 cf. Articles of Hamas in German at: http://usahm.info/Dokumente/Hamasdeu.htm

* 52 http://www.welt.de/politik/ausland/article13567609/Mahmud-Ahmadinedschad-will-Israelausloeschen.html

* 53 THE DEATH PACT—How National Socialism and Islamism formed an alliance in Germany and together plotted the Holocaust, with permission from the author: Rosamund Stresemann, November 2011.

* 54 www.originofnationsorg/Great _German_Nation/germany/history_of_germany.htm

* 55 Los Angeles Times.com/news/nationworld/la-fg-germany-europe-201228,02973408.story

* 56 The Downing Street Years, by Margaret Thatcher, pp 790-791.

Chapter 9

* 1 Penguin Books, New York, 1979, Mary Kaldor, "*The Disintegrating West.*"

* 2 Excerpts taken with permission from pages 96-98 EUROPE'S FULL CIRCLE —Corporate Elites and the New Fascism by Rodney Atkinson, published by Compuprint, Publishing, Newcastle upon Tyne, Great Britain.

* 3 Dr Tony Corn, Excerpt from: "The Real Politic behind the European Financial Crisis." Small Wars Journal, November 29, 2011.

* 4 Financial Times, May 22, 1995.

* 5 The Economist, August 24, 2002

* 6 www.revivalscotland.com/jesuit_europe.html

* 7 THE TWO BABYLONS—the Papal Worship proved to be the Worship of Nimrod and his Wife, by Rev. Alexander Hislop, published by S. W. Partridge & Co. [A. & C. Black Publishers Ltd] 35, Bedford Row, London, U.K.

* 8 First Principals of the Reformation, Martin Luther, Concerning Christian Liberty III on the Babylonian Captivity of the Church.

* 9 Antiquities of the Jews 1:iv:2.

* 10 Heidel 1963: 18.

* 11 see Heidel 1963 34ff.

* 12 Babylonians and Assyrians—Life and Customs, by Professor A.H.Sayce, P. 168.

* 13 Babylonians and Assyrians—Life and Customs, by Professor A.H.Sayce, P. 172.

* 14 July 25e, 2005/12:00am, (Catholic NewsAgency)

* 15 July 25e, 2005/12:00am, (Catholic News Agency)

* 16 CAN Catholic News Agency.

* 17 Vatican body asks U.N. to 'end Israeli occupation'- Reuters 10.23.10.

* 18 For more detailed information read: The Origin of Nations and The Great German Nation, by Craig M White.

* 19 Antiquities, I, ix, 1

* 20 Antiquities, I, x, 1.

* 21 Leonard Cottrell -The Anvil of Civilization

* 22 Oppenheim L. *Ancient Mesopotamia* 164:66

* 23 Plotrovsky, 1969:86

* 24 'IM Deutschen Landen' (P.69) by Joseph K L Bihl.

* 25 The Germans: Double History of a Nation, by Emil Ludwig, 1941, p.12

* 26 www. originofnations.org/Great-German - Nation/german/history-of-germany

* 27 The Gathering Storm, P. 591

* 28 Ibid., P. 606.

* 29 The SIPRI Arms Transfer Database.

* 30 Deutsche Presse-Agentur Gmbh (Hamburg, Germany) Distributed by MCT Information Services.

* 31 www.algemeiner.com/2012/06/26/german-court-outlaws-ritual-circumcision/

* 32 Holy Roman Empire, by Professor Friedrich Heer, page 26,translated by Janet Sondheimer, published by George Weidenfeld and Nicolson Ltd, London © 1968.

* 33 11th edition, vol. 20, article Otto I.

* 34 Holy Roman Empire, by Professor Friedrich Heer, page 7, translated by Janet Sondheimer, published by George Weidenfeld and Nicolson Ltd, London © 1968).

* 35 Holy Roman Empire, by Professor Friedrich Heer, page 3-4, translated by Janet Sondheimer, published by George Weidenfeld and Nicolson Ltd, London © 1968.

* 36 Excerpts from: Meat in Due Season, Third edition, by J.G. Messervy-Norman, Published by LuLu, U.S.A. 2008

* 37 Holy Roman Empire, by Professor Friedrich Heer, page 67,translated by Janet Sondheimer, published by George Weidenfeld and Nicolson Ltd, London © 1968.

Chapter 10

* 1 Genesis 15:9-10; 17-21, commentary & emphasis added.

* 2 George Santayana, The Life of Reason, Vol. One, 1905.

Chapter 11

* 1"Christian Minorities in the Middle East." Ibid, June 1994. p.7.** "Oh little town of Bethlehem." Ibid, Feb. 1995, p.6.

2 Al Jazeera, June 5th 2009

* 3 Source: The Religion of Peace.com.

* 4 Ann Leslie Daily Mail, August 11, 2005.

* 5 Source: Muslim Brotherhood's "Explanatory Memorandum on the General Strategic Goals of the Group," entered into evidence by the Department of Justice in the 2008 Holy Land foundation terrorism-finance trial. Archived at the NEFA FOUNDATION.)

* 6 Source: Undated Muslim Brotherhood Paper entitled, "Phases of the World Underground Movement Plan." Archived at; <u>SHARIAH: THE TREAT TO AMERICA</u>

* 7 Frontpagemag.com2012/02/29why-is-obama-in-bed-with-the-muslimbrotherhood/print/

* 8 Washington's Schizophrenic Approach towards the Muslim Brotherhood.

* 9 Yoseph Qaradawi, (Spiritual leader of the Muslim Brotherhood).

* 10 Andrew C McCarthy, "Sistani and the Democracy Project – A useful measure of the divide between 'To Hell with Them' and 'Anything Goes'" (National Review Online, March 20, 2006).

*11 Iranian student News agency, October 26, 2005, cited by Middle east Media Research Institute, October 28, 2005.

*12 Reza Kahlili - WND/2012/02/ ayatolla-kill-all-jews-annihilate-israel

*13 David Lev, IDF Intel Chief: 200,000 Missiles aimed at Israel - Arutz Sheva, www.IsraelNationalNews.com

*14 Israel, Get Ready For More Obama Leaks by John Bolton, Jewish World Review April 4, 2012

*15 Merrill D Peterson, ed., Jefferson Writings, (New York: Literary Classics of the United States, Inc., 1984), Vol. IV, p 289. From Jefferson's Notes on the State of Virginia, Querry XVIII, 1781.

*16 David Horowitz; www.unitedisrael.org/blog/2008/01/04/george-washington-an-american-joshua

*17 The above is a compilation of extracts from an article by Rabbi Jonathan Cahn entitled "EIGHT HARBINGERS OF JUDGMENT

Chapter 12

* 1 Authorized Selichot, second edition, P. 400-401 by Abraham Rosenfeld, published by Judaica Press, INC., New York, N.Y.,19